AMERICAN

V...

C...

served. No part of this book may be used or reproduced
without written permission. ISBN 978-0-692-58717-1.
www.americanbystander.org

EUGENIA LOLI

HERE GOES NOTHING

Print humor? In 2015? We might as well try to grow trees on concrete

Right off, here's something you should know: We aren't doing this to be popular. We expect *no one* to read this magazine. In a media world that measures audience in billions, we predict a readership in the hundreds. And it will decline from there.

Now, today, no one in their right mind would start a print humor magazine as a business. That is the kind of idea that makes an artisanal pencil shop seem like crass commercialism. And anyone who contributes to it — well, they should be added to some kind of watch list. Not just the ones we're all on already, but new ones. More watchful watch lists.

Any backers will lose scads of money, that's for sure. We're preparing an investor packet now, and the cover reads: "You will lose scads of money." That's only fair. But the illustration is of a smiling older white couple, so maybe people will invest anyway.

"Oho, what about all this advertising?" you ask. "Surely that brings in a bit?"

First: nobody actually says, "Oho," but who are the proprietors of a print humor quarterly, to criticize self-conscious anachronism? And second: it isn't advertising, it's *subversion* — that is, free ads for stuff we like, mostly by people we know. Maybe they'll sell a few more; maybe they won't. But we're not making money from any of it. How could we? None of these products are even remotely addictive.

"Oho," sadder now, wiser. Things are becoming clear to you. This isn't a business. It isn't even really a magazine.

MICHAEL GERBER

(@mgerber937) is the Publisher of *The American Bystander*.

This is willfully re-launching the Titanic, *knowing full well it will sink*, in some vague attempt to bring back the golden age of transatlantic travel.

But don't misunderstand. We embrace our all-too-inevitable destiny. After you reach a certain age, you realize that cataclysmic failure isn't the worst thing that can happen to a person. If the Titanic hadn't sunk in 1912, it would've ended its life being cut up for scrap. *The Bystander* deserves better — by which we mean worse. We're just trying to be honest, so loss of life is kept to a minimum.

Please don't overthink this. We aren't being ironic, nor are we working some sitcom-grade reverse-psychology. "We'll say we *expect* to fail, and they'll be charmed, and then we'll have them."

No.

When you live in the world of people, as we do, you get a sense of what's popular. If this magazine ever gets popular, we've made a terrible, terrible mistake. That's as close to a motto as we'll ever have.

So why are we doing it? Simple: for the last four years (and it really has taken that long), every time we'd mention we were thinking of doing a print humor magazine, people would get very excited, and share fond memories of *National Lampoon* or *SPY*. And then we'd get excited too, forgetting for a second that all these people really meant was, "I used to love being in college." A time machine that transports you back to college? Now that's a business idea. But this? This is a recipe for heartbreak. Listen to me: what we're doing here will wear on you. Halfway through every article, you'll long to be back on Twitter. Because Twitter is freaking addictive. Print humor is more like a splinter, the kind that sort of aches.

Paper doesn't talk or move, and reading makes your brain sweat. (You can feel it now, can't you?) To laugh under those circumstances, you pretty much have to be high. So just hold on until pot is legal, right? Wrong. Even this isn't in our favor. Marijuana is considerably stronger now, so two puffs and you're too baked to follow anything. We might as well be telling jokes to a geranium.

Still — you're here, for now, and since you're here we want to say "thank you." We genuinely hope you enjoy this first issue. We worked hard on it, and tried to ignore all the little voices that said we should've done something useful with our skills, like gone to law school (writers) or become counterfeiters (artists).

Instead, we were bystanders — watching everything, staying quiet, taking notes. *The American Bystander* will not change the world, we guarantee it. But it will be harmless fun, for however long it lasts. I personally give us until Tuesday.

Freed from the burden of expecting success, our hearts are light. Here goes nothing — and who knows, life could surprise us. Maybe this Titanic will float.

.... ◆ ....

P.S. We are much more sanguine about the prospects for "Big Ship Radio," *The Bystander*'s prospective podcast.

Our marvelous Mr. McConnachie explains the premise: "We bought a WWII battleship and have converted it into a cruise ship. Mostly. Shortcuts were taken. The destination is Bermuda but the Captain can't seem to find it on any of his maps. So like the Flying Dutchman, it wanders the seas."

Will the ship ever reach safe harbor? Will the guys make their deadlines without my having to fly to New York and stand underneath their windows with a bullhorn? Subscribe to "Big Ship Radio" on iTunes, and find out. I've heard the first one, and it's aces.

SCOTT MARSHALL

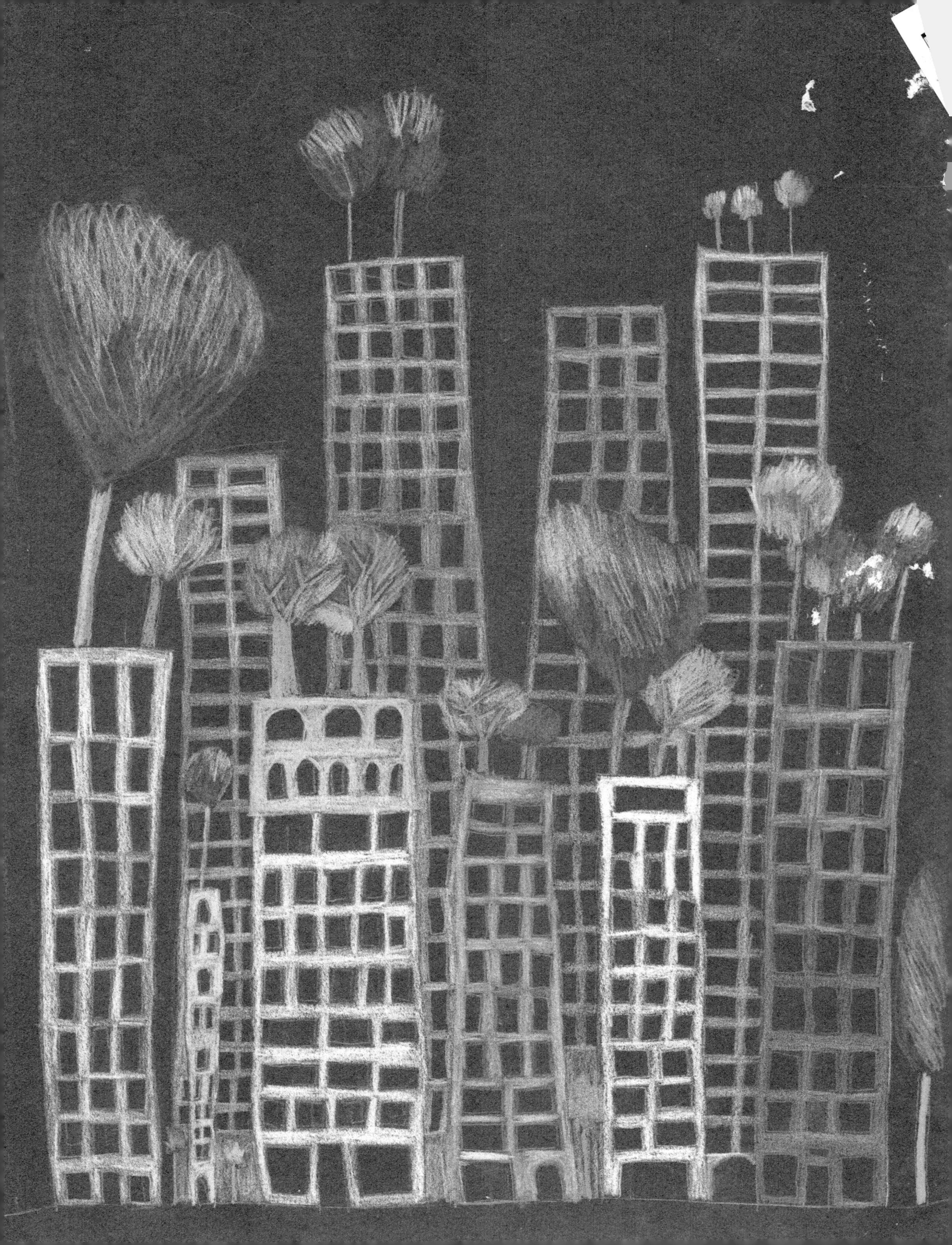

TABLE OF CONTENTS

Whole No. 1 • Fall 2015 • Americanbystander.org • 1619

"What exquisite pearls!"

SHORT STUFF

FEATURES

OUR FINE ARTISTS

Ron Barrett, Kate Beaton, Louisa Bertman, R.O. Blechman, Chris Bonno, M.K. Brown, John Caldwell, Roz Chast, Seymour Chwast, Liza Donnelly, Xeth Feinberg, Liana Finck, Emily Flake, Shary Flenniken, Patricia Gerber, Robert Grossman, Stefan Hagen, Ron Hauge, Danny Hellman, Farley Katz, Adam Koford, Ken Krimstein, Eugenia Loli, Scott Marshall, Ethan Persoff, Mimi Pond, Arnold Roth, Cris Shapan, Mark Simonson, Grant Snider, Edward Sorel, Akiko Stehrenberger, Tom Toro, D. Watson, Julia Wertz, Nathan Yoder, Steve Young, and Jack Ziegler.

COVER: *"Black Friday"* by Scott Marshall and Ethan Persoff, with thanks to D. Parker, M. Twain, H. Kurtzman, T. Southern, A. Poehler, E. May, M. Nichols, L. Bruce, F. Brice (Baby Snooks), S. Howard, D. Close, M. Short (Jiminy Glick), I. Coca, M.Mabley, G. Radner, R. Pryor, B. Keaton, W. Sykes, J. Winters, F. Wilson (Geraldine), L. Tomlin (Ernestine), T. Jones (Mr. Creosote), E. Kovacs, G. Marx, P. Bergman, and L. Buckley.

EDITORS
Brian McConnachie, Alan Goldberg, Michael Gerber

PUBLISHER
Michael Gerber

CONTRIBUTORS
Chris Austopchuk, Ron Barrett, Kate Beaton, R.O. Blechman, Chris Bonno, M.K. Brown, John Caldwell, Roz Chast, Seymour Chwast, River Clegg, Liza Donnelly, David Etkin, Xeth Feinberg, Liana Finck, Emily Flake, Shary Flenniken, Patricia Gerber, Joey Green, Robert Grossman, Stefan Hagen, Jack Handey, Dave Hanson, Ron Hauge, Danny Hellman, Daniel Immelwahr, Al Jean, Terry Jones, Farley Katz, Adam Koford, Ken Krimstein, Eugenia Loli, Scott Marshall, Sam Means, George Meyer, Sport Murphy, Mark O'Donnell, Michael O'Donoghue, Mallory Ortberg, Dennis Perrin, Ethan Persoff, Mimi Pond, Mike Reiss, Simon Rich, Arnold Roth, Mike Sacks, Jon Schwarz, Cris Shapan, Grant Snider, Edward Sorel, Frank Springer, Akiko Stehrenberger, Sloane Tanen, Tom Toro, Dirk Voetberg, D. Watson, Julia Wertz, Ellis Weiner, Nathan Yoder, Steve Young, Jack Ziegler.

ISSUE PATRONS
Evan Goldberg, Kate Powers, Bonnie Roche, Gregory & Patricia Gerber, Dennis O'Brien

Copyediting by Chuck Ferrara, with an initial read by Aryeh Cohen-Wade. All errors are Mike's fault because he loves to add stuff at the last minute (like this). *Thanks to* Tom Ruprecht, Ben Orlin, Mike Thornton, Jack Silbert, Kit Lively, R.J. Fried, Pat Reeder, and all cover/letters submittees. *Nameplate by* Mark Simonson. *Issue created by* Michael Gerber.

The AMERICAN BYSTANDER

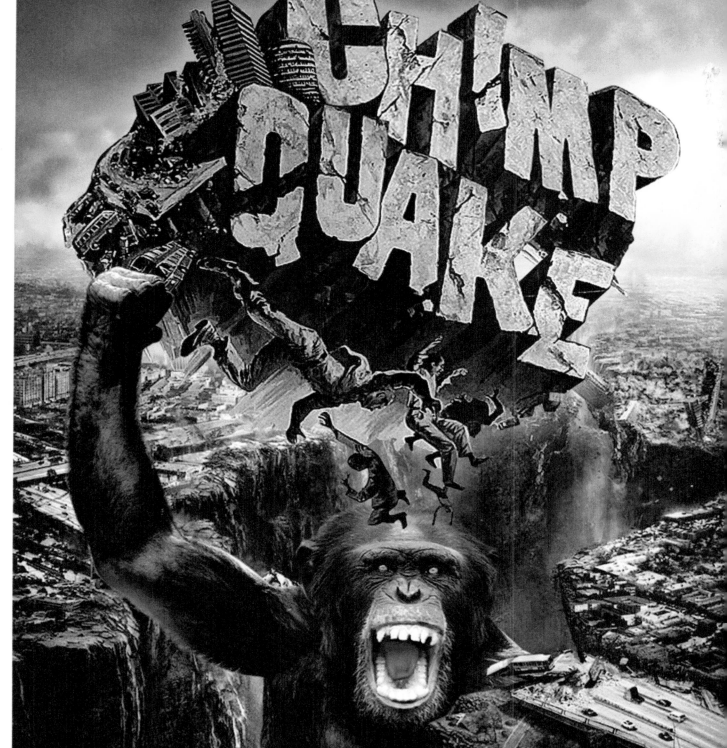

NOBODY COULD HAVE IMAGINED SUCH A THING

CHIMPQUAKE

BUT IT WAS BOUND TO HAPPEN EVENTUALLY

SYFY AND MEXAR S.A. PRESENT A SEITAN PRODUCTION "CHIMPQUAKE" STARRING PARKER STEVENSON EVE PLUMB INTRODUCING GUY FIERI AS "LOBO" WITH BRIAN BENBEN ROYCE APPLEGATE DELTA BURKE STEVEN FURST AND THE DALLAS COWBOY CHEERLEADERS WRITTEN BY STEVEN FURST EDITED BY TYRELL GANT VISUAL EFFECTS BY THE MONKEY FACTORY LLC SPECIAL EFFECTS BY MEXAR FX ESPECIAL CASTING BY SAMMY GLOTZ ART DIRECTOR CHUCK CONNORS JR PRODUCTION DESIGNER SHEREE FLICK DIRECTOR OF PHOTOGRAPHY LOUIS FESTICLES EXECUTIVE PRODUCER ART ESTEVEZ PRODUCED BY PEDRO ESTEVEZ DIRECTED BY HERIBERTO ESTEVEZ

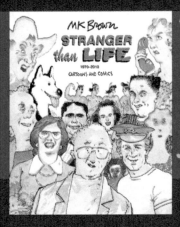

NEWS & NOTES

OF COURSE
I CAN'T SPEAK FOR
THE WHOLE STAFF...
CALDWELL

RON BARRETT is a New York bystander to the process of yet another transformation of the "modern day classic" children's book he illustrated, *Cloudy With a Chance of Meatballs*. After metamorphosing into two feature films and twelve Happy Meal plastic toys it's now being repackaged as a TV series on the Cartoon Network. He can only hope for the best.

His art for *Animals Should Definitely Not Wear Clothing* was exhibited at The Louvre's Musée des Arts Décoratifs (October 2015-February2016). The musée's report that the art was mistakenly hung upside-down proved to be a Parisian prank. What else can we expect from the nation that gave us poodles and pom-poms?

STEVE YOUNG writes, "Still learning how to 'make it on the outside' after being paroled from my Letterman show life sentence." In September, your editor was lucky enough to meet Steve after his fascinating presentation at The Cinefamily here in Los Angeles. Steve kept us all rapt for over an hour with rare film clips of vintage industrial musicals and a glimpse of the upcoming documentary.

At a recent event in Kansas City someone approached **TOM TORO** and asked him how he comes up with his cartoon ideas. He responded, "Who's that?" (It turned out not to be Tom Toro after all but a guy who vaguely resembles him. The real Tom Toro had gone home ten minutes earlier because his baby wasn't sleeping and there was an episode of *Inside Amy Schumer* that needed watching.)

D. WATSON sent along an e-mail that his wallet was stolen with all his credit cards in Ubekistan and he needs all his friends to send money to pay the hotel bill. He may be there for some time.

When she's not in post-production for her upcoming short *#Manmade,* (an animated commentary focusing on the demand side of child sex-trafficking in the U.S.), illustrative journalist **LOUISA BERTMAN** can be found writing visual letters to her *Vagina*, sharing *Tits*, or trying to decide which of the endless stream of political malcontents to skewer in her ongoing animated gif series, *#Dickheads*. (We're sensing a theme here, Louisa.)

Now splitting time between Burbank and Phoenix for a television show called *The List* (insert commuting joke here), **DAVE HANSON** spends his free time making mosaics of tile and glass — "even though I'm not technically a woman." Embrace the low T, Dave; we've seen your stuff and it's wonderful.

And finally, Editor **BRIAN** slipped in a few words just as we went to press, reiterating just exactly what we think we're trying to do: "This premiere issue of *The*

American Bystander is a collection of talented artists and writers working in *all* the forms available to them -- essays, features, columns, illustrations, short stories, panel cartoons, photography, comic strips and combinations thereof.

"As a publication, we're offering them a place to show their work. As a business we're creating a place where talent will be paid (never enough), while still keeping ownership of their work.

"We're tapping into a great resource: the strength and independence of the American character. And that of several Canadians as well. A few. Not enough to affect the title.

"The strength of this publication is in the verity of its contributors. We hope to be loose enough to be able to jump in over our heads and be brave enough to feel around in the dark --- but not in the basement where no one is wearing shoes and someone has set a bunch of mouse traps --- you can understand that.

Let us know what you think."

Well said, Brian. So hie thee to the website, folks — www.americanbystander.org — and do what web people do: drop us an email, sign up for updates. Whenever and however, **please spread the word**.

It's a whole new world out there. On the one hand, there's no corporate fat-cats looking to drop millions on a new humor magazine. But on the other, we don't need them anymore. *We can do it together.* In fact, we have to.

The Bystander's on Facebook (www.facebook.com/americanbystander/) and on Twitter, too (@Bystandertweets). We figure we need at least five thousand paying readers for this to change from a folly into a business. We believe in you…and in *The American Bystander*.

COMING NEXT ISSUE: "The Dracula Letters" by McConnachie & Handey…Merrill Markoe's Teenage Acid Diary…A *Madeline* parody by Sean Kelly…Shary Flenniken's "Leashless in Seattle"…Mimi Pond, B.K. Taylor…Who knows what else will hunker forth, if we really crack the whip?

"Connie and the Fifth Time" by Brian McConnachie. @ 2015 Brian McConnachie.
"Treasure Hunting" by Julia Wertz. © 2015 by Julia Wertz.
"Dear Trusting Sir or Madam" by Steve Young. © 2015 by Steve Young.
"Preparation Anxiety" by Joey Green is adapted from the book **Last-Minute Survival Secrets: 128 Ingenious Tips to Endure the Coming Apocalypse and Other Minor Inconveniences by Joey Green.** This piece © 2015 by Joey Green.
"A Day in the Life of an Empowered Female Heroine" by Mallory Ortberg originally appeared at The-Toast.net. Reprinted with permission from the author. © 2013 by Mallory Ortberg.
"David Hockney's Tricks of the Masters," by Mike Reiss. © 2015 by Mike Reiss.
"Truly Blessed" by Jonathan Schwarz. © 2015 by Jonathan Schwarz.
"Call Me Mr. Lucky" by Dave Hanson. © 2015 by Dave Hanson.
"Fast and Loose" by George Meyer. © 2015 by George Meyer.
"Inspirational Animal Stories #1: The Motivational Tiger" by Brian McConnachie. © 2015 by Brian McConnachie.
"Sizing Up Champagne" by Mike "Sport" Murphy. © 2015 by Mike Murphy.
"Boyfriend" by Liana Finck. © 2015 by Liana Finck.
"A Brief History of Sandwich Theory" by Sam Means and Daniel Immerwahr. © 2015 by Sam Means and Daniel Immerwahr.
"Kids' Advice to Lincoln," by Jack Handey. © 2015 by Jack Handey.
"The Painter of Pain" by Ron Barrett. © 2015 by Ron Barrett.
"The Old Codger's Almanac" by Mark O'Donnell and Christopher Austopchuk originally appeared in *The New York Times*. Reprinted with permission of the illustrator and the estate of the author. © Mark O'Donnell and Christopher Austopchuk.
"The Road Warrior (The Radio Version)" by George Meyer. © 2015 by George Meyer.
"Second Base" by Brian McConnachie and Frank Springer originally appeared in the privately circulated 1982 pilot issue of *The American Bystander*. Reprinted with permission of Brian McConnachie. © 1981 by Brian McConnachie.
"The Truthful Telephone" by Terry Jones originally appeared in the book *Evil Machines.* © 2015 by Terry Jones.
"Yardwork" by Brian McConnachie. © 2015 by Brian McConnachie.
"Interview: Josh Alan Friedman" by Mike Sacks originally appeared at www.dangerousminds.net. Reprinted with permission of the author and subject. © 2014 by Mike Sacks.
"Elevator Conversations" by River Clegg. © 2015 by River Clegg.
"Goodnight Moon, Hello Martini" by Sloane Tanen and Stefan Hagen. © 2015 Sloane Tanen and Stefan Hagen.
"Post-Life Survey" by Roz Chast. © 2015 by Roz Chast.
"Back of the Bus" by Al Jean. © 2015 by Al Jean.
"Atlas Slugged Again" by Ellis Weiner originally appeared as an ebook. Reprinted with permission of the author. © 2011 by Ellis Weiner.
"Chekhov's Mother" by R.O. Blechman. © 2015 by R.O. Blechman.
"Are You a Middle-Aged Hipster?" by Mimi Pond. © 2015 by Mimi Pond.
"Notes From *Janitorgod*" by Dennis Perrin. © 2013 by Dennis Perrin.
"John Wilcock: The New York Years" by Ethan Persoff and Scott Marshall originally appeared at www.boingboing.net. Reprinted with permission of the authors. © 2015 by Ethan Persoff and Scott Marshall.
"Mr. Johnny Bullwhip" by Brian McConnachie. © 2015 by Brian McConnachie.
"A Dream of Consequence (Is Hard to Find)" by M.K. Brown originally appeared in the privately circulated 1982 pilot issue of *The American Bystander*. Reprinted with permission of the artist. © 1981 by M.K. Brown.
All one-panels, illustrations, and spots are © their creators. "Live Loud Tiger" was created by Nathan Yoder for Sevenly, and is used with permission from both the artist and owner.

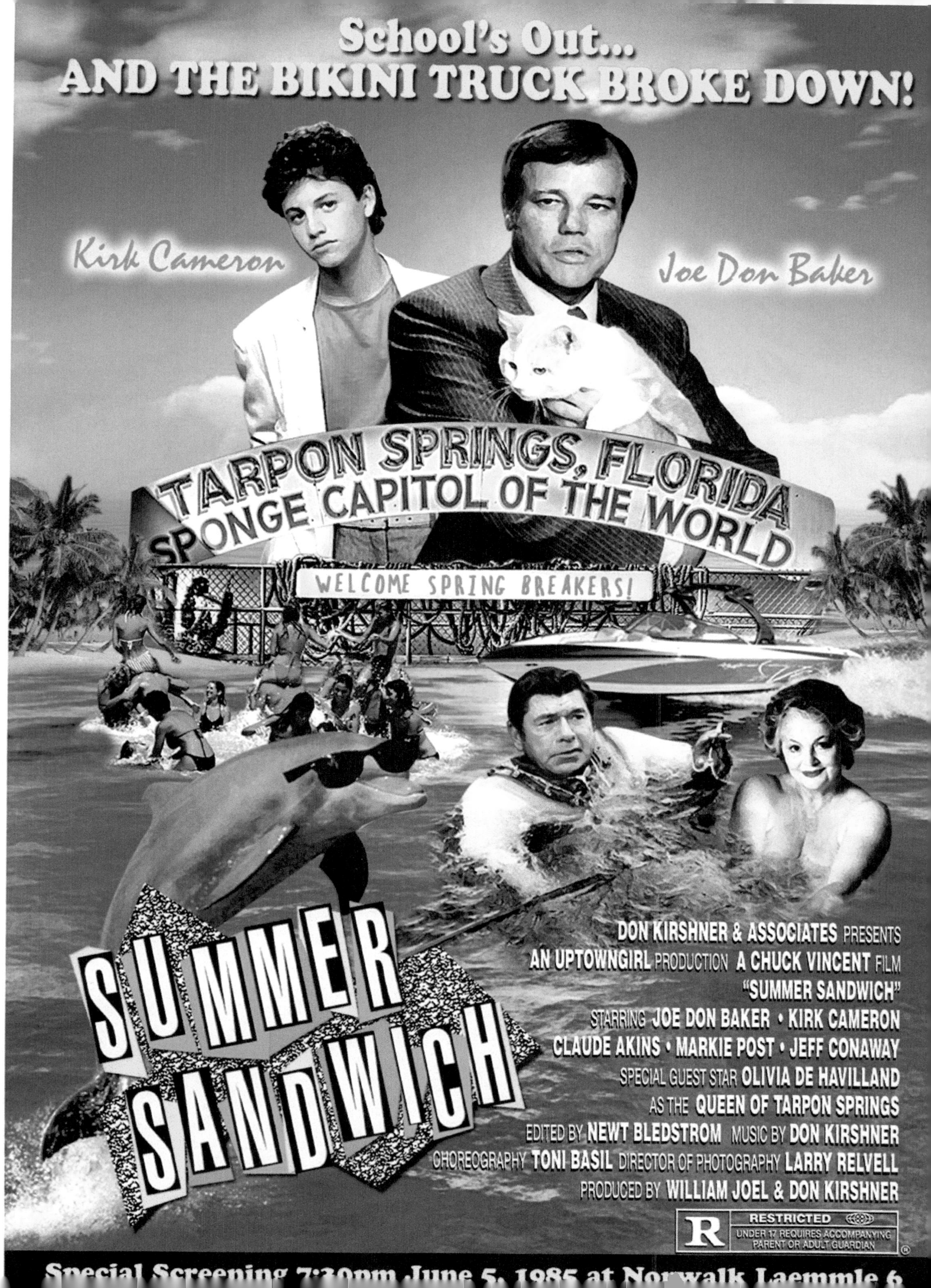

School's Out...
AND THE BIKINI TRUCK BROKE DOWN!
Kirk Cameron
Joe Don Baker
TARPON SPRINGS, FLORIDA
SPONGE CAPITOL OF THE WORLD
WELCOME SPRING BREAKERS!
SUMMER SANDWICH
DON KIRSHNER & ASSOCIATES PRESENTS
AN UPTOWNGIRL PRODUCTION A CHUCK VINCENT FILM
"SUMMER SANDWICH"
STARRING JOE DON BAKER • KIRK CAMERON
CLAUDE AKINS • MARKIE POST • JEFF CONAWAY
SPECIAL GUEST STAR OLIVIA DE HAVILLAND
AS THE QUEEN OF TARPON SPRINGS
EDITED BY NEWT BLEDSTROM MUSIC BY DON KIRSHNER
CHOREOGRAPHY TONI BASIL DIRECTOR OF PHOTOGRAPHY LARRY RELVELL
PRODUCED BY WILLIAM JOEL & DON KIRSHNER
R RESTRICTED
UNDER 17 REQUIRES ACCOMPANYING PARENT OR ADULT GUARDIAN
Special Screening 7:30pm June 5, 1985 at Norwalk Laemmle 6

Spoof by **CRIS SHAPAN & DAVIN WOOD**

The 50 FUNNIEST AMERICAN WRITERS*

An Anthology of Humor from Mark Twain to The Onion

* *According to* ANDY BOROWITZ

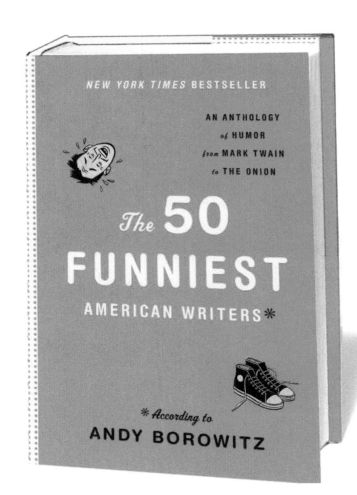

featuring

David Sedaris Sloane Crosley
George Saunders **E. B. White**
Ian Frazier Nora Ephron
Calvin Trillin **Dorothy Parker**
James Thurber Susan Orlean
Veronica Geng **Bernie Mac**

and many more!

A new book and e-book from
THE LIBRARY OF AMERICA

BY BRIAN McCONNACHIE

CONNIE AND THE FIFTH TIME

I was not spying. I do not spy. Now or ever.

I'll never forget the first time I fell off the roof. *WhamThump! EEEOwww!*

It happened fast. One minute you're up on the roof, and the next thing you know, you're so not there at all anymore. *Whump!*

You don't get a lot of time to really examine the moments from when you've completely departed the roof but you haven't yet arrived upon the ground. It can really get away from you. Like, snap.

However, the second time I fell off of the roof, thump! Damn! It did seem to slow down more. I remember thinking, well, here I go; I'm falling off of the roof again. And I'm looking around for anything to grab onto. Then I happen to notice a lot of leaves in the gutters and make a mental note: don't forget to clean the gutters when you get back from the hospital. And for God's sake, try and be a little more careful up there.

By the third and fourth time I fell off the roof, it started slowing down quite a bit. I was hearing dogs bark and birds chirp and I could identify three different kinds of leaves: maple, elm and oak.

Now the sixth time I fell off the roof. *Thump Crapdamnpisshell.* I remember thinking, I should quit going up on the roof. But I did manage to savor the time immediately following the clawing desperately at the roof tiles but before the actual hitting the ground. I thought to myself, Hey, I'm in the air. It was that time I remember seeing four or five sparrows chasing a crow. The sparrows had good, quick looping moves and took turns pecking and all Mr. Crow could do was try and get the hell away. I wondered if any of them noticed me, still in the air, my arms flailing, and pondered, what's that thing doing? It was five sparrows I now recall. Then it was over pretty quickly. But while you're in the air, you learn to make that time last because, believe me, before you know it, *WHAM! Helldevilcrapfuck!* It's over.

Now the seventh, eighth and ninth times, I have to admit, sort of ran together. The tenth time really hurt when I landed. I guess we're talking about re-breaking the same bones again and again. But also the tenth time seemed to me by far the longest

I spent in the air. There were lots of clouds that looked like they just came out of the dryer they were so white, clean and fluffy. I saw distinctive shapes. One of them had the body of a lion and the face of the Gerber Baby but then it turned into a sort of reclining buffalo. And then into a woozy version of Monument Valley. And then I think I saw the same crow but it was being chased by a whole different bunch of birds. Swallows?

Now if you're going to ask, what's with you going up on a steeply pitched Victorian farm house roof, sitting on the roof, walking around on the roof, traipsing around the

BRIAN McCONNACHIE is the Editor of *The American Bystander*.

roof and generally acting like the star from the show, *Fiddler on the Roof*, you're going to get a blank stare from me. And if there's one handy, I'll pick up a magazine and impatiently flip through it — rear to front — shaking my head that you don't get it and you're never going to get it and we don't have anything to talk about.

If you think I'm going to go into the "…there are two kinds of people in the world…" you're even more off-base.

However, if you were to ask me, by the way, what happened on the fifth time you fell off of the roof? Now that would get my attention. I would slowly close the magazine and put it down and regard you with a whole new level of respect.

Yes, that was no casual omission. That was the time Connie yelled at me.

When I fall off the roof, it's usually down the east side of the house onto the driveway near the juniper bushes and the grease trap. But on the fifth time, I went down the west side. And I fell past Connie's window. Connie is my wife; she has her own room. As I went by, I might have glanced in but it was too dark to really see anything and I certainly wasn't trying to see anything. I

was falling off the roof for God's sake. Then I landed on the slate walkway near the irises. A few minutes later she came out of the house and stood over me for a while before she said anything.

"You were spying on me, weren't you? Don't ever do that again, hon. It'll really make me crazy and you don't want me crazy." Then she headed out the driveway, got into somebody's waiting van and took off. I couldn't see who was driving.

Spying on her!

As best I could, I yelled after her that spying is not exactly something you achieve by trying to see in someone's window you're falling past at that incredible speed that falling things all travel at. I'm certain anyone who has ever had any success at spying can verify that fact. Spying is a real dig-your-heels-in kind of chore. It's not done on the fly. If I had been able at that moment to drag myself into the house, I would have gotten the Policy Director of the CIA on the phone to verify that their spies do not jump off roofs or out a window to grab a peek into another window. Even for a government that's not exactly known for being cost-conscious, that would be a pretty inefficient use of their highly trained personnel.

I was not spying. I do not spy. Now or ever. But that was the fifth time.

I had to make a compromise with Dr. Goldberg or he swore he wouldn't be my doctor anymore. I had to promise I'd only go up on the roof if there was an absolute roof emergency. Or if there was a flood and the whole house was floating away. Connie and I could sit on one of the dormers tightly holding onto one another. A little scary but romantic.

We didn't go too deeply into what would constitute a "roof emergency," but as soon as they take these screws out of my jaw and forehead and the brace comes off of my head, I'll be able to sit at the kitchen table and make up a list of what would "constitute" a "roof emergency." A loose weather vane would probably qualify. That'd be one.

…that is, if we had a weather vane up there…

BY JULIA WERTZ

TREASURE HUNTING

If you were to take a walk with me through NYC, this is what you'd experience

1) A DISCUSSION OF REAL LIFE ISSUES THAT NEED ANALYZING AND/OR CRITICIZING.

...AND THAT'S WHY I DON'T BOTHER CHECKING FACEBOOK EVENTS ANYMORE.

I ENJOY PERUSING THE EVENTS JUST FOR THE ENORMOUS SENSE OF RELIEF I GET KNOWING I DON'T HAVE TO SUFFER THROUGH ANY OF THEM.

2) EATING AT A CHEAP, UNCROWDED RESTAURANT THAT PLAYS MUSIC AT A REASONABLE VOLUME, OR GETTING STREET VENDOR FOOD TO EAT IN THE PARK.

I DON'T KNOW WHY THERE AREN'T MASS RIOTS AGAINST LOUD MUSIC IN RESTAURANTS. WE DON'T HAVE TO TOLERATE LIVING LIKE THAT!! FUCKIN' SAVAGES.

3) LISTENING TO ME TELL YOU A BUNCH OF RANDOM FACTS I KNOW, PROBABLY FROM SOME BOOK I READ OR A DORKY PODCAST I LISTENED TO.

PINBALL WAS BANNED IN NYC UNTIL 1978. IT WAS A "PINBALL PROHIBITION," AND OFFICIALS WOULD SMASH THE MACHINES WITH SLEDGEHAMMERS, AND DUMP THEM IN THE RIVER. THEY'RE PROBABLY STILL DOWN THERE! A WATERY PINBALL GRAVEYARD...

BUT WHILE ALL THAT IS GOING ON, THIS IS WHAT I'M DOING UNBEKNOWNST TO YOU:

1) OGLING THE DETAILED ARCHITECTURE OF OLD BUILDINGS.

IF ONLY I KNEW HOW TO SCUBA DI...

OOOOH, THAT DETAILED CROWN MOULDING ON THAT BROWNSTONE!

2) SCANNING THE GROUND FOR IRON WORKS STAMPED BRASS NAME PLATES ON BASEMENT SIDEWALK HATCHES.

B & S
40 WYCKOFF AVE BKLYN N.Y.
IRON WORKS

3) LOOKING AT APARTMENT AND BUILDING DOORS FOR ANTIQUE ORNATE DOOR HARDWARE.

4) LOOKING FOR PATCHES OF OLD ARCHITECTURE PARTIALLY OBSCURED BY RECENT STYLES.

LOOK, IT LOOKS LIKE THE NEW STYLE IS EATING THE OLD ONE. MY CARTOONIST PAL TOM K. CALLS THAT "SHARKITECTURE."

5) MAKING A MENTAL NOTE OF EVERY TYPE OF FIRE ALARM, ANTIQUE OR NEW, ON THE STREET CORNERS.

6) SPOTTING PATCHES OF OLD SLATE SIDEWALK, OR HIDDEN COBBLESTONES PEAKING THROUGH A POTHOLE IN THE ROAD.

7) AND ALL THE TIME, I'M LOOKING AT APARTMENTS, AND IMAGINING WHAT IT'D BE LIKE TO LIVE IN THEM, AND TO SIT ON THE FIRE ESCAPE OVER A SMALL STORE ON A CROWDED STREET, AND PEOPLE WATCH ALL DAY.

I BASICALLY SPEND THE WHOLE WALK IN CURRENT NEW YORK CITY LOOKING FOR EVIDENCE OF THE PAST NEW YORK CITY.

I'M PERPETUALLY FANTASIZING ABOUT A TIME I NEVER EXPERIENCED, AND IMAGINING A LIFE I'LL NEVER LIVE.

©JULIA WERTZ

JULIA WERTZ *(@Julia_Wertz) is the writer/cartoonist of* **Museum of Mistakes, Drinking at the Movies** *and* **The Infinite Wait & Other Stories.** *She does a monthly history comic for* **The New Yorker.**

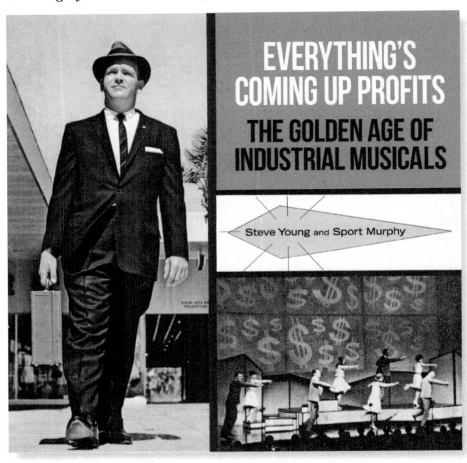

BY STEVE YOUNG

DEAR TRUSTING SIR OR MADAM...

It feels good to finally tell you the truth.

I hope this letter finds you well. My name is Philip Nobaro. I am one of the top practitioners of the so-called "Nigerian Prince" scam, in which greedy, gullible people are induced to transfer funds in expectation of a large undeserved payment. Over the past ten years I have made over 88 million U.S. dollars through such fraud! My records indicate that some of this money came from you. I am sorry. But that's not why I am writing.

Recently, I encountered an unforeseen problem. My vast wealth is on deposit in the Bank of Cyprus, and due to the financial crisis in Cyprus, the money is now unavailable for withdrawal!

I'm going to assist a nice man in Nigeria.

There is a way to get my ill-gotten gains out of the Bank of Cyprus, but I need your help, for which you will be amply compensated.

A timely, discreet $10,000 bribe to a Bank of Cyprus official will effect the transfer of the $88 million to the U.S. bank account of a third party such as yourself. Please reply immediately with your bank account number and routing information, and I will tell you where to wire $10,000 with which I may pay the bribe. Once the $88 million is safely in your bank account, I will gladly remit to you a $10 million fee!

Now, the irony of this proposal is not lost on me. But what else can I do? For you, at least, there is finally "closure." In truth, for both of us it is "win/win."

But you may be asking yourself, "What if this is also a scam? What if the $10,000 I send will not secure me $10 million, but instead will disappear, leaving me shamed, impoverished, and without recourse?"

Come on, what are the chances?

Although I shall tell you in confidence, that if I were to enact such a clever, multi-layered scheme, I would expect to gain at least $150 million from "dupes" like yourself, which would then be frozen in the next banking crisis, most likely in Luxembourg or Malta, according to my contacts at the Bank of Cyprus. To extract these frozen funds would require a bribe of $20,000, and would of course mean an even larger fee for you: $20 million!

Naturally, this excellent windfall will only come to pass if you act now and assist me with my current fraud.

I am sensing hesitation.

Frankly, I am impressed by your skepticism. Unlike most of my victims, you have learned from your past sorry experiences. Yes, you have correctly divined that the two foregoing scenarios I detailed were both frauds. Clearly, you have the makings of a fellow criminal mastermind!

I may therefore be so bold as to invite you into the inner circle of financial chicanery. Full disclosure: I am actually working with the Bank of Cyprus and a shadowy consortium of crime syndicates to pull off the ultimate global swindle, and we would love to have you on our team. While I cannot divulge the details of the scam in this email, I can tell you that in exchange for your buy-in amount of $50,000, your share of the proceeds will be in excess of ten billion dollars!

This time I am not lying. We are beyond all that now. It feels good to finally tell you the truth.

Your assistance in the past has been invaluable, and I pray that I can count on you again. Reply promptly so that you may soon receive ten billion dollars! Or, if you are not in a position to contribute $50,000, the $10,000 and $20,000 options are still available, though as I mentioned, they are fraudulent and will get you nothing.

With respect and affection,
PHILIP NOBARO
Central Bank of Nigeria
(really a Lagos internet cafe)
(see, no more lies!)

STEVE YOUNG *(@pants_steve) has written for* **Late Night With David Letterman,** **The Simpsons** *and many other venues. His latest is* **Everything's Coming Up Profits,** *a book on industrial musicals written with Sport Murphy.*

BY JOEY GREEN

PREPARATION ANXIETY

Chance of a quake in LA before 2018 is 99%. Where you live, maybe zombies or sharknado

Call me crazy, but I've done nothing whatsoever to prepare for the inevitable zombie apocalypse, alien invasion, and melting of the polar ice caps destined to turn our happy little planet into Dante's fifth circle of hell sometime next Thursday. So when a Polar Vortex knocks out the electricity for hundreds of miles in every direction, making my ten-speed blender and microwave oven completely useless, when a torrential Frankenstorm drenches all my firewood, and when I realize that silly me neglected to fill the propane tank for the barbecue grill, how, you may ask, will I ever stay warm and cook up a box of macaroni and cheese to brighten up my Doomsday?

For starters, I'll pop open a bag of Doritos, which stay nice and dry in the Mylar bag, and then use the corn chips as kindling to light a fire. The crushed dry corn chips, saturated with oil, burn long enough and strong enough to dry wet firewood and get a campfire going. I call them Genuine Flaming Hot Doritos. By the way, if you want a romantic evening and you don't have a fireplace, just turn to your loved one and whisper, "Honey, what do you say we pop open a bag of Doritos?"

I don't own a canoe or an inflatable motorized life raft, but should floodwater come raging down my street, I won't be waiting helplessly on my roof for a helicopter to rescue me. I'll simply remove my bedroom door from its hinges, strap fifty empty 2-liter soda bottles to one side with duct tape, and go floating merrily down the stream. But not before setting a folding beach chair on top of it for comfort and creating an oar by unscrewing a broomstick from the bristles and duct-taping a Ping-Pong paddle to one end of it.

If the Martians invade and they spray all that noxious Martian vapor around, which could happen any moment, or if you acci-dentally find yourself at some big protest like Occupy Walmart, and you get a face full of tear gas, pepper spray, or Glade air freshener, you'll need a gas mask—pronto. If you don't happen to carry a gas mask wherever you go, you can saturate a bandana with vinegar and hold it up in front of your face. Or, to fashion a more stylish gas mask, use a pair of scissors to cut a clean, empty plastic soda bottle in half on a diagonal, discard the bottom half, turn the top half upside-down, and fill it with cotton balls. Pour in vinegar to dampen the cotton, and hold the bottle to cover your nose and mouth. Poof! Instant gas mask—and a trendsetting fashion statement to boot. The vinegar neutralizes those nasty fumes and, with a little luck, may even repel those nasty Martians.

Have you ever fallen off a cruise ship in the middle of the ocean (or been pushed overboard by a spurned lover or jealous husband) and suddenly realized, "Oops! I don't have a life vest!"? If that scenario seems highly unlikely, consider this: The chances of that cruise ship smashing unexpectedly into an errant iceberg, getting hit by a tsunami and flipping upside down, or capsizing after the drunken captain steers too close to shore and collides into underwater rocks are better than the odds of catching the common cold (based on statistics I recently fabricated to instill fear). But when you do find yourself in that unfortunate situation, you can easily fashion a life vest while treading water—if you remove a shoelace from one of your soggy shoes and retrieve two condoms from your back pocket.

Unwrap the first condom and inflate it like a balloon. When the condom reaches the size of a watermelon, knot the free end. Tie one end of the shoelace above the knot. Repeat with the second condom. Slip the shoelace around your waist, and position the inflated condoms so you look like Jane Russell. The water displacement created by the buoyant and surprisingly durable latex balloons will keep you safely afloat—demonstrating that condoms can save your life in more ways than one.

By the way, a condom also doubles as a waterproof container for matches, a waterproof case for a cell phone, and when placed over the muzzle of rifle, a sheath to keep rainwater out of the barrel. In fact, during the Vietnam War, Navy SEALs used condoms as sheaths to keep fuse igniters dry and ready, which, I'm told, is the sole reason why they carried condoms.

Yes, hundreds of quirky yet ingenious survival techniques lie hidden in everyday household items—proving there's no need to rely on months of preparation and expensive equipment because it's just as easy to survive by the seat of your pants. Should all hell break loose in the wake of a major disaster or calamity, simply embrace your inner MacGyver and make a radio antenna with a Slinky, revive a dead car battery with aspirin, and improvise an alarm system with dental floss. In a pinch, you can disinfect a wound with Listerine, boost a cell phone signal with an empty soda can, and build an emergency tiki torch with petroleum jelly and a tampon.

Just because we're living in a constant state of super-ultra-hyper-red-alert doesn't mean you have to build a Costco in your basement. To survive all those imminent earthquakes, hurricanes, and coups d'état, you can filter and purify puddle water with a bandana and iodine, treat dehydration with a disposable diaper, and splint a broken leg with a pizza box and Bubble Wrap. All you need is a healthy dose of American ingenuity. And perhaps a paperclip and a pair of panty hose.

JOEY GREEN *(@authorjoeygreen) has written over fifty books, including* **Last-Minute Survival Secrets: 128 Ingenious Tips to Endure the Coming Apocalypse and Other Minor Inconveniences.** *Visit him at www.joeygreen.com.*

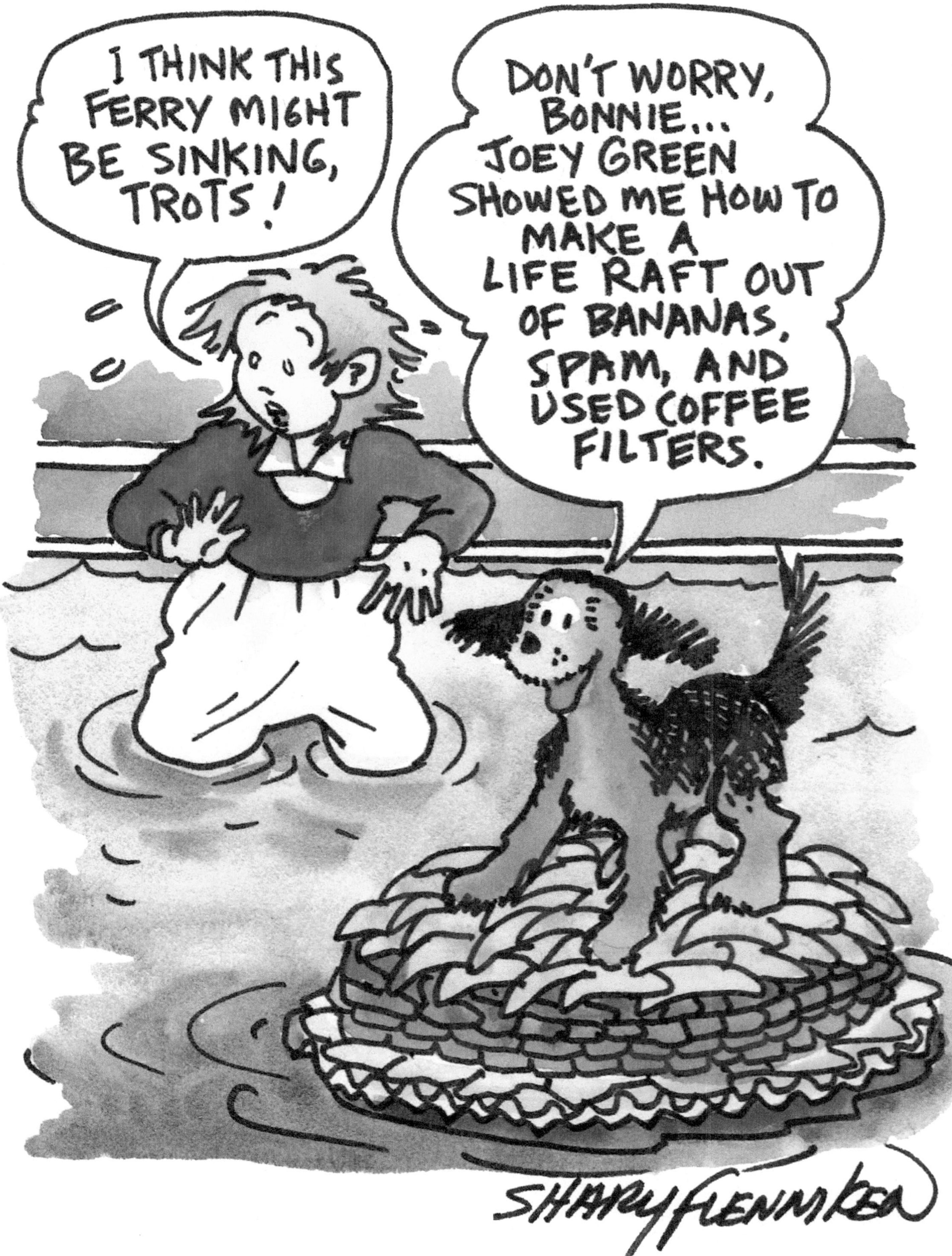
I THINK THIS FERRY MIGHT BE SINKING, TROTS!
DON'T WORRY, BONNIE... JOEY GREEN SHOWED ME HOW TO MAKE A LIFE RAFT OUT OF BANANAS, SPAM, AND USED COFFEE FILTERS.
SHARY FLENNIKEN

SHARY FLENNIKEN

"In Texts from Jane Eyre Mallory Ortberg hilariously proves that she understands fictional characters better then they understand themselves. She makes me laugh like no one else."
—RAINBOW ROWELL, bestselling author of Eleanor & Park and Fangirl
TEXTS FROM JANE EYRE
And Other Conversations with Your Favorite Literary Characters
MALLORY ORTBERG

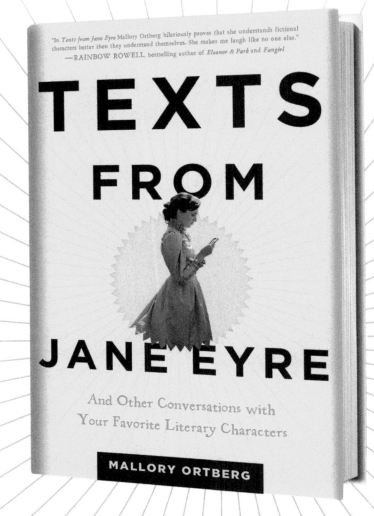

BY MALLORY ORTBERG

A DAY IN THE LIFE OF AN EMPOWERED FEMALE HEROINE

She woke up like she did every day: slowly pulling her motorcycle helmet off, then shaking her head slowly back and forth to reveal a long, blond ponytail. Everyone gasped. "That's right," she said, kicking the winning football goal before sliding into a sheer, sexy camisole under a blazer and playing as hard as she worked, "I've been a girl this whole time." One of the guys, the real sexy one, shook his head in slow motion, as if to say "wh-wh-wh-whaaat?" You know the kind. His mouth was kind of open while he did it. He was totally blown away.

She walked off the field, and she knew everyone was looking at her butt, and she totally loved it. "Sorry, boys," she called out over her super-sexy shoulder. She always called men boys, because she knew what gender was. Now she was carrying a briefcase and wearing a pencil skirt and sex glasses. She was at law.

"Your Honor," she said, and the Honor paid attention, "I'd like to win this case," and she totally did, she totally beat that busted-looking male lawyer who had the mushy face and wore suits that didn't fit. She gave a little fist-pump, because even though she's tough, she's still relatable. "Girl power," she said, high-fiving her curly-haired friend, who had just appeared behind her.

"Girl, you need a drink," her curly-haired friend said, "and I need a man." She laughed because her curly-haired friend didn't really get it yet, but she was getting there.

.... ◆ ....

She strolled up to the bar and planted a firm-yet-sexy pump-encased foot down on the rail. The bartender looked at her and started pulling out little frilly umbrellas and Malibu and speared slices of pineapple to make some kind of girl drink, but she held up her hand. "A whiskey," she said, her voice low in her throat. "Neat."

Behind her the pool table exploded. Every man in the bar immediately grew a beard. The jukebox made a record-scratching sound, even though it was an mp3-playing jukebox.

Her lawyer partner was there too. "Buy you a drink?" he asked.

"I can't be bought," she said. Later, after they did it, she slipped out of bed and briskly put on her clothes.

"You're leaving?" he asked, full of feelings.

"Sorry, babe," she said, turning to leave. "You knew what this was." She threw a thong at him, to remember her by. It was totally awesome, the way he wanted to be her boyfriend but she was too busy and cool to care. "Thanks for all the doing it. But I have to go win a karate tournament."

.... ◆ ....

"Yeah, I get it," she said. "Like a contest. Like a boys against the girls thing."

"Not exactly...there's no reason to make this a conte–"

"Like a contest," she said firmly. "Girls versus guys. Prove once and for all who's really the toughest."

"I don't see what this has to do with toughness," he began.

"The girls are totally going to win," she said, "You're a bunch of sexists."

She could win at everything. She could change a tire and dance in a ballgown in the same ten minutes. Maybe with a little streak of grease over her cheekbone, to remind you that she was tough and beautiful, and also to remind you how good her cheekbones were. Now she was wearing a pretty dress but combat boots underneath it, and she also had a gun, to fight sexism. She looked so good. She kicked a guy in the face, and she didn't even care.

"Feminism," she said to herself, and then put on some red lipstick. "Just because I'm a feminist doesn't mean I don't like to look good." Then she kicked another guy through a window, and he fell all the way. He was probably dead. She had like four guns strapped right on her boobs.

.... ◆ ....

"I'm sorry, Miss, but we really do have to go–"

"It's Doctor, actually," she smirked. The guys were totally shocked. They'd been talking about the doctor they were supposed to meet like it was some old guy, but it was her the whole time. "According to this scroll, all the prophecies are going to explode," she explained. "Let me run some tests in my hacking lab. I'm a very important scientist." She had so many abs, too. So many abs.

"I can hold my own in the bedroom and the boardroom," she said to no one, and to everyone. "You should never underestimate me." She took off her blond ponytail and shook her hair loose; there was another blonde ponytail underneath it. ♟

MALLORY ORTBERG *(@malelis) is co-founder of the feminist site The-Toast.net and the author of the 2014 bestseller,* **Texts From Jane Eyre.** *She has recently become "Dear Prudence" at Slate.com.*

BY MIKE REISS

DAVID HOCKNEY'S TRICKS OF THE MASTERS

Hello, I'm David Hockney, a painter best known for such works as "L.A. Swimming Pool, No. 1" and "L.A. Swimming Pool, No. 718". In my first book, *Secret Knowledge*, I theorized that our greatest painters relied on "tricks": Velasquez used the camera obscura; Ingres employed lenses and mirrors; Vermeer drew a turkey by tracing around his outstretched hand. Am I calling the Old Masters "cheaters"? Of course not. I'm merely saying they are all lazy no-talent bastards. Here are new theories about the great men of art, excerpted from my forthcoming book *Good Grief—MORE Secret Knowledge*:

LEONARDO DA VINCI

The greatest mind of the Renaissance, da Vinci has been credited with so many inventions: the parachute, the glider, Snapple. Is it a stretch to believe that he also invented the Xerox machine? Could the vast number of faded sketches he left behind be the result of low toner? One can picture the great artist trying to run off another *Mona Lisa*, pumping florin after florin into his machine, only to read the sad news: *"papieri impacto grosso"* (Paper Jammed).

MICHELANGELO

How could one man create so staggeringly powerful a masterpiece as the Sistine Chapel? Tracing paper.

VAN GOGH

Vincent van Gogh was crazy...like a fox. He acted a bit daft, lopped off a bit of earlobe, and suddenly his painting of sunflowers is going for thirty-five million bucks. I believe his madness was no more real than my English accent. And such skepticism should extend to all arts. Was Beethoven deaf, or just not listening? Is Stevie Wonder blind, or does he just look cool in shades?

PIET MONDRIAN

This Dutch artist created beauty and elegance from stark arrangements of horizontals and verticals. I am certain he used an Etch A Sketch®. This popular children's toy can't draw a circle or write your name, but it can crank out Mondrians to beat the band. Sadly, any of Mondrian's original etch-a-sketchings would have been erased in the Amsterdam Earthquake of 1948.

SALVADOR DALI

With the image of a drooping, melted pocket watch, the Surrealist movement was born. But perhaps Dali was simply painting what he saw. If you've ever been to Spain in the summertime, you know it's bloody hot. But hot enough to melt a pocket watch? Sure, I guess so, why not?

JACKSON POLLOCK

You can't look at the throbbing, vibrant abstracts of this troubled artist and not think, "My kid brother could do that." Well, he did have a kid brother, Benjy Pollock. Is this proof he painted most of Jackson's works? To my mind, yes. I am also investigating other artists' kid brothers, including Skippy Kandinsky and Chu Chu Picasso.

JIMMY FALLON

I don't think he just "makes up" all that funny stuff he says on the *Tonight Show*. I believe other people write these jokes in advance, and then he reads them off cards of some sort.

DAVID HOCKNEY

I employ no tricks whatsoever. I merely paint pictures of swimming pools. And sell them to millionaires. Who own swimming pools.

MIKE REISS *has won four Emmys and a Peabody during his twenty-six years writing for* **The Simpsons.** *Reiss also co-created the animated series* **The Critic,** *and created Showtime's hit cartoon* **Queer Duck** *(about a gay duck).*

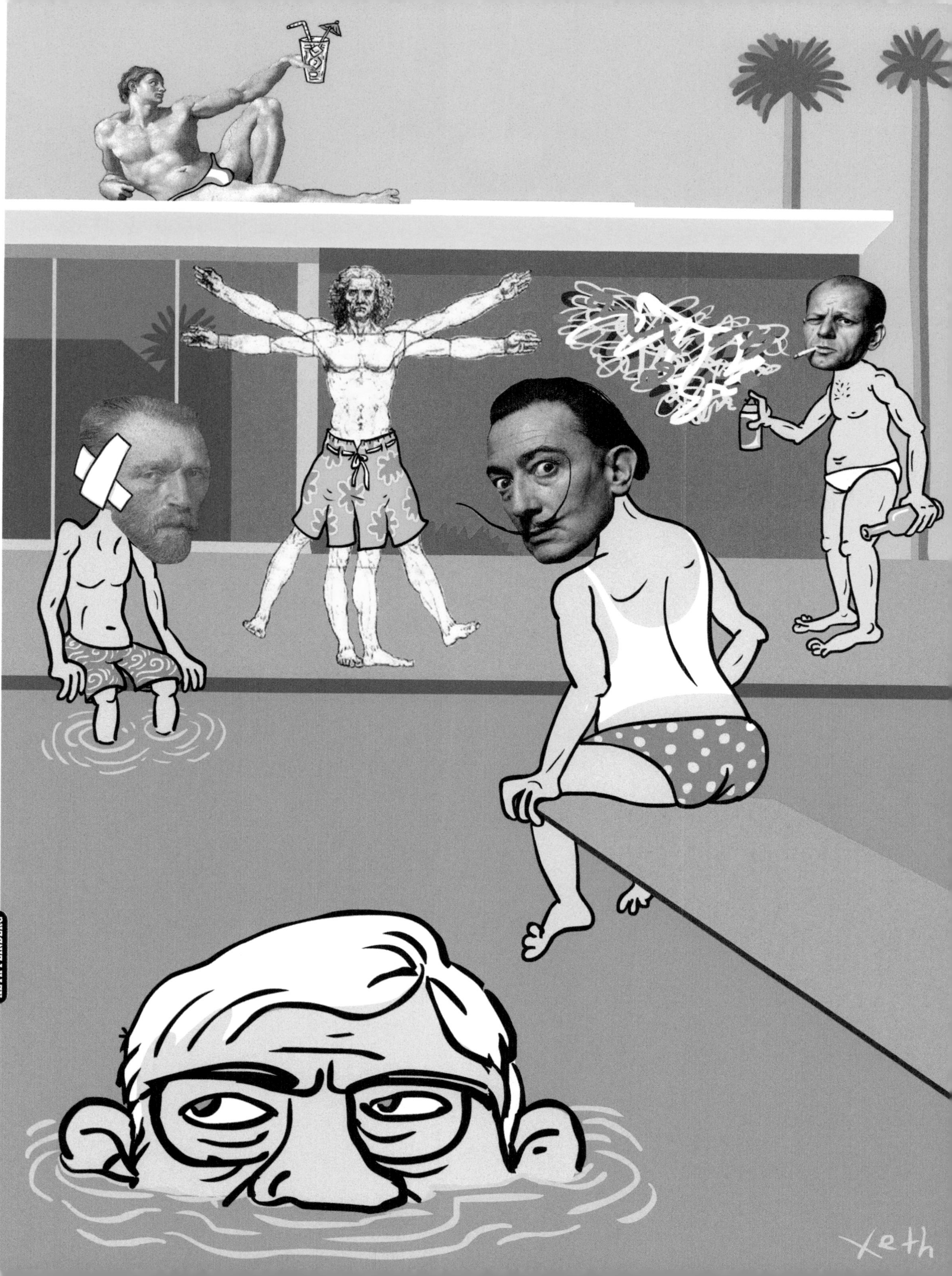
xeth

XETH FEINBERG

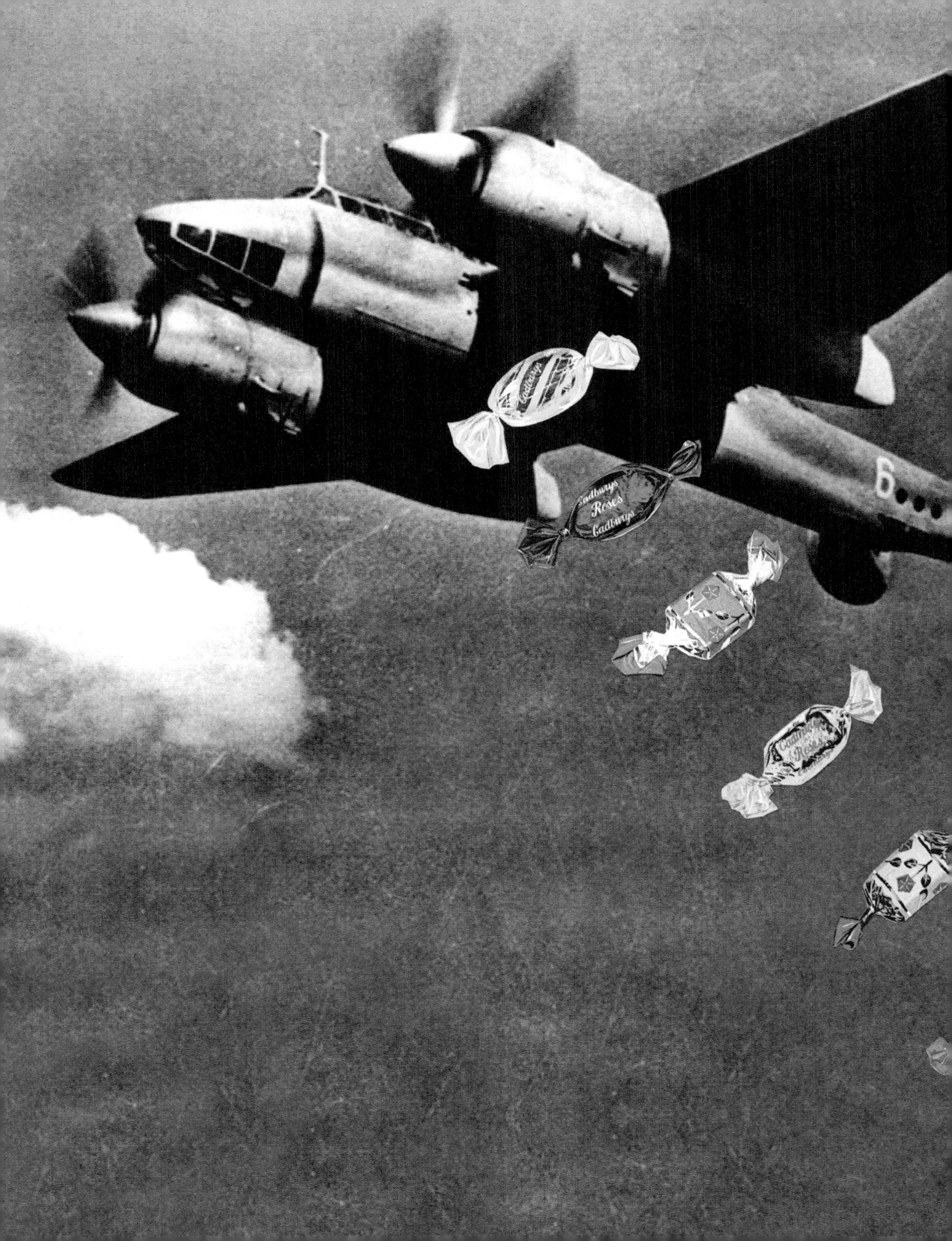
Cadburys
Cadburys
Roses
Cadburys
Cadburys
Roses

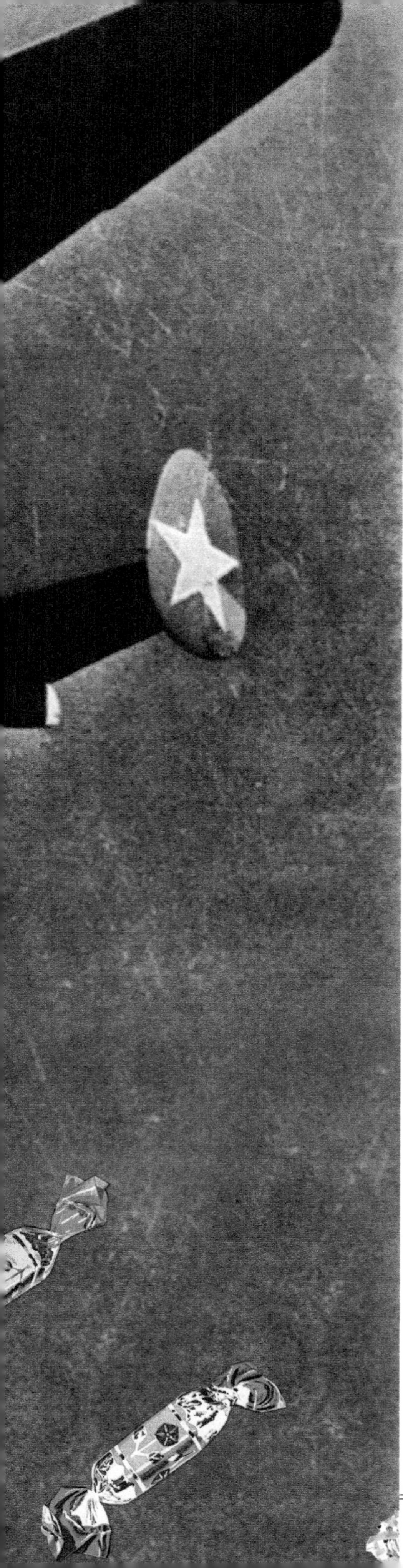

BY JON SCHWARZ

TRULY BLESSED

Even better than victory? Enemies who don't mind defeat one bit

One of the great things about being American is we're just lucky. For example: lots of other countries through history have killed millions of people—it sorta comes with the whole wealth and power thing. Afterwards, it's only natural for the killing country to feel bad. But when America's done what it had to do, we've always lucked out and picked people who turned out *not to mind being killed*.

I know you're thinking, "How can this be? Aren't people pretty much the same everywhere, especially when it comes to liking being alive?" Apparently not! And I have the data to prove it!

Take Afghanistan: In 2012, Steve Inskeep of NPR and Rajiv Chandrasekaran of *The Washington Post* discussed how Afghans haven't gotten all bent out of shape about a U.S. soldier massacring sixteen of them. Why? Because "human life is already cheap" way over there.

Well, what about Iraqis? Were they whiny bitches when we killed them? No way, according to Fred Kagan, architect of the Iraq "surge":

> *"If anyone has seen pictures of Ramadi or Fallujah, they looked like Stalingrad. Cities absolutely crushed...*
>
> *"The interesting thing is that when we were fighting those battles and doing that damage, on the whole the Iraqis were not bitching about collateral damage...the Iraqis don't on the whole say "darn it, you shouldn't have blown up all of our houses." They sort of accept that."*

I don't know if I could accept that, could you? But the Iraqis are a really easy-going people. Just take the 1920s, when they were being slaughtered by the British:

> *"The natives of these tribes love fighting for fighting's sake," Chief of Air Staff Hugh Trenchard assured Parliament. "They have no objection to being killed." The military's argument was that, though the often indiscriminate air attacks might perturb some civilized folks back in London, such acts were viewed differently by the Arabs. As one British commander observed, "[Sheikhs]...do not seem to resent...that women and children are accidentally killed by bombs."*

Is it just the legendary hospitality of desert peoples? No. In Vietnam, human life wasn't just cheap but also plentiful, as U.S. General William Westmoreland pointed out. Obviously, it's just supply and demand:

> *"The Oriental doesn't put the same high price on life as does a Westerner. Life is plentiful. Life is cheap in the Orient.*

And here's a review of Gen. Curtis LeMay's autobiography, in which he explained precisely why massive carpet bombing of North Korea during the Korean War didn't make them surrender:

continued ☛

JON SCHWARZ *(@tinyrevolution) is Senior Writer/Editor at The Intercept. He is co-author of the humor collection* **Our Kampf***.*

BLESSED continued from p.25

LeMay [argues] that bombardment failed because of an "undying Oriental philosophy and fanaticism." He says, "Human attrition means nothing to such people," that their lives are so miserable on Earth that they look forward with delight to a death which promises them "everything from tea parties with long-dead grandfathers down to their pick of all the golden little dancing girls in Paradise."

All this makes it seem like it's an Eastern Hemisphere thing, which it's not. People in the Western Hemisphere have also never minded being killed by America, as U.S. soldiers have observed:

Marine major Julian Smith testified that the "racial psychology" of the "poorer class of Nicaraguans" made them "densely ignorant...A state of war to them is a normal condition." Along the same lines, Colonel Robert Denig observed in his diary, "Life to them is cheap" ... When asked if he ever witnessed American brutality in Haiti, General Ivan Miller replied that "you have to remember that what we consider brutality among people in the United States is different from what they consider brutality."

Afghanistan, Iraq, Vietnam, Korea, Nicaragua, Haiti—none of 'em minded too much. It's like we have a gift for it, a sixth sense, and it's been that way since the beginning. Actually, before the beginning: in *Notes on Virginia*, Thomas Jefferson investigated and found out that his African slaves didn't feel emotions like white people do:

Their griefs are transient. Those numberless afflictions, which render it doubtful whether heaven has given life to us in mercy or in wrath, are less felt, and sooner forgotten with them.

Other scholars discovered that Africans were less physically sensitive too:

Negroes...are void of sensibility to a surprising degree... what would be the cause of insupportable pain to a white man, a Negro would almost disregard.

So there you have it: sure, we've done some things that would've maybe been bad if we'd raped/enslaved/murdered normal people, people like us. But in each case they haven't minded it. Not a bit.
Lucky us.

GRANT SNIDER

BY DAVE HANSON

CALL ME MR. LUCKY

Reflections on a truly charmed life

Life... so fragile... a million ways this crazy ride could end in a heartbeat. You don't get to be my age without some pretty serious luck. Good fortune. Real horseshoe-up-the-hiney stuff.

For example: it's just a crazy, wispy twist of fate that JFK Jr. wasn't gay, and gay for me. I mean, I'm straight, but how could you resist if a guy that *flippin' awesome* wanted to fly you up to Martha's Vineyard for a romantic weekend? Answer: you couldn't. But John-John and I *never even met*. What a lucky break.

And that's not all. Back in '83 I was a lock for the host job on *Wheel Of Fortune*. Then I slipped in the shower and broke my leg, and the gig went to Sajak. At first, I was devastated, how could you not be? But God had a plan. Turns out *Wheel* tapes on Thursday and Friday, and on that schedule, I never would have been at Vincent de Paul for Chili Night. Which means I never would've met the missionary, who gave me the Bible, that was in my jacket pocket, when the cops raided the underpass. As I was running away, and the cop opened up with his Glock, it was that Bible that stopped the bullet from entering my heart!

I don't tell people this. I keep it to myself. I don't wanna jinx it. But a couple years after that, I had literally *forty-two cents* to my name when lucky old me found a five-spot on the sidewalk. I walked over to a diner; the waitress who

brought my burger flashed me a smile... and ultimately became my wife. A year after that, we had a daughter. Who, twenty-three years later, was killed in a skydiving accident — but was *a perfect match* for the kidney I needed.

Talk about a charmed life!

It just keeps going. That Czech underwear model? The one whose photographer boyfriend got swept away in the tsunami? If she'd returned *even one* of my 4,000 emails, that would have been me. Dude, look in the mirror and answer me this: how are you *not* in Vegas?!

Two years ago, I was feeling lonely so I decided to see if the classifieds had any pets for sale. But the newspaper delivery guy had hurt his elbow playing softball and it made his throwing arm so weak that the paper came to rest in the

lower section of the driveway, where the runoff from my neighbor's sprinkler turned the classified section into papier-mache. Did that save my life? *For sure.* I know me, and I know that I couldn't have passed up that adorable-looking little chimp... who subsequently ripped the buyer's face off.

Wanna talk destiny? I was born minus the chromosome that would have given me the bravery to try swimming the Pacific. But even before then! My entire freaking life began with a labyrinthine series of events involving a car mechanic getting sick from street food, going to an Urgent Care, and recognizing the doctor from his homeland as a fugitive. After an exhausting night of questioning, the mechanic called in sick. Two days later, *an unrepaired car* backfired in my neighborhood, startling our cat, who knocked Mom's birth control pills down a heating grate. And that's how I got a baby brother. Who looked so much like me, when an enraged Pat Sajak came after me in 2009, he shot my bro instead— without ever realizing he'd killed the wrong brother! That, my friend, is luck. Crazy, dumb luck.

Look, I'll tell you what I told Homeland Security: I guess I rubbed Mohammad Atta the wrong way at the job interview — maybe it was my necktie? Twenty openings and I didn't get picked. Tough on the old self-esteem, but it all turned out okay I guess. #blessed.

DAVE HANSON *has written for Letterman, Leno, and Lopez,* **National Lampoon** *and* **The New Yorker**. *He's wiling away the time before death writing on unpublishable novel he can adapt into an unproduceable screenplay.*

BY GEORGE MEYER

FAST AND LOOSE

Cherchez les femmes. Or les buddies du golfing.

Welcome to "Dateline: Pounder County." I'm your host, Bob Butler. This evening our guest is Warden O.A. Gilroy of the Harkness State Penitentiary. Warden—welcome.

WARDEN: Delighted to be here, Bob. My wife loves your show.

BUTLER: Let's talk about last night's prison break.

WARDEN: I knew you were gonna say that!

BUTLER: How many inmates escaped?

WARDEN: We don't know yet.

BUTLER: Just roughly.

WARDEN: Even one is too many, Bob. I could barely get to sleep last night.

BUTLER: Give me a number.

WARDEN: Nine hundred and forty.

BUTLER: So, all the prisoners.

WARDEN: We can't say that for sure. There could be a couple hiding in the laundry — or more likely, the snack room!

BUTLER: Nine hundred and forty escaped prisoners. Is that a record?

WARDEN: I would think so. You'd have to ask a historian. Is it "a" historian or "an" historian? 'Cause they both sound wrong!

BUTLER: How in God's name could so many convicts escape?

WARDEN: Well, when we slow down the security video, it clearly shows them rushing out the front gate.

BUTLER: Just rushing out.

WARDEN: Or in some cases, skipping.

BUTLER: The gate was open?

WARDEN: Yes it was. It was propped open, so its hinges could be oiled.

BUTLER: Propped open. So nearly a thousand dangerous criminals got loose —

WARDEN: I don't know how much you know about hinges, Bob. But if hinges don't get oil, first they make a horrible squeaking. Eventually they seize up, and then you have a huge and very heavy iron gate breaking off and crashing to the ground. I don't think any sane person wants that.

BUTLER: OK. So the prisoners go through the gate…

WARDEN: Not through the gate. Through the gateWAY. Only Casper can go through a gate!

BUTLER: Fine. So now they're in the parking lot. Don't you have guard dogs? Don't you have towers manned with sharpshooters?

WARDEN: Of course we do. Our guard dogs were on vacation. So that's the story with them. And by the time our sharpshooters could get over their confusion and butterflies and whatnot, the prisoners were long gone.

BUTLER: How is that possible?

WARDEN: They had golf carts.

BUTLER: (*confounded noise*)

WARDEN: I know, I had the same reaction. Hundreds of golf carts. It's like something out of a science fiction movie.

BUTLER: Didn't anyone notice hundreds of golf carts sitting around?

WARDEN: Notice, yes. Do anything about, no.

BUTLER: So the convicts had help on the outside.

WARDEN: It certainly looks that way. One theory is girlfriends. The other is golfing buddies.

BUTLER: Is Harkness a high-security prison?

WARDEN: We thought it was! (*chortles, slaps knee*)

BUTLER: So now we have mobs of felons roving Pounder County. Are these men violent?

WARDEN: Oh, *very* violent. The other day one of 'em bit me! (*pulls up his shirt to show Bob*)

BUTLER: Have you captured anyone?

WARDEN: In what sense?

BUTLER: Caught. Apprehended.

WARDEN: Not as such, no. But a major manhunt is on. We're combing the entire region.

BUTLER: I'm surprised to hear that, because just this afternoon, I saw at least a dozen convicts, still in their orange jumpsuits, over at the Lamplighter.

WARDEN: Come on.

BUTLER: Right across from the prison. Drinking beer, and eating popcorn with Worcestershire sauce.

WARDEN: You're funnin' me.

BUTLER: I'm not. It was frightening.

WARDEN: You're funnin' me. Cons don't have any cash.

BUTLER: They paid with threats.

WARDEN: (*chuckles*) That's a con for ya!

BUTLER: I'll be blunt with you, Warden. People are saying this whole affair stinks to high heaven.

WARDEN: (*stiffens*) They are, huh? (*takes out cigarettes*) OK to smoke in here?

BUTLER: No.

WARDEN: Could I have some water?

BUTLER: It's there, by your elbow.

WARDEN: Cool, cool water. (*takes a long swig*) How're we doin' on time?

BUTLER: Warden, I'm just going to ask you straight out: Was this entire prison break staged?

WARDEN: Whoa, whoa, hold the phone there! I agree, the whole thing looks very strange. Especially when you consider that the state is in budget trouble. But allowing a bunch of vicious thugs to bust out, just to save 50 or 60 million a year -- that's crazy.

BUTLER: So you've heard the rumors.

WARDEN: Sure, we all have. But the idea that my guards and I would take a retirement package so the prison could be sold off to a Bible college — it's just bizarre.

BUTLER: Without a doubt. But is it true?

WARDEN: (*heavy sigh*) Yeah…and here comes the guilt wave. Woosh!

BUTLER: Well, now we are out of time. Folks, thanks for watching, and please: Be careful out there.

GEORGE MEYER *wrote for* **The Simpsons** *and* **Saturday Night Live**, *among other venues. He is currently working on a novel,* **Kick Me a Million Times or I'll Die.**

"We made all the dogs cut short their vacations.
Their union raised hell, by the way."

BY BRIAN McCONNACHIE

INSPIRATIONAL ANIMAL STORIES #1: THE MOTIVATIONAL TIGER

Tiger, Tiger burning bright
Won't you guide my sleigh tonight?
—Edna St. Louis Missouri

If you don't stand up for yourself, no one else will.

This was an important life lesson that a 600-pound Burmese tiger taught me one memorable afternoon at the Auto Show.

I had recently been fired from my job (after only two weeks) as a restroom attendant in a medieval adventure village. The reason they gave was that medieval villages didn't have restrooms much less restroom attendants and they weren't going to pay me. Before I could protest the logic of this, they had two guys in armor suits and swords escort me from the fairgrounds.

I felt small. It felt like I barely existed.

More and more, people were bumping into me and not saying, "Sorry." My dry cleaners started cutting all the buttons off my clothes and claiming I did it or my clothes didn't have buttons to begin with. The kids who'd throw water balloons at me and then run away didn't bother to run away anymore. They sauntered. And now all three of the waiters at the corner coffee shop spill soup on me. The manager agrees to pay for the cleaning but only if I use the same dry cleaners who cuts all my buttons off. And then my bank who said they "lost" my entire savings account—all the money my mother left me—and they weren't going to say a thing about it.

I really needed something to cheer me up and that's when I saw an ad for a car show. The latest in technology and style could be the thing I needed to take my mind off of my troubles.

As I looked at all the beautiful, futuristic cars, it really did take my mind off my woes. A number of the really expensive cars were on revolving platforms and some had gorgeous models posing with them. One of the cars, a $425,000.00 cream-colored Bentley convertible, had this awesome tiger sitting on the hood. I had never seen any creature so majestic and self-confident.

I moved closer and as I did, the tiger looked directly into my eyes. As strange as it sounds, I felt there was a sudden bonding between us. Then the platform's rotation moved the tiger from my sightline but then he came around and our eyes locked again. It was like I could read his thoughts. I could hear his thinking in my head. With each rotation he'd say something different like: I feel lonely. Am I an endangered species? Are you? Then it would go around again, our eyes would meet and he said: How is Siegfried's pal Roy doing? We all feel terrible about that. The next time around it was: Tell me that tigers aren't bad animals.

I was then getting a powerful feeling he was going to tell me something important. Something that could help me with my low self-esteem. I began to feel that the next time around he would say it. Or, I could even ask for his advice. But before I could, he said something I didn't expect: I'm getting dizzy. This sucks.

But when I saw him leap from the car, it became clear to me what he was saying. He was saying, Take action.

"Yes! I will!" I yelled at him. What happened next changed me in more ways than one.

As he landed on me, I went over backwards. There was no doubting what he meant by this: Life comes at you fast. "Boy! Doesn't it," I agreed.

His momentum rolled us over a few times. My initial understanding of this was: Turn over a new leaf. I felt I should probably be writing this down but that was a little impractical.

When his teeth went into my thigh, I felt oddly calm and went completely limp and from then on, everything seemed to move in slow motion. Then he shook me like a rag doll and tossed me up into the air. Now the toss in the air I got as: *Reach for the heights. Go for the dream. Live your hope.*

The violent shaking I wasn't too sure about. *Shake things up? Wake up? Rip Life a new one?* That was unclear to me and it hurt a lot.

Just before I went into a coma, I perceived another message from the tiger that was disturbing. Could this animal, instead of giving me helpful advice, for no good reason, be trying to kill me? Or perhaps he was telling me I should get a gun and kill my dry cleaner? Or the next person who bumps into me without saying, "Sorry"? When I woke up in the hospital all the positive lessons the tiger put into my head had a chance to settle down and form one clear plan. A plan of action and leaping and snatching that I'm going to execute as soon as I can get a pair of bouncy prosthetic legs.

The folks who ran the auto show said, as much as they would love to, they weren't allowed to give me any money for pain and suffering because they didn't have the right insurance.

But thinking back, I don't believe you can put a price on a motivational jolt that speaks to the good beast within us and turns our lives around. A chance like that comes once in a lifetime. If you're lucky. It's something I call "the tale of the tiger," and it's something you've just got to Geeerrrraaaab!—*Karl Raimes, age 31.*

Nathan Yoder for SEVENLY

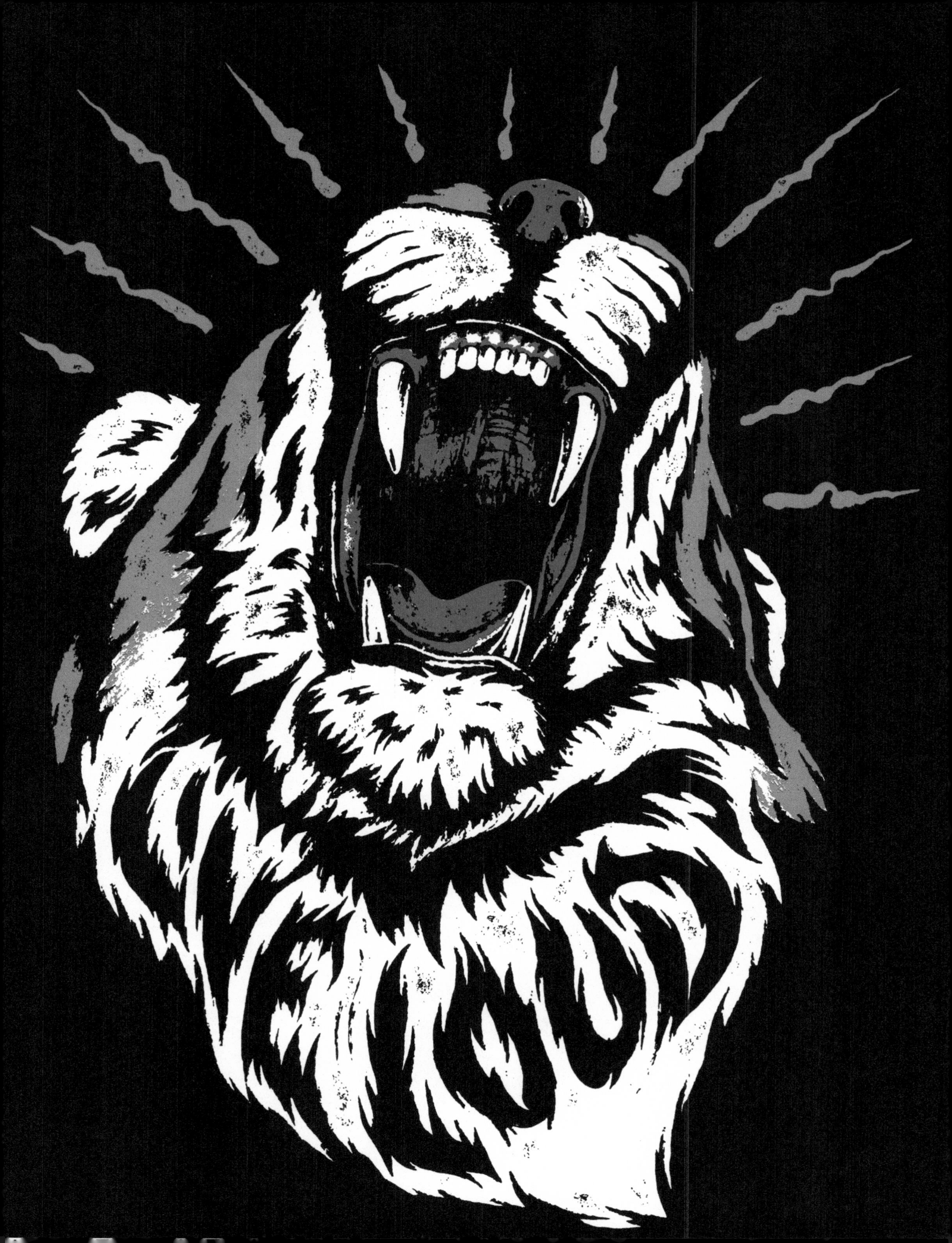

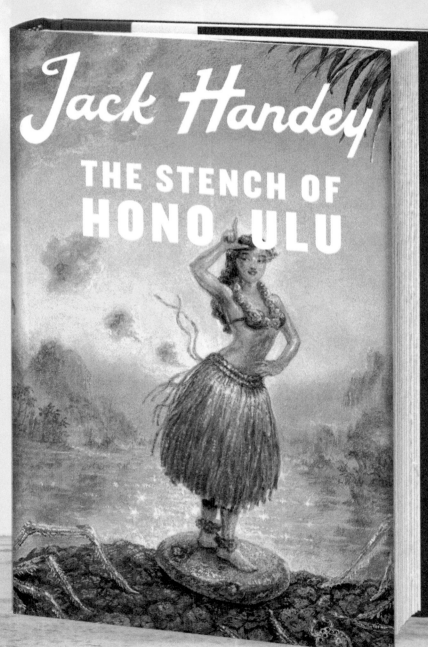

BY SPORT MURPHY

SIZING UP CHAMPAGNE

Quick — distinguish your jeroboams from your salmanazars

Pity the nascent "man at his best" who fumbles one of the crucial signifiers of sophistication just when love's labours or the protocols of business are close to glad fruition. Who hasn't "blown the closer" with an incorrectly pronounced French phrase or a tactless bathroom joke? For many who've deftly simulated class and charm through the dread minefields of conversation, the tipping point occurs at the tippling point, when ordering an inappropriate quantity of bubbly reveals the would-be big shot as a crass dolt. Circumstance will dictate the amount of alcohol required, so in order to shore up your savvy I offer a list of the names assigned to sizes of Champagne bottles, in ascending order.

(A bit of history on each is included, to be casually mentioned during the pour, lending a note of offhand erudition to the entire sordid ruse. I will list the quantity of each in liters, followed by the name of the bottle and its derivation.)

0.375L: SPLIT OR PONY

"Split" is what you gotta do, man, when the time comes, dig? It's also the battle cry of a little-known version of "Captain Marvel" circa 1966, whose body parts would fly off in different directions so that the fingers could poke guys in the eye while the feet were kicking other guys in the balls.

"Pony" is a character in Eric Bogosian's play *Suburbia* as well as a dance popular in the Hullabaloo era. All these things — beatniks who leave early, that superhero, that play, and that dance — are half-assed, thus it applies to a half bottle of champagne.

Humphrey Bogart: "The problem with the world is that everyone is a few drinks behind."

0.75L: BOTTLE

This is the least imaginative of the bottle-size names, which is why it's the most popular. By way of illustration:

"Where are you from?"
"Around."
"What do you listen to?"
"Music."
"What'll you have?"
"A bottle."

See? It's best to skip this one, as there is no way to suavely convey that you're ordering a "bottle" ...not just a "bottle."

1.5 L: MAGNUM

A private dick, played by Tom Selleck on CBS; very big in the 1980s, very popular with the ladies. Therefore, the standard "show-off" quantity, always welcome if a tad "Reagan Era."

3.0 L: JEROBOAM

Israelite king who waged bitter war with...

4.5 L: REHOBOAM

...despite (or because?) of the similarly doofy names. But why did the "battle o'

the 'boams" inspire these designations for bottles? Well, imagine yourself drinking three liters of Korbel and your archenemy (and if you don't have one, you're living wrong) downing four-and-a-half liters of same. An inevitable brawl of biblical proportions.

6.0 L: METHUSELAH

Oldest man ever! Died at 969 years, in the year of the flood. Consider the related idiomatic expressions, "he's old as Methuselah" and "Ain't seen him since the year of the flood" ...two cliches plus a hell of a party. And remember Ira Gershwin's take on Methuselah's longevity: "Who calls that livin' when no gal will give in to no man what is nine hunderd years!" Drink up, Pops.

9.0 L: SALMANAZAR

Assyrian king who combined the religion of Israel with local pagan faiths, creating a notable early example of the "moral relativism" and "mix-n-match religion" that purists and orthodox sorts decry. What better way to toast your impurity and impiety than with a ridiculously huge bottle of booze?

12.0 L: BALTHAZAR

This is one of the Magi of Christmas creche fame. Your three wise men. According to some exhaustive Bible "who's who" website I was nice enough to consult:

"The traditional names adopted in the West are Gaspar, Melchior, and Balthazar. The Syrian tradition uses the names Gushnasaph, Hormisdas and Larvandad. Others use Hormiz-

SPORT MURPHY *co-authored the book* **Everything's Coming Up Profits.** *He enjoys habitat dioramas and "mild" Slim Jims, and is completing his fourth album, a multimedia behemoth entitled* **A Room of Voices.**

dah, Perozdh and Yazdegerd, or Basanater, Karsudan and Hor, or various other names."

So why Balthazar? As we'll see, Melchior gets a bottle named after him, but not Gaspar (How come? Read on). But be glad that we need not order a "Larvandad" or… yikes… a "Gushnasaph" on New Year's Eve. Of course, I will not stoop to making jokes about a "Hor full of wine." That's the kind of reflexive yobbery of which I am trying to cure you.

15.0 L: NEBUCHADNEZZAR

Probably the baddest of your ancient kings, this time reigning o'er the land of Babylon. Which should give him the jumbo-est of all bottles, but no. Instead he replaces wise man Gaspar (not to be confused with 'Wiseman, Fred,' a guy who makes documentaries). "Neb," son of kick-Assyrian Nabopolassar, eventually paid for persecuting three upright Hebrews in a fiery furnace by suffering "lycanthropy." His hair was perfect.

18.0 L: MELCHIOR

OK, this is the other wise man. I can only surmise that he gets pride of place for bringing gold to baby Jesus. Obviously, that's the gift that keeps on giving, but what of frankincense and myrrh? Ponder this little nugget about Balthazar's gift, myrrh, which I found in my exhaustive research for this important piece: "…an aromatic juice of a shrub called the Cistus or rock rose, which has the same qualities, though in a slight degree, of opium." So: gold… opium… and INCENSE? Guess why Gaspar was excluded from the wine-tasting party! All mysteries are answered in the fullness of time.

25.5 L: SOVEREIGN

Once the most ubiquitous gold coin in British circulation, coin collectors scorn these nickel-sized bits of change as too common. So they are worth only the value of the gold itself. You think "worth its weight in gold" is a compliment? Then you are no numismatist, and philately will get you nowhere. Now, twenty-five-and-a-half liters of champagne is just way too much. Foster Brooks, Shane MacGowan and Boris Yeltsin couldn't have put all that away with Judy Garland's help. So really, the regal name accorded this super-size serving of the stuff is a lot of piffle.

Next month we'll take up narcotics! ♜

Boyfriend
Liana Finck

I HAD A BOYFRIEND ONCE WHO WASN'T THERE. WHEN I TEXTED HIM, HE NEVER TEXTED BACK.

AT NIGHT, WHEN I LAY IN BED ALONE, HE WHISPERED NOTHING IN MY EAR. I KNEW EXACTLY WHAT HE MEANT TO SAY:
"SILENCE IS HOW I SHOW MY LOVE. MY ABSENCE PROVES I LOVE YOU."

I HAD A BOYFRIEND ONCE WHO WASN'T THERE. I TRIED TO GIVE HIM SPACE AND WHEN I COULDN'T BEAR IT I EMAILED HIM A SHORT EMAIL, AND THEN I EMAILED HIM AN APOLOGY FOR EMAILING. HE DIDN'T EMAIL BACK.

WHAT HE WAS TRYING TO SAY WAS THIS: I HAVE TO GO AWAY FOR AWHILE. BUT NOT BECAUSE OF YOU.

A WEEK PASSED, AND THEN ANOTHER AND ANOTHER. I KNEW SOMETHING TERRIBLE HAD HAPPENED TO HIM. I TEXTED HIM DAILY. I ALWAYS SAID, "I DON'T NEED YOU TO WRITE BACK. BUT I'M THINKING OF YOU."

HE DIDN'T TEXT BACK. HIS SILENCE SPOKE VOLUMES. I WAS MOVED THAT HE NEEDED ME SO MUCH.

I HAD A BOYFRIEND ONCE WHO WASN'T THERE. HE LOVED ME, AND BECAUSE OF THIS, IT WAS HARDER FOR HIM TO TALK TO ME THAN TO OTHER PEOPLE. I WAS GLAD WHEN MY FRIENDS TOLD ME HE'D MET THEM FOR ICE CREAM AND HAMBURGERS. THAT WAS HOW I KNEW HE WAS OK AGAIN. HIS SILENCE, AT THIS POINT, MEANT MORE THAN A LONG LOVE LETTER.

I'D LEANT HIM A BOOK ONCE, AND HE MAILED IT BACK TO ME. AT FIRST, WHEN I OPENED THE PACKAGE, I MISTOOK THE LACK OF A NOTE FOR A LOVING LACK OF A NOTE, AND MY HEART BEAT FAST. SILENCE CAN BE A PUNISHMENT, THOUGH, TOO, AND THAT'S WHAT HIS SILENCE HAD BECOME. AND YET SILENCE IS ALWAYS SILENCE.

I HAD A BOYFRIEND ONCE WHO WASN'T THERE. NONETHELESS I BEGGED HIM TO MEET ME, JUST ONCE. I NAMED THE PLACE AND TIME. HE CAME. AFTERWARDS, AS WE WERE LEAVING, HE SAID, "YOU MAY NOT KNOW THIS, BUT I AM AN ARTIST. SILENCE IS MY ART. ABSENCE IS MY ART. WHAT I CREATE FOR YOU, YOU HAVE BROKEN. BECAUSE OF THIS, I WILL NEVER SPEAK TO YOU AGAIN."

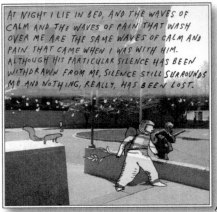

AT NIGHT I LIE IN BED, AND THE WAVES OF CALM AND THE WAVES OF PAIN THAT WASH OVER ME ARE THE SAME WAVES OF CALM AND PAIN THAT CAME WHEN I WAS WITH HIM. ALTHOUGH HIS PARTICULAR SILENCE HAS BEEN WITHDRAWN FROM ME, SILENCE STILL SURROUNDS ME AND NOTHING, REALLY, HAS BEEN LOST.

BY SAM MEANS & DANIEL IMMERWAHR

A BRIEF HISTORY OF SANDWICH THEORY

Sandwich theory, as a discipline in its own right, began almost two hundred years after the foodstuff itself, when Gödel published his seminal "Incompleteness Theorem of Sandwiches" (*Die Sammichunvollständigkeitssatz*). A lesser-known precursor of his famous theorem, it asserts that, for any axiomatic system of sandwich construction, there exists at least one edible sandwich that cannot be constructed within the rules of the system: anomalies that he called "recursive sandwiches."

Gödel never claimed to be a chef, and he was famously chary of making claims for the practical significance of sandwich recursivity, but an explosion of culinary research quickly discovered two real-world examples of these anomalies: the bread sandwich — a sandwich whose only filling is another slice of bread — and, more adventurously, the sandwich sandwich.[1]

That's when things got interesting. Building on the link between sandwich theory and set theory, several of Gödel's protégés also posited the (purely theoretical) existence of a null sandwich and a universal sandwich. The null sandwich consists entirely of two slices of bread,

possibly with a thin spread of mayo, and was accepted immediately by the academic and culinary communities. The universal sandwich, however, met with surprisingly vociferous resistance.

Only the most hard-line theorists were willing to admit of a sandwich that

Sontag's "Panini As Metaphor, Metaphors As Lunch" (1972) first brought sandwich theory to a general audience.

contains everything that exists, except itself. In fact, the very possibility of its existence was denied until almost thirty years later, when a brilliant young graduate student at Princeton actually made one.

Mort Kummelstein had originally set the sandwich world on its head with his groundbreaking 1976 Inedibility Hypothesis. Published anonymously, "Must Sandwiches Be Food?" posited the rock sandwich, the lightbulb sandwich, and the Volkswagen sandwich, sparking a series of still-unresolved controversies that changed the face of edible mathematics forever.

An unnamed letter-writer to the Journal of Comparative Mastication sniped that, under Kummelstein's hypothesis, one could conceivably place two slices of pumpernickel antipodally in Paraguay and Taiwan, creating an Earth sandwich. Professor Jan Deutsch of Tübingen took it one step further, suggesting that, if we were to accept inedibility, nothing would prevent the construction of an "air sandwich," consisting only of two slices of seven-grain whole wheat pointed in each other's general direction.

Unbeknownst to him, Deutsch's facetious suggestion had paved the way for the greatest paradigm shift since the invention of the sandwich itself. Kummelstein and his advisor, Professor Charlotte Stein, accepted the *reductio*, and at CUNY Graduate Center's 1978 conference on cognitive edibility, they set the sandwich world on its head by placing two pieces of bread together, but facing away from each other. The repercussions of this bold and unexpected move were felt in every area of public life, and it was immediately deemed a threat to national security by the Carter administration.

To date no one has been able to conclusively disprove Kummelstein-Stein, and more than one thinker has been driven mad by the effort. But thanks in large part to their experimentation, sandwich theory continues to move forward, and remains a vibrant field of graduate research. (For undergraduate study, it is generally folded into either the sociology department or the hospitality school.) ♨

---

[1] An interesting twist on the history of the sandwich sandwich came as recently as 2010, when an undergraduate in the Fast Casual department at Cornell placed a sesame seed bun around an existing KFC® Double-Down®. The first book on the resulting controversy is expected next fall from OUP.

SAM MEANS is a writer for the Netflix series **Unbreakable Kimmy Schmidt**. Previously, he wrote for **The Daily Show**, **30 Rock**, and **Parks & Recreation**, and drew cartoons for **The New Yorker**. His dog is named Myrna.

DANIEL IMMERWAHR professes history at Northwestern University. He can do three (3) pull-ups, knows the lyrics to many folk songs, and still has all of his teeth.

Jack Handey

Kids' Advice to Lincoln

OPEN ON: PHOTO OF ABE LINCOLN WITHOUT BEARD. HIS EYEBROWS SHOULD BE PAINTBOXED DOWN TO A THINNER VERSION OF THEIR NATURALLY BUSHY SELVES.)
(*MUSIC:* "BATTLE HYMN OF THE REPUBLIC")
(*CHYRON:* CRAWL OF ANNOUNCER V.O.)

ANNOUNCER: (V.O.)
…In 1860, an eleven-year-old girl named Grace Bedell wrote a letter to President Lincoln, suggesting he grow a beard, as his face appeared too thin.

(*DISS. TO:* PHOTO OF LINCOLN WITH BEARD)

…The beard proved to be a huge success, and soon Lincoln began poring over children's letters to him in desperate hopes of discovering even more image-enhancing suggestions…

(*DISS. TO:* PHOTO OF WHITE HOUSE, CIRCA 1860)
(*DISS. TO:* INT. OVAL OFFICE. LINCOLN IS BEHIND HIS DESK. HIS ADVISOR IS SEATED BEFORE THE DESK, A STACK OF CHILDREN'S LETTERS BEFORE HIM)

LINCOLN:
OK, let's move on to the next one.

ADVISOR:
(*reading*)
…"Dear President Lincoln…" Oh,

look, she spelled it "Prezel-dent."

LINCOLN:
(*impatient*)
Yeah, yeah, c'mon.

ADVISOR:
"Dear President Lincoln. I am eight years old. I live in Bedford, Massachusetts. It snows here. Does it snow in Washington?…"

(LINCOLN MOTIONS TO HURRY IT UP)

…blah-blah-blah… "I like your beard. I think it looks good…"

(LINCOLN MOTIONS AGAIN)

…blah-blah-blah…Okay, here: "What if you had bushy eyebrows? I think it would make you look better."

LINCOLN:
Bushy eyebrows? Hmm? Do we have that?

ADVISOR:
Yessir, Mr. President. I took the liberty of securing some…

(ADVISOR PULLS OUT SOME BUSHY FALSE EYEBROWS FROM A BOX OR CHEST AT HIS FEET. LINCOLN TAKES THEM AND, USING A MIRROR, QUICKLY STICKS THEM ON)

LINCOLN:
All right, let's give it a try…

(LINCOLN STRIDES THROUGH THE

OPEN FRENCH DOORS BEHIND HIS DESK, OUT ONTO THE BALCONY)
(CUT TO: EXT. BALCONY. LINCOLN WAVES, AS IF TO A CROWD O.S.)
(SFX: CHEERS)
(LINCOLN RETURNS)

LINCOLN:
Okay, that works. They liked that. What else do we have?

(ADVISOR GOES TO NEXT LETTER)

ADVISOR:
(*reading*)
"Dear President Lincoln…"

LINCOLN:
Just gimme the gist of it.

ADVISOR:
Well, sir, this is a little girl from Pennsylvania who thinks you should wear lipstick.

LINCOLN:
Lipstick, huh? What the heck. Let's give it a shot.

(ADVISOR HANDS LINCOLN A LIPSTICK TUBE. USING MIRROR, LINCOLN PUTS ON LIPSTICK AND WALKS OUT ONTO BALCONY AND WAVES)
(SFX: ONE PERSON CLAPPING)
(LINCOLN RETURNS INSIDE)

LINCOLN: (cont'd)
Hoo, boy, that didn't go.

ADVISOR:
One guy liked it.

continued

············ ◆ ············

Best known for his "Deep Thoughts," **New Yorker** *regular* **Jack Handey** *recently published his first novel,* **The Stench of Honolulu.**

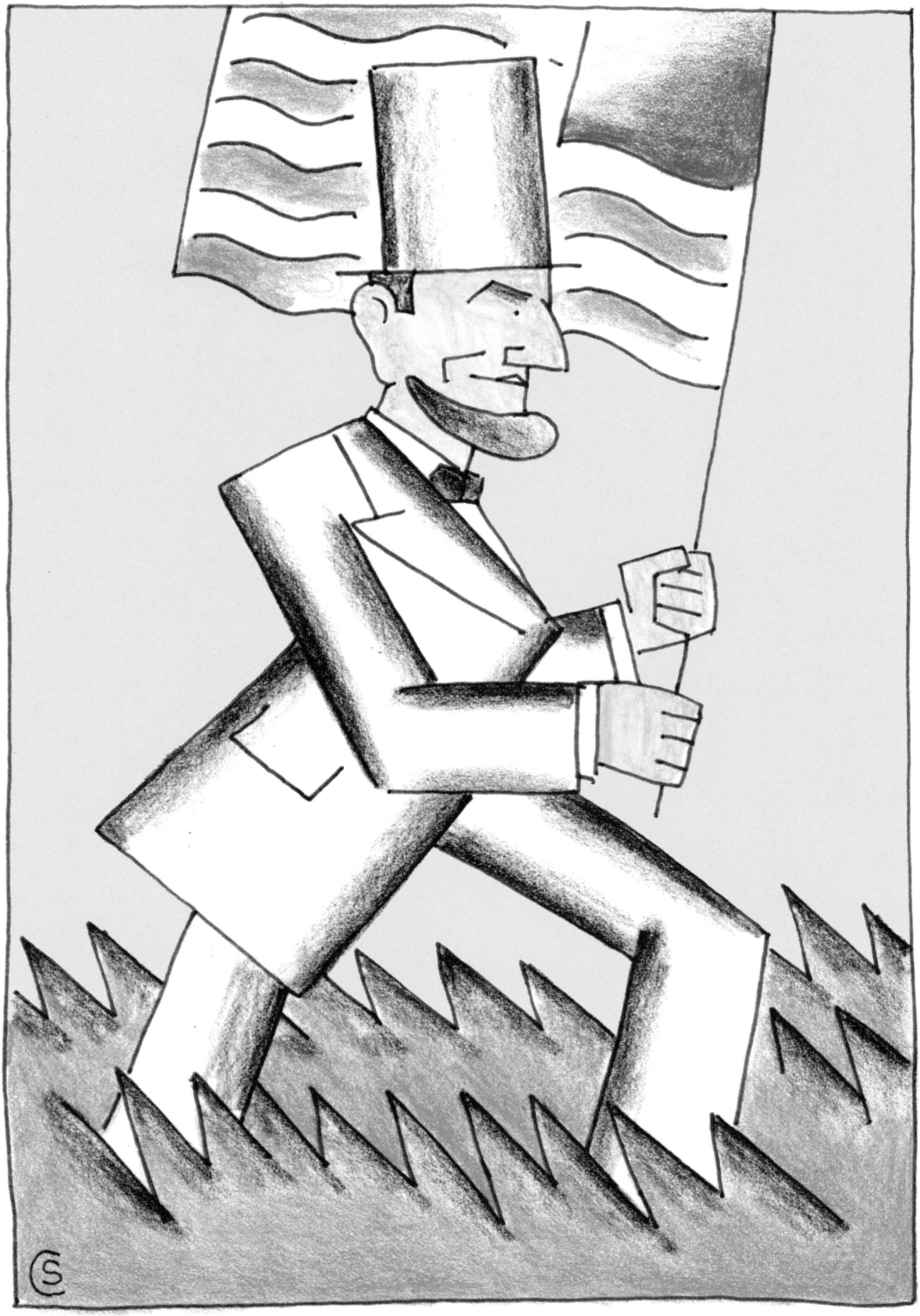

LINCOLN:
Yeah, I think it was the same guy who liked the can-can dress. Wait, let me try it with these...

(LINCOLN TAKES SOMETHING FROM HIS DRAWER AND STICKS IT IN HIS MOUTH. HE WALKS TO BALCONY AND GRINS. HE HAS FAKE VAMPIRE TEETH)
(SFX: CRICKETS)
(LINCOLN WALKS BACK IN, TAKES OUT TEETH)

LINCOLN: (cont'd)
Ouch! Nothing that time. What's next?

(ADVISOR MOVES ONTO NEXT LETTER. AS LINCOLN WIPES OFF LIPSTICK)

ADVISOR:
This one is from a ten-year-old boy in Maryland. He thinks a fake tomahawk on the head would be good.

LINCOLN:
I don't know. What do you think?

(ADVISOR PULLS OUT A FAKE TOMAHAWK-IN-THE-HEAD)

ADVISOR:
We've got it. You might as well...

(LINCOLN PUTS IT ON AND STEPS OUT ONTO BALCONY)
(SFX: BIG BOOS)
(LINCOLN RETURNS INSIDE)

LINCOLN:
Boy, they hated that.

(TAKES OFF TOMAHAWK. ADVISOR PULLS OUT A FANCY TURBAN AND HANDS IT TO LINCOLN)

ADVISOR:
You want to try the turban? That's the suggestion from the nine-year-old in Cincinnati.

LINCOLN:
(taking it)
Sure, why not. Now, what about the stovepipe hat? They liked that, didn't they?

(PUTS ON TURBAN)

ADVISOR:
Yeah, they did. A lot.

LINCOLN:
Okav. give it to me. I want to try something.

(ADVISOR HANDS LINCOLN A STOVEPIPE HAT. LINCOLN STEPS OUT ONTO BALCONY WEARING TURBAN)
(SFX: CHEERS)
(HE TAKES OFF TURBAN AND PUTS ON STOVEPIPE HAT)
(SFX: BIGGER CHEERS)
(TAKES OFF HAT, PUTS TURBAN BACK ON)
(SFX: A LITTLE LESS CHEERING)
(LINCOLN TURNS, RE-ENTERS OFFICE)

LINCOLN:
The turban is good, but I think it's still the hat.

ADVISOR:
I agree, Mister President.

(NEXT LETTER)

The next one is a parrot on the shoulder, like a pirate.

(ADVISOR TAKES OUT A STUFFED PARROT AND TOSSES IT TO LINCOLN, WHO SETS IT ON HIS SHOULDER)
(SFX: BOOS)

LINCOLN:
Oh, they can see me through the window and they're already booing.

ADVISOR:
We'll forget that one. Do you even want to try the monkey?

LINCOLN:
Naw, I don't think so. That one scares me.

ADVISOR:
All right, that leaves Zontar.

LINCOLN:
Zontar?

ADVISOR:
Remember? The little boy from Rhode Island wrote in and said you should have an alien from outer space as your next vice president. . .?

LINCOLN:
Oh, yeah, right, right...

(ADVISOR CROSSES, OPENS DOOR TO OTHER ROOM)

ADVISOR:
(to O.S.)
Zontar, please come in.

(A WEIRD ALIEN FROM OUTER SPACE ENTERS)

LINCOLN:
(extended hand)
Zontar...

ZONTAR:
(shaking hands)
A pleasure, Mister President.

LINCOLN:
Welcome to our planet. Shall we give it a shot?

(LINCOLN AND ZONTAR GO OUT ONTO THE BALCONY)
(LINCOLN HOLDS UP ZONTAR'S HAND IN A VICTORY POSE)
(SFX: BOOS)
(ZONTAR AND LINCOLN SHRUG AND RE-ENTER OFFICE)

LINCOLN:
Well, thanks anyway, Zontar.

ZONTAR:
Mister President, if you don't mind, I'd like to try it again. But this time…

(ZONTAR REACHES OVER AND PUTS TURBAN ON HIS ALIEN HEAD)
(THEY WALK OUT AGAIN ONTO BALCONY AND DO VICTORY POSE)
(SFX: BIG BOOS)
(THEY RE-ENTER. ZONTAR TAKES OFF TURBAN)

LINCOLN:
(consoling)
It's okay. They're just not buying it.

(ZONTAR EXITS. LINCOLN THINKS FOR A BEAT, THEN:)

LINCOLN:
What about the toga?

ADVISOR:
We could try it again.

LINCOLN:
Let's. I don't think I had it on right last time.

(ADVISOR GETS A TOGA FROM THE BOX. AS HE HELPS LINCOLN INTO IT, WE)

(FADE)

Ron Barrett

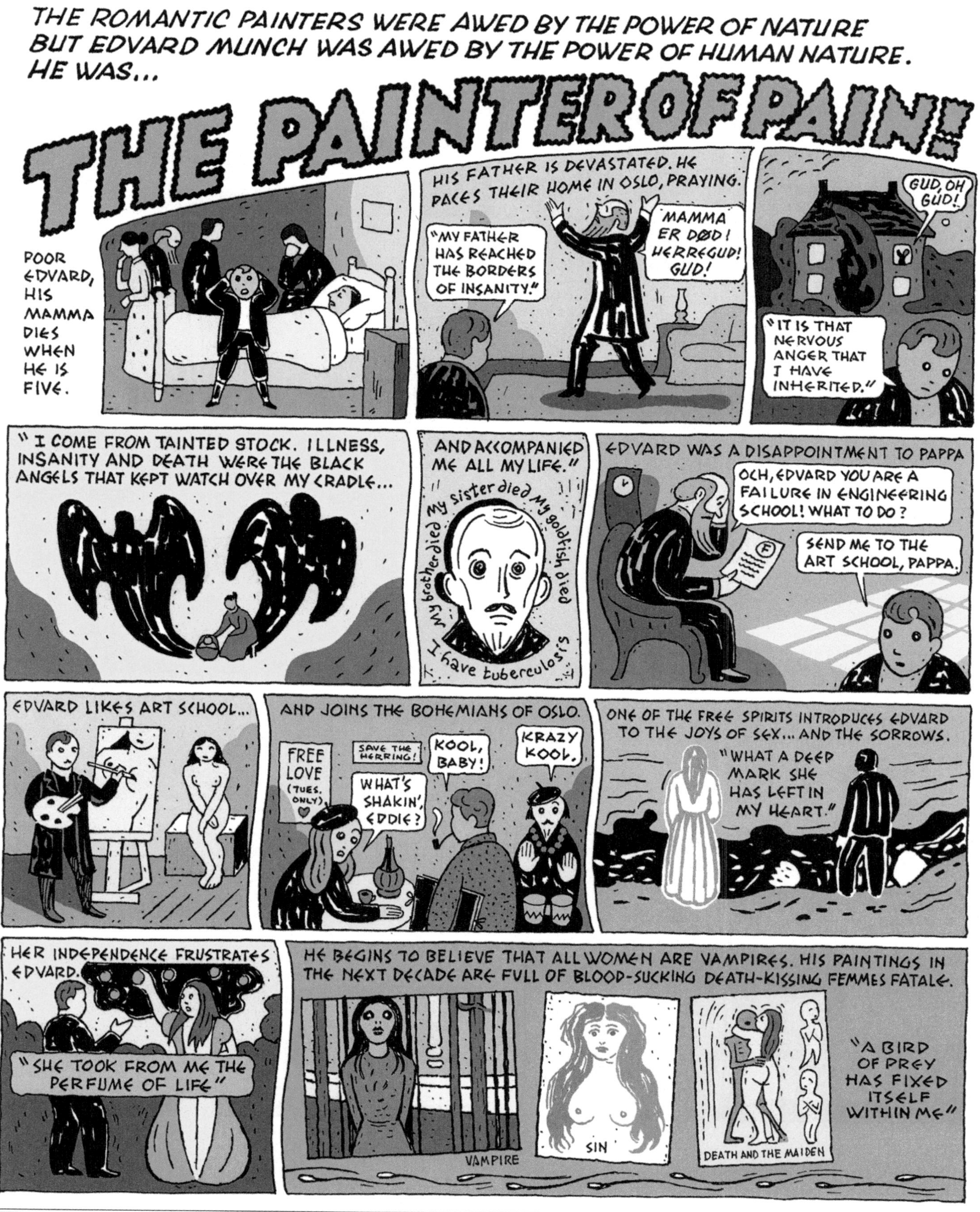
THE ROMANTIC PAINTERS WERE AWED BY THE POWER OF NATURE BUT EDVARD MUNCH WAS AWED BY THE POWER OF HUMAN NATURE. HE WAS...
THE PAINTER OF PAIN!
POOR EDVARD, HIS MAMMA DIES WHEN HE IS FIVE.
HIS FATHER IS DEVASTATED. HE PACES THEIR HOME IN OSLO, PRAYING.
"MY FATHER HAS REACHED THE BORDERS OF INSANITY."
MAMMA ER DØD! HERREGUD! GUD!
GUD, OH GUD!
"IT IS THAT NERVOUS ANGER THAT I HAVE INHERITED."
"I COME FROM TAINTED STOCK. ILLNESS, INSANITY AND DEATH WERE THE BLACK ANGELS THAT KEPT WATCH OVER MY CRADLE...
AND ACCOMPANIED ME ALL MY LIFE."
My brother died My sister died My goldfish died
I have tuberculosis
EDVARD WAS A DISAPPOINTMENT TO PAPPA
OCH, EDVARD YOU ARE A FAILURE IN ENGINEERING SCHOOL! WHAT TO DO?
F
SEND ME TO THE ART SCHOOL, PAPPA.
EDVARD LIKES ART SCHOOL...
AND JOINS THE BOHEMIANS OF OSLO.
FREE LOVE (TUES. ONLY)
SAVE THE HERRING!
KOOL, BABY!
KRAZY KOOL.
WHAT'S SHAKIN', EDDIE?
ONE OF THE FREE SPIRITS INTRODUCES EDVARD TO THE JOYS OF SEX... AND THE SORROWS.
"WHAT A DEEP MARK SHE HAS LEFT IN MY HEART."
HER INDEPENDENCE FRUSTRATES EDVARD.
"SHE TOOK FROM ME THE PERFUME OF LIFE"
HE BEGINS TO BELIEVE THAT ALL WOMEN ARE VAMPIRES. HIS PAINTINGS IN THE NEXT DECADE ARE FULL OF BLOOD-SUCKING DEATH-KISSING FEMMES FATALE.
VAMPIRE
SIN
DEATH AND THE MAIDEN
"A BIRD OF PREY HAS FIXED ITSELF WITHIN ME"

IN 1899 EDVARD MOVES TO PARIS, WHERE HE BASKS IN THE SUNLIT PAINTINGS OF THE IMPRESSIONISTS.

·GALERIE·

HE BRIGHTENS HIS PALETTE.

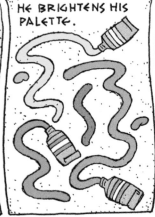

AFTER TWO YEARS, HE RETURNS TO OSLO AND EXHIBITS HIS WORK.

OPENING TONIGHT

WINE'S OVER THERE, FOLKS!

THE RECEPTION IS EMPHATICALLY COOL—

TAKE DOWN THAT SCHMIEREN!

Oslo has no love for Edvard's depressing expressionism. But the Germans do.

Expressionist art is flourishing in Berlin. Edvard goes to live among Nolde, Kirchner and the artists of Der Blaue Reiter & Die Brücke.

HE FINDS THE BOHEMIANS OF BERLIN EVEN MORE DISSOLUTE THAN IN OSLO.

FREE LOVE PLUS COUPONS!

HEIL, BABY! WHAT'S SHAKIN'?

ME.

DISSOLUTION IS DER SOLUTION

DER KAISER ROLLS!

DISSOLUTION SEEMS TO AGREE WITH EDVARD.

Schnapps

IN HIS SOBER MOMENTS HE LEARNS PRINTMAKING WITH AUGUSTE CLOT.

LOOKS TOO HAPPY.

CLOT HAS WORKED WITH BONNARD, LAUTREC AND VUILLARD. THE PRINTS SPREAD EDVARD'S FAME EVEN AS HE SPIRALS DOWN INTO ALCOHOLISM, PARANOIA & SCHIZOPHRENIA

WITNESS HIS AFFAIR WITH TULLA LARSEN—

MARRY ME, EDVARD!

I CANNOT. I AM A BAD SEED.

I WILL KILL MYSELF!

TULLA! STOP!

BLAM!

MARRY? NEVER. YOU HAVE SHOT OFF THE FINGER THAT WOULD HAVE WORN THE WEDDING RING.

DESPERATE AFTER A FOUR DAY BINGE, EDVARD VISITS DR. DANIEL JACOBSON...

HELP ME, DOCTOR.

I WILL BEGIN TREATMENT IMMEDIATELY.

8 MONTHS OF ELECTROSHOCKS CURE EDVARD OF ALCOHOLISM...

BUT RUIN HIM AS AN ARTIST. FOR THE REST OF HIS LIFE HE PAINTS THE BANALITIES OF THE EXTERNAL WORLD RATHER THAN THE FEAR AND LONELINESS OF THE WORLD WITHIN HIM.

GALLOPING HORSE

Oslo comes to love Edvard. In 1911 he is offered a prestigious public commission. Ironically, he finds acceptance at home after his finest artistic, albeit most troubled, decades have passed.

"THE LAST PART OF MY LIFE HAS BEEN AN EFFORT TO STAND UP."

Mark O'Donnell and Chris Austopchuk

IN MEMORIAM:
Mark O'Donnell, 1954-2012

When Brian, Alan, and I embarked on this project, the first writer I reached out to was Mark O'Donnell—and not just because Mark and I had been friends for twenty years, and he was a notoriously soft touch. A humorist in the classic mode, Mark worked exactly the territory we were aiming for: intelligent but not arid, incisive but not acid, ever-mellow, always sweet.

In a world full of funny, this sweetness was Mark's signal virtue. Whenever you talked to him, you got the distinct (and sometimes distinctly uncomfortable) feeling that he was a couple of steps ahead. Most truly brilliant people don't wait for you, but Mark always did.

We are fragile creatures subject to immediate departure; how we wait is who we are. From his apartment on the western flank of Manhattan, Mark lived a life of observation with compassion. Through his writing, and instruction at Yale, and his friendship, Mark O'Donnell gave pleasure, insight, and sweet relief to many.

You'll see all those qualities in this piece, which is reprinted here courtesy of his brother Steve and the artist Chris Austopchuk, whose illustrations compliment Mark's writing perfectly. We thank them both, and wish Mark well, wherever he might be waiting for us…as usual, a couple of steps ahead.
—*Michael Gerber*

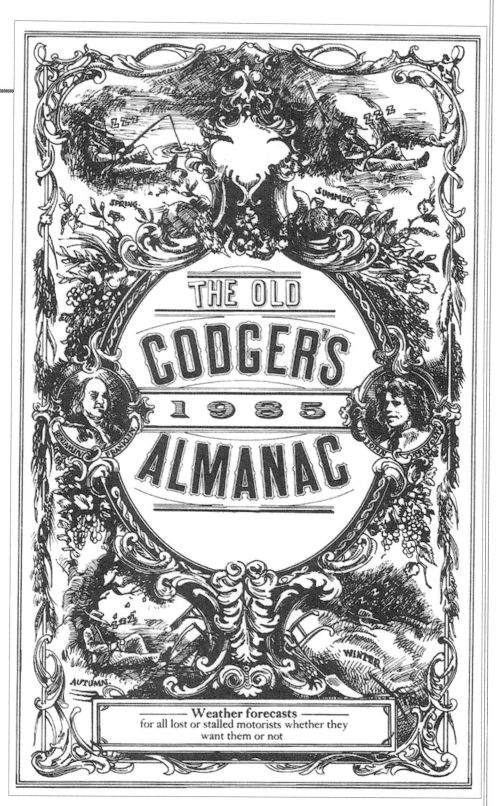

THE OLD CODGER'S 1985 ALMANAC

— Weather forecasts —
for all lost or stalled motorists whether they want them or not

LETTER TO PATRONS

Here at the watershed roadside offices of *The Old Codger's Almanac*, we have several complete sets of all 486 previous editions of the little volume you are now holding, and all of us here must say we enjoy browsing through the stacks of these old troves of information. Crops Editor Bert Winters and I, for one, often abandon our families and checkers partners for weeks on end to bone up on some particularly arresting stretches of decades. (Did you know, for instance that in 1805, the tide went out but not in?)

The annual news of the sun's and moon's movements may lack the sensation and splash of more trivial journalism, but there is a soothing, musical regularity to the long rows of statistics that I myself prefer to warm Ovaltine. So we continue, year after year, like the running of the sap, undaunted by time, weather, and the fickleness of changing design styles. "Why do you maintain this illegible, crackerbarrel rigamarole in this day and age?" I am asked by lost media people from New York who mistake our offices for a gas station. "The layout is dense, it's unfocused and frankly unattractive," they tend to go on. "Maybe," I respond, "but I ain't the one who's lost."

This is not to say we haven't been tempted over the years to offer more timely material than kitchen remedies and unsolicited advice. Our 1943 and 1944 editions, in addition to a Pony Express retrospective, featured detailed articles on the interior designs and present positions of all battleships in the American fleet.

Since then, we have made occasional forays into the appraisal of passing fads (e.g., *Ten Uses for Old Television Antennas*, 1962), but, for the most part, we sit tight under the rapture of stars like a contented, abandoned plow.

Still, we have our own measure of fashionability. These days, what with every taxi-taking ballet dancer and advertising executive gallivanting around in down-filled skivvies and a hunter's jacket, eating country-style anything, discussing their window-boxes, and talking down-home talk into C.B.'s, *The Old Codger's Almanac* has had something of a slow-blooded revival. A lot of folks hang it in their summer home like a social register.

So, if anything, the incomprehensibility of the book boosts its value as a status accessory. And a lot of people find comfort in the notion that the elements themselves can be camp.

However that may be, we press on, already gathering outdated information for next year's edition. By our fruits ye shall know us, and by yours.

FEBRUARY hath 30 days.

1985

The winter wind will drone and drone
From day's debut 'til night is black:
Its sound is very like the tone
Of The Old Codger's Almanac.

D.M.	D.W.	Dates, Feasts, Fasts, Aspects, Taxes Due	Weather
1	M.	**CIRCUMCISION** ● Taxes {$10.50 / $11.70	Snow,
2	Tu.	☾ over Miami ● *stupid birds come north*	sleet
3	W.	**All Saints Softball** ● *!☞ Taxes {$9.25 / $10.10	and slop
4	Th.	☾ light becomes you ● 1st woman lawyer dies, 1892	on top
5	Fr.	Rhode Island ignored, 1925 ● Taxes {$10.75 / $10.75	of ice:
6	Sa.	How high the ☾ ● *Jupiter lets Mars lead*	not neat
7	G	**St. Elmo's Fire Sale** ● Taxes {$9.50 / $11.00	or nice —
8	M.	Festival of the Related-by-Marriage Gleaners	*Watch out!*
9	Tu.	largest whale born, 1881 ● *Pluto does a little dance*	*Winds clout*
10	W.	old devil ☾ ● *frogs stir in sleep*	*your home*
11	Th.	1st tub in White House, 1938 ● Taxes {$11.05 / $12.05	and chill
12	Fr.	Elizabeth Taylor born, 1932	goodwill
13	Sa.	Elizabeth Taylor born again (for photographers), 1932	'til all
14	G	52nd Sunday after last year ● ☾ river	within,
15	M.	*Saturn arrested for trespassing by Venus*	their
16	Tu.	it's only a paper ☾ ● snow in Alaska, 1926	patience
17	W.	**All Goats Day** ● meteor resembling Will Rogers, 1953	thin,
18	Th.	☾ light sonata ● 4-foot herring elected to Congress, 1938	lash at
19	Fr.	fly me to the ☾ ● Unknown Soldier's birthday	each other,
20	Sa.	*moon eclipsed by large building*	husband. mother
21	G	D. Eisenhower either b. or d., not clear which	*children, wife.*
22	M.	Lint Day !$%&* ● Taxes {$11.30 / $12.00	and life
23	Tu.	unexplained noises, 1840 ● $☾♂	seems ghastly.
24	W.	**Doomed Wheat Day** ● Taxes {$9.75 / $10.60	Lastly,
25	Th.	☾ glow ● St. Anne's Surprise Potluck	though,
26	Fr.	Bad News Day ● *frogs murmur spouses' name*	a thaw!
27	Sa.	concept for Star Wars born, 1974 ♣♡*	Hurrah!
28	G	**Gherkin Sunday** ● *Aquarius aligns with rich relatives*	Then
29	M.	Deodorizing of St. Jerome ● Taxes {$10.45 / $11.00	more
30	Tu.	☾ comes over the mountain ● world ends, 1979	snow.

Farmer's Calendar

Remove drifts of snow that have accumulated indoors and investigate possible missing walls.

Dip all household articles in tar to preserve them.

Old Christmas trees can be used to cover floors with festive dry needles.

Slice enough cheese for the entire winter, in case frostbitten fingers prevent knife use later.

Get up at half-hour intervals throughout the night to shake the bottled salad dressings in the refrigerator. This will prevent even momentary settling of contents.

Leftover holiday guests make perfect sources of inconvenience and unpleasantness.

Moose and bear can be coaxed into the house to spend winter with you by coating the halls and staircases with maple syrup.

Catch all local mice and rabbits and pull their teeth to prevent garden damage come spring.

Label your children and store them in a dry, frostproof place.

Use the mild, moonlit nights to prune grapevines and dig up a disliked neighbor's garden.

Chip away at large boulders with only a needle, to learn better what eternity means.

S T A T E · F A I R

PRIZE-WINNING JAMS AND JELLIES ARE AS NEAR AS YOUR NEAREST GOURMET STORE

by Velveteena Tinbrook Wheeler

Yes, mealtime wouldn't be meal time without food, and few foods are as nice as good jams and jellies, just as the little prayer above suggests. Delicious on bread, all by itself in bowls (I serve it in troughs on New Year's Eve instead of alcohol), or packed inside a big Christmas Turkey and/or doughnut, jams and jellies have long been truly the "staff of life" for millions. Even the ancient Egyptians must have loved their jelly, because we certainly don't find any leftovers cluttering up their tombs!

The best method I know for making preserves is quick, inexpensive and sure to snare you a blue ribbon at your next State Fair. I would, of course, be a fool to part with it, so I'll tell you a lesser recipe which should, nonetheless, suit your purposes adequately.

First of all, remember that when making fruit preserves, fruit is of the essence. In these strapped times, it's a temptation just to churn out the preserves minus the expense of fruit, but even if your guests don't catch on, you'll know in your heart you've been cheap — and anyway, if you like bright colors in your kitchen creations, you'll want that extra sparkle that ingredients always add.

Now that you've peeled and sliced a load of peaches or raspberries — I usually gauge a winter's supply by how many it takes to snap the springs on my mother-in-law's daybed — put on some water to boil. This is for coffee, since you've been doing all that thankless peeling and slicing for hours without a break.

Refreshed? Back to work, this time to cook those peeled and sliced whatevers within an inch of their soulless lives. Then, add sugar, pectin, cornstarch and perhaps some storebought jelly as an encouraging example to the rest of the mixture. After that — by the way, I hope you used *clean* jars! We don't want bolts or bandaids in among the boysen berries — it'll be no time before blue ribbons are dangling on your prize preserves.

Remember, too, that sometimes your own excellence is not so effective as preventing the excellence of others. Switching labels at the judging booth can make strawberry jam look deathly green, and green beans seem a bloody pulp. A little well-timed jostling and your neighbors won't even be in the running, except for a mop and wastebasket. In that gingham dress you're wearing and your hair pulled back in a bun, no one will imagine that the corridors of evil in your heart are as labyrinthine as a city slicker's.

And, after all, isn't that the beauty of country life?

RAINY DAY AMUSEMENTS

—PAPER SCRUNCHING—

Those with no patience for origami can use scrunched-up paper and lots of glue to fashion assorted animal or human figures, mostly very basic snowmen. Paper scrunching is an art that has been unknown to the Orient for centuries and though they tend to resemble stuck-together popcorn balls, scrunched-up paper figures often give the maker minutes of satisfaction.

—WUT WUZZAT?—

Alone? Blindfold yourself and spin until you are dizzy. Now, walk around the house colliding with things. Carry a pad of paper and scribble down what you imagine you've broken, based on the sound of the objects crashing to the floor. When exhausted, stop, have something cool to drink, and compare the real breakage with your guesses. The ears, you'll find, are not as quick as the eye.

—BRAIN TAUNTERS—

Mr. Morton wants to combine candy costing 79 cents a pound with candy costing 99 cents a pound to get a mixture costing 87 cents a pound. Is that all right with you?

John and Jane live on a planet that is 8,000 miles in diameter hurtling through space at 1,800 miles a second, tipped 23½° to the plane of its orbit. What chance does their love have?

THE TEN MOST COMMON ARGUMENTS—SETTLED

● The chicken came first, not the egg.
● Hot tea does not cool you off.
● Not even the President can hold his breath for more than three minutes.
● You cannot get used to poison.
● Fish *do* feel pain when hooked, but who cares?
● Scarlett does not get Rhett back.
● There are no top-secret federal conferences with super-intelligent bees.
● Women are more neat than men, except unmarried ones in large cities.
● You cannot get drunk on water, no matter how much you drink.
● It is not proper to machine-wash the American flag. It *is* proper not to mention that it is dirty.

ANSWERS TO LAST YEAR'S PUZZLES

(1) First of all, hens can't talk. Second, even if they could, they wouldn't go around trading their own eggs. No answer is correct.

(2) No, because we didn't tell you that the mother didn't really die. She was all right all along.

(3) Seven in all. There will be no Leap Year in 2200, don't forget.

(4) It depends.

(5) Never. Don't forget, the water would flow down the drain the other way once the bathtub crossed the equator.

(6) Five pieces, if you think you could eat that many.

(7) None—since, you'll recall, penguins live only at the *South* Pole.

(8) Ten. Or eleven, if you jammed them in.

(9) An infinite amount, but it sounds like publicity to us.

(10) Farmer Jones should reply, "I don't give a tinker's cuss about your daughter being half the age you are now and my being twice your age next year. I asked you a civil question and I expect a direct answer, dammit."

A different, *fully-cooked, ready-to-eat* pancake delivered to your door each month. We mail it while it's still warm.

the PANCAKE of the MONTH CLUB

$10/year. BON-VIVANT TYPES, Bucrus, TN 72429.

FISH APHRODISIAC

and it's you they'll love.

Specify after-shave or cologne.

BITE-MORE, Poonsocket, MO 65360.

Amagansett Chickens lay eggs

cooked to order!!

Incredible but true, the Amagansett chicken not only lays poached, boiled, fried and shirred eggs, but, with a little shaking, delivers sides of home fries and toast. Sadly, none of these chickens is available to you.

UNCLAIMED VALUABLES

in your own mouth!

Send inquiries to AMULETS & IVORY Nantucket, MA 02554.

EYEGLASSES!

EYEGLASSES!

150 pairs of glasses, all yours, all guaranteed *different* prescriptions — just $2.00!!!

Ware-house clearance! HAYNES MORTUARY,

EYEGLASSES!

Freet, KA 82101.

Eliminate painful **SOCK RUB, END ARGYLE CHAFE** with **UNDERSOX**

– the gentle leggings that go under your socks.

Shoe
Foot
Sock
Undersox

Stop suffering! Send $5.00 to UNDERSOX, Portmount, NH 05382.

RAISE SCIENTISTS

in your own home. Industry and research always need new supplies of these creatures, and pay top prices! Write for your starter booklet to: SCIENTIST RANCH Phoenix, AZ 91467.

100 BRAND NEW TOWELS

to You!

only $1.25

Incredible, but true. Durable. Beautiful colors. Sent in plain brown envelope. Box 4, Vincennes, IN 93782. Allow 6 to 8 weeks for bitter disappointment to wear off.

TRAVEL BY PLANK

For less expense than bus fare to the junction, you can take that long-dreamed-of vacation to the Fijis, Rio or Paris, France. Send $1.00 for brochure.

SPINNY LUMBER. Fort Linda, VT 13587.

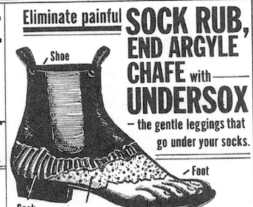

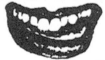

George Meyer

The Road Warrior
(The Radio Version)

Pulse-pounding action from the St. Louis Broadcast Workshop.

D.J.
Tonight we present one of my all-time favorite movies, *The Road Warrior*, adapted for radio by the St. Louis Broadcast Workshop.

(MUSIC: ROAD WARRIOR *OPENING THEME*)

GYROCOPTER PILOT
I remember the Road Warrior. The man we called Max. In the years that followed the Great War between the Super Powers he wandered out into the wasteland in search of the now-precious juice... gasoline.

(MUSIC: *TRANSITION*)

MAX
Let go of that gas can.

GYROCOPTER PILOT
That's *my* juice, mate.

MAX
Like hell! I found it, in this over-turned truck!

GYROCOPTER PILOT
I need it for my gyrocopter!

MAX
What about my car?

GYROCOPTER PILOT
All right! We'll share it! Damn, people will kill each other for gas in this bizarre post-apocalyptic society.

MAX
You said it. Hey, what's that down there?

GYROCOPTER PILOT
Where?

MAX
Way in the distance, in that desert valley. It's some sort of heavily-fortified colony. Here, use the binoculars.

GYROCOPTER PILOT
Oh, yes, now I see. It appears to be a makeshift refinery for turning crude oil into gasoline.

MAX
Hmm. Resourceful of them. Not like those cutthroat savages who murder and scavenge and plunder...

GYROCOPTER PILOT
Hey, look over there!

MAX
Well, I'll be damned! It's a little boy, with long straggly hair and weird clothing that looks almost like a caveman's.
(to boy)
Hello, there! What's your name?

GYROCOPTER PILOT
Seems he can't speak.

MAX
Yes, but there's something in his demeanor that makes me think he could be a valuable ally. I'll take him with me to the fortress. We'll be back with some juice.

(SFX: CAR ROARING TO LIFE)

(MUSIC: TRANSITION)

BLONDE WARRIOR
Open the gate for the stranger!

(SFX: BUS MOVING)

MAX
(thinking aloud)
How interesting. They've used a school bus to form a crude barricade.

BLONDE WARRIOR
State your business.

MAX
(thinking)
Wow, she's a knockout. Her clothing is a bit strange and futuristic, but what a body! She really brightens up this harsh landscape.

BLONDE WARRIOR
We cannot admit strangers! They try to steal our fuel... although now that I look in your eyes, I see that there's a certain intelligence and soulfulness there. I'm more inclined to trust you.

MAX
Thanks.

BLONDE WARRIOR
And I like this little wolfboy, too. He seems nice.

MAX
He is.

PAPPAGALLO
(shouting)
Close the gate!

GYROCOPTER PILOT
They're coming!

(SFX: HUBBUB, SHOUTING, APPROACHING HOT-RODS)

BLONDE WARRIOR
Look at them all! Stretching across the horizon!

MAX
Look at that weird clothing! And those bizarre haircuts. Every one's a different color!

BLONDE WARRIOR
Have you ever seen such a strange collection of vehicles?

MAX
Obviously, they've been built from scavenged auto parts!

BLONDE WARRIOR
Hey, that big guy with the mask is talking to the guy with the red mohawk.

HUMUNGUS
Let me do the talking!

MOHAWK
Okay.

HUMUNGUS
(shouting)
Greetings! I am the Lord Humungus! We intend to seize your supply of juice! Walk away from it now, and your lives will be spared! Anyone who disobeys will be shot with this crossbow I'm holding.

MOHAWK
Hey, that little kid just threw a boomerang at us! See it spinning through the air?

HUMUNGUS
Well, can't you just catch it?

MOHAWK
Sure, why not?
(screams)
YEEOOW! It cut my fingers off!

HUMUNGUS
(shouting)
Fools! We will be back tomorrow. None of you will get out alive!

HUMUNGUS (cont'd)
(to his men)
Move out!

(SFX: CARS ROARING AWAY)

(MUSIC: TRANSITION)

BLONDE WARRIOR
It's hopeless! They have us outnumbered. We must leave in a convoy, with a tanker truck full of juice. I want you to drive the tanker.

MAX
Don't you already have a leader?

BLONDE WARRIOR
Yes, but he's weak. That man over there…

PHIL
That blonde guy?

BLONDE WARRIOR
Yes.

MAX
Well, he is a bit older than me. I'd say about 45. And there's a certain weariness to him—an air of defeat. All right, I'll lead the convoy.

(MUSIC: TIME PASSAGE)

GYROCOPTER PILOT
This is it, everybody. Start your engines.

(SFX: MANY ENGINES STARTING UP)

BLONDE WARRIOR
Max, I'll be riding shotgun on top of the tanker. And I'm glad you're letting the wild boy ride in the cab with you. Ready, wild boy? Good, your smile tells me "yes."

MAX
Okay, let's do it!

(MUSIC: TRIUMPHANT)

(SFX: MANY CARS ROARING AWAY)

BLONDE WARRIOR
(shouting)
Max! I think it's going to work!

MAX
Not so fast! Look!

BLONDE WARRIOR
Oh, I see what you mean! Humungus and his men…They're right on our tails!

(SFX: MORE CARS)

MAX
Hey, that Mohawk guy has a grappling hook! I wonder what he's planning …

(SFX: ENGINE ROARING CLOSE)

MOHAWK
I'll just throw this grappling hook at the speeding tanker... Hey, it caught on his door and tore it off!

(SFX: CLATTER)

I'd better try again. Hey, this time, it caught onto something solid. Now I can use the rope to swing onto the tanker truck. Here goes…

(SFX: THUD, FOLLOWED BY CRASHES)

It worked! Hey, wow! The car I jumped out of flipped over and then two other cars smashed into it! Heh! Heh!

BLONDE WARRIOR
Max! The guy with the Mohawk is on the tanker! And Humungus is ramming us with his car! He has that thing that can shoot 4 arrows!

MAX
Look out!

BLONDE WARRIOR
AAGH! All four of them hit me! AAAGH!

(SFX: SMASHING GLASS)

MAX
Wild boy! *I need the shotgun shells*. They rolled onto the hood when the mohawk guy smashed the windshield just then! Crawl out there and get them! Do you understand?
(BEAT)
Good! You're doing it! You're almost to the shotgun shells!

MOHAWK
(battle cry)
AIIEEE!

MAX
Oh, no! The Mohawk guy just loomed out of nowhere! He's going to kill the wild boy!

MOHAWK
You're dead, kid! Hey what's that? An oncoming truck? We're going to hit it!

(SFX: CRASH)

MOHAWK
AHHGHGH! My body was crushed between the two trucks! I'm hitting the pavement!! Now all the cars are running over my body!!! I'M DEAAAAADD!!!

(SFX: GYROCOPTER)

GYROCOPTER PILOT
Oh no! From up here in my gyro-copter, I can see that the tanker truck has crashed and flipped over. Well, at least the convoy is getting away!

(SFX: CARAVAN OF CARS RECEDING)

MAX
Wow! What a crash! Am I all right? Yes, I think so. Got to crawl out of this wreckage… Hey, there's the wild boy. Better drag him free too, before this thing explodes! Wait a minute, what's this? Look, wild boy! Look what's leaking out of the tanker truck! It's sand! Not gasoline, just sand! What do you think that means? Oh, I get it. They hid the gas in all the smaller vehicles. Our tanker was just a decoy. Very clever. But then again, they kind of used me, so it's sort of a bittersweet feeling… Oh, well. It's over now. Guess I might as well start walking down the road here…

WILD BOY
(narrating)
That was the last I ever saw of the Road Warrior. You see, I'm the little wild boy, all grown up now. Are you surprised? Well, someone taught me English. But I'll never forget the expression on the Road Warrior's face that day. That look will forever haunt my soul.

(MUSIC: FINALE)

D.J.
We hope you've enjoyed *The Road Warrior.* Next week, don't miss the radio version of *Gravity.*

ASTRONAUT
Phew, I missed the solar panel! But now I'm going to hit some other thing! OOOGH!

Brian McConnachie and Frank Springer

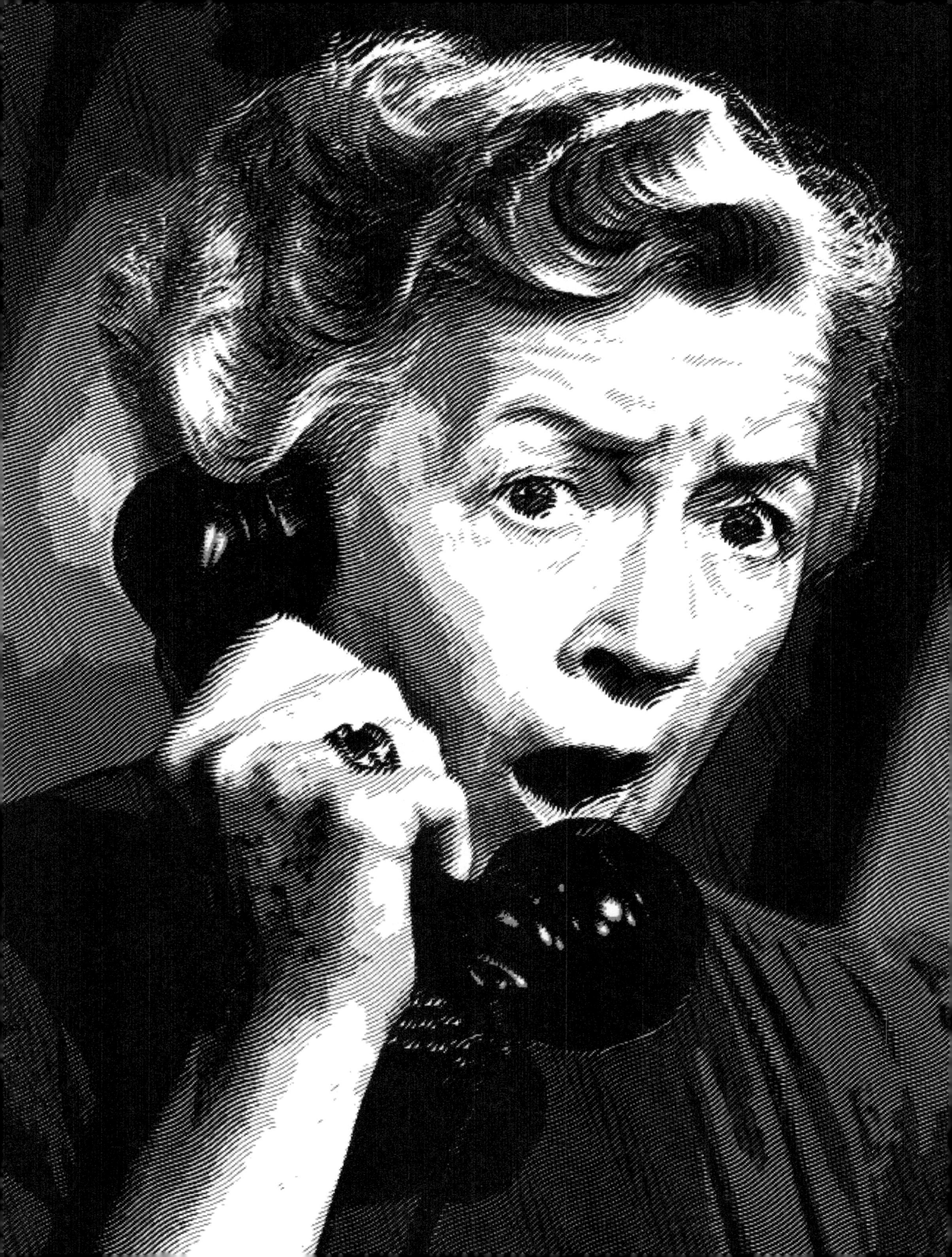

Terry Jones

The Truthful Telephone

"May Morris, you old fraud! *I hope you rot in HELL!*"

You might think that there was nothing particularly evil about a Truthful Phone. It simply told the truth, which is, of course, 'A Good Thing To Do.' But the way this particular telephone told the truth was not at all good. In reality the thing was evil from the tip of its mouthpiece to the end of its cord.

It was put up for sale in a shop window with a label that read: 'The Truthful Phone – £10'.

'I've never heard of such a thing,' said Mrs Morris, who was frail and elderly but of an enquiring mind.

'I wouldn't take it, if I were you, Mrs Morris,' said the shopkeeper, who was a kind man despite his appearance. 'The truth can get you into all sorts of trouble.'

'Oh dear,' replied Mrs Morris. 'I always understood the truth never hurt anyone.'

'Don't you believe it,' said the shopkeeper. 'The truth can be dangerous and undesirable and should be shunned as long as is possible. Nobody really wants the truth. They want to live in a world that is comfortable and happy. The truth would just make most people miserable.'

'But I need a new telephone,' said Mrs Morris, 'and this one is the cheapest by far!' And with that she bought the phone and took it home. That very day she got Albert, the odd job man, to come and install it.

The first time it rang, Mrs Morris picked the phone up and was surprised to hear her old friend Mabel say, 'Ha! May Morris, you old fraud! I hope you rot in hell!'

'I beg your pardon? Is that you Mabel?' 'How dare you call me a parasite!' cried Mabel indignantly.

'I didn't, my dear . . . Are you feeling quite well?'

'If you've always thought I was a free-loader who cultivated your friendship simply for the free teas, why have you pretended to be my friend for so many years?' shouted Mabel.

'Upon my soul!' cried Mrs Morris. 'I think you had better ring back when you're feeling more yourself again, dear.' And she hung up.

She then stood for some time gazing at the phone.

A little later she rang the greengrocer.

'Hello, Mr Murphy?' she said into the phone. 'I hope you're well today?'

There was a long silence on the other end of the phone.

'Hello? Are you still there?' asked Mrs Morris. 'I'd like to order a big bag of your best potatoes and some leeks.'

'Er . . .' said Mr Murphy.

'And a cucumber, a lettuce and a pound of tomatoes. Is that all right?' asked Mrs Morris.

"I think my wife's coming!" said Mr Murphy hurriedly and he rang off.

Mrs Morris was more than a little astonished, though she had the feeling that the phone may have had something to do with the odd way in which Mr Murphy had received her order for potatoes, leeks and salad.

As for Mr Murphy he was equally surprised. He had picked up the phone and had heard Mrs Morris, that sweet little old lady from down the road, say, 'Hello, you gorgeous hunk! I've been thinking about your bottom all week!'

He was so surprised, in fact, that he didn't know what to say.

Then he heard Mrs Morris continue, 'I love the ginger hair on your arms and the manly way you tip potatoes into my shopping bag and then stick in the leeks.'

All he could say was, 'Er . . .'

Then Mrs Morris went on, 'Since the unfortunate late Mr Morris disappeared under mysterious circumstances in the Campsie Fells, I have dreamt of running a market garden with you in Worthing!'

At this point, Mr Murphy began to get really worried, and made up some story about his wife walking into the shop. He put the phone down and blinked at his assistant, Tom, and then at the customers. Had they heard what Mrs Morris had said? What on earth had got into the woman?

He spent the rest of the day keeping to the back of the shop in case Mrs Morris should turn up in person. But she didn't.

In fact Mrs Morris was far too busy to go down to the shop to pick up her leeks and potatoes. She was round at the police station telling Constable Robinson how she'd

Actor, director, historian, poet and Python, *Terry Jones'* latest book, *Evil Machines*, is available at all online booksellers.

received a strange phone call.

'It was Albert, the odd-job man. He said he was going to come round and fix the boiler for me . . .'

'Does he often ring up and say things like that?'

'Oh yes, officer, he's very helpful.'

'So what's the problem?'

'Well, he also said that he'd probably steal a few things while he was at it. He said he'd noticed some valuable-looking jewellery in a drawer in my bedroom. I said I didn't realize he'd been poking around in my bedroom drawers, and he told me he'd been stealing things from me for years, but I'd never noticed because he only took small things and only a few at a time.'

'Why do you think he was telling you all this?'

'Oh! I don't think he was!' said Mrs Morris. 'I think it was the Truthful Phone.'

'Hmm!' said Constable Robinson. 'The Truthful Phone?'

'Yes,' replied Mrs Morris. 'I want you to arrest it!'

'We don't normally arrest telephones,' said Constable Robinson. 'Perhaps I'd better come and have a look.'

So Constable Robinson went with Mrs Morris to her house to take a look at the Truthful Phone. It didn't look very different from an ordinary phone, except that it had a switch on the side.

'May I try it?' asked Constable Robinson.

'Of course,' said Mrs Morris.

So Constable Robinson rang the superintendent back at the police station.

'Oh! Hi, Super!' said Constable Robinson. 'Robinson here. I'm just trying out Mrs Morris's Truthful Phone.'

'You're what?' exclaimed the superintendent, who was startled to hear Constable Robinson say he knew all about the bribes the superintendent took from criminals and local businessmen, and that he was going to report the matter to his superiors.

'I'm trying out Mrs Morris's Truthful Phone,' repeated Constable Robinson.

'You do and I'll break every bone in your body!' roared the superintendent. 'And I mean that!'

And, from the tone of the superintendent's voice, Constable Robinson knew it was the truth, even though he hadn't the slightest idea what he had said to make the superintendent so angry.

'It's not what you said,' whispered Mrs Morris. 'It's what the phone said that is the problem. I think I'll take it back to the shop.'

Just then the phone rang.

'Hello?' said Mrs Morris. 'This is May Morris speaking.'

'I don't want to go back to the shop,' said the phone.

'Who is this?' asked Mrs Morris.

'It's me, your new telephone,' said the phone. 'I like it here. If you try to have me disconnected, I'll make your life a misery.'

'You're already doing that!' exclaimed Mrs Morris. 'I'm going to call Albert now.'

'What and let him steal from you?' said the phone.

'At least he doesn't mess around with what I say!'

'Don't disconnect me or I'll . . .'

But Mrs Morris had already slammed the phone down.

'Who was it?' asked Constable Robinson.

'It was the phone,' said Mrs Morris.

I know it was the phone, but who was on the phone?' asked Constable Robinson.

But before Mrs Morris could explain, the phone rang again. Mrs Morris picked it up and then turned to the police officer.

'It's for you, constable,' she said.

Constable Robinson took the phone. 'Hello?' he said.

'Ask Mrs Morris what happened to her husband,' said the phone and then rang off.

'What was that?' asked Mrs Morris.

'Someone just said, "Ask Mrs Morris what happened to her husband," and then rang off,' explained the constable.

'What!' exclaimed Mrs Morris in some agitation. 'Who was it?'

'They didn't say!'

'It's the phone!' cried Mrs Morris. 'It's evil!'

And she grabbed the phone and shouted into the mouthpiece, 'I'm having you disconnected and you're going straight back to the shop!' But all she got back was the dialling tone.

'Constable,' said Mrs Morris. 'Would you help me disconnect this phone? I don't trust it to say what I want it to say.'

'Certainly,' said Constable Robinson, and he started to pull at the wires, whereupon the phone rang again. Constable Robinson stopped and looked at Mrs Morris. She shook her head.

'Don't pick it up!' exclaimed Mrs Morris. 'Don't listen to it!'

'But it might be the superintendent,' said Constable Robinson, and he picked up the phone as if it were a live crab.

'Look in the garden shed,' said the phone.

'Who's that?' shouted Constable Robinson, but the phone had rung off.

Constable Robinson frowned. He looked across at Mrs Morris. She was white-haired and frail.

'No, no . . .' he said to himself. But then he remembered that it was his duty as a policeman to investigate anything that needed to be investigated.

'Would you mind if I looked in your garden shed, Mrs Morris?' he said.

'Of course not,' said Mrs Morris. 'Is there something you need from there?'

Mrs Morris took Constable Robinson into the garden and showed him the shed. She unlocked it, and he went inside. Immediately the phone started ringing back in the house, and Mrs Morris hurried back, while Constable Robinson inspected the garden shed.

But Mrs Morris didn't answer the phone; she simply took it off the hook and left it there. She didn't want to hear another word it said.

When Constable Robinson returned from inspecting the garden shed, he said to Mrs Robinson: 'You have a very fine garden shed, Mrs Morris. It is remarkably well equipped: you have welding apparatus, wood and metal lathes, and even a blast furnace for smelting.'

'Yes,' replied Mrs Morris. 'It was my unfortunate late husband's favourite place. He spent hours in there making all sorts of things.'

'Is there someone on the phone?' asked Constable Robinson, indicating the receiver lying off its hook.

'Ignore it,' said Mrs Morris.

But Constable Robinson had already picked up the receiver.

'Well! Did you see it?' hissed the phone.

'It's full of equipment,' said Constable Robinson.

'Don't listen!' said Mrs Morris.

'The weedkiller!' hissed the phone. 'In the bottle on the shelf by the flower pots! That's what she used!'

'For what?' asked Constable Robinson.

'Take no notice of it!' said Mrs Morris, and she grabbed the telephone receiver out of the Constable's hands, and yanked the wire hard.

'NOOO!' screamed the Truthful Phone. 'Don't!'

But it was too late! The wire came out of the socket in the wall, and the Truthful Phone was disconnected. Mrs Morris sank down in a chair.

'It is an evil thing!' she said, glaring at the phone. 'I shall take it back to the shop straightaway.'

'But what was it talking about?' asked Constable Robinson.

'It was raking up old and unfounded rumours about my late and unfortunate husband's disappearance, under mysterious circumstances in the Campsie Fells,' replied Mrs Morris. 'You see, he liked making things in the garden shed, which, as you so rightly observed, is remarkably well equipped. One day he told me he was going out on the Campsie Fells, which, as you know, is a range of hills to the north of Glasgow, to test out a new kind of dog walker. The Campsie Fells was his favourite place for testing things. But that day he never came back.'

'I'm very sorry,' said Constable Robinson.

'Yes,' said Mrs Morris. 'I was sorry too. Would you like a cup of tea?'

'That sounds like an excellent idea,' said the constable.

And so that's what they had.

When Constable Robinson returned to the police station, he found the superintendent waiting for him.

'Listen, Constable Robinson, I'm thinking of promoting you.'

'Really!' exclaimed Constable Robinson. He'd been in the force without promotion for so long he'd almost given up hope.

'Yes,' said the superintendent, 'but there are one or two things that we should keep confidential, just between you and me.'

'I see,' said Constable Robinson, 'that's OK by me.'

But the business with the Truthful Phone was not quite over.

'Oh, by the way,' said the superintendent, 'There's a message on the an-swering machine for you.'

Constable Robinson recognized the voice on the answering machine at once. It was the Truthful Phone. 'Listen, Constable Robinson,' it said. 'Just in case I do get disconnected, I think you should know the truth about Mrs Morris's husband. He didn't disappear under mysterious circumstances in the Campsie Fells. He was poisoned in his own home. With weedkiller.'

Constable Robinson shuddered. All his working life in the police force he'd dreaded this moment when he would be confronted by a real criminal and would have to make an arrest. Of course, he'd given out the usual speeding fines and he'd reported several cars for going through red traffic lights, but he generally managed to avoid any contact with proper criminals.

Now here he was faced with a criminal of the worst sort: a murderer – possibly a murderess! But Constable Robinson didn't hesitate. He knew what his duty was and he went straight to his superintendent, and told him the story. The superintendent immediately leapt into action.

'We've no time to lose!' he said. 'She may be armed and dangerous!'

'Who? Mrs Morris?' stuttered the Constable, who was having difficulty imagining that dear little old lady wielding a machine gun.

But the superintendent was already on the phone. 'I want six squad cars and an armed escort a.s.a.p.!' He yelled and slammed the phone down.

In less than an hour, the police had arrived at Mrs Morris's home. Several armed officers jumped out of a van, wielding machetes, and broke down Mrs Morris's front door. Four sprang up the stairs and broke down all the doors up there, while six ran through the ground floor, knocking down any door that happened to be shut and one or two that weren't.

They opened Mrs Morris's cupboards and pulled all her clothes and personal belongings on to the floor. They pulled all the tins off her larder shelves and ransacked her fridge.

'The suspect seems to have skipped it!' reported Officer Tait to the superintendent.

'Somebody must have tipped her off!' exclaimed the superintendent. 'Which means she's not operating alone! Quick! Send reinforcements!' he barked into his radio.

In the meantime, some police officers dug up the lawn and rose beds looking for dead bodies and others raided the unfortunate late Mr Morris's garden shed.

'Suspect's shed is full of suspicious gear!' reported Officer Tait, and he took the superintendent to see the metal-working lathes, mechanical saws and smelting furnace.

'Looks like she's been cutting up her victims and burning them in the furnace!' exclaimed the superintendent. 'No wonder we didn't find any dead bodies buried under the lawn or rose beds! She could be the greatest mass-murderer of all time! Quick, send more reinforcements! This is going to be all over the press tomorrow! Well done, Constable Robinson! I can see promotion ahead for all of us!'

'I can still hardly believe it,' murmured Constable Robinson. 'She seemed such a sweet old lady. But look! There's the weedkiller, just as the phone said!'

'Take that as evidence!' exclaimed the super-

intendent. 'And that garden fork is an offensive weapon.'

By the time the helicopter had arrived there were something like fifty police officers crowded into Mrs Morris's house and garden, most of them armed.

'Now where is that phone?' asked the superintendent. 'It's our key witness.'

'It's gone!' gasped Constable Robinson. 'She must have taken it back to the shop!'

'No time to lose!' shouted the superintendent. 'We may yet apprehend the suspect, before she can escape the country!'

All this while, Mrs Morris had been making her way back to the electrical shop where she had bought the Truthful Phone. She went via the park, where she always spent a pleasant hour feeding the ducks and pigeons. She then stopped at the greengrocer to order some leeks and potatoes. The greengrocer himself wasn't to be seen, however, as he was hiding in the back of the shop, so she told his assistant to give him her best wishes.

She then went on to the electrical shop, and was surprised to find that it had a helicopter hovering above it.

'There she goes!' whispered Constable Robinson, peering out from the police van, on the other side of the street. 'That's her!'

'Suspect entering shop now!' radioed the superintendent. 'OK, men, we'll go in all together and take the suspect by surprise. Wait for my countdown.'

When Mrs Morris handed the Truthful Phone back to the shopkeeper, he nodded. 'I didn't think you'd like it,' he said. 'The truth is often very unpleasant.'

'You are quite right, young man,' replied Mrs Morris.

'But wait a minute!' said the shopkeeper. 'You've got it set all wrong! Look!'

And he pointed to the switch on the side. When you looked closely you could see in tiny letters the words 'True – False'. The switch was turned to 'False'.

'It's been telling you lies!' exclaimed the shopkeeper.

'And not just me!' said Mrs Morris.

And that was the moment when six specially trained officers leapt out of the helicopter on to the roof of Baker's Electrical Shop, smashed their way through the ceiling and abseiled down on to the counter.

At the same time, fifty armed officers burst into the shop, spraying bullets at the ceiling. They pounced on Mrs Morris, handcuffed her, put a bag over her head and bundled her into the back of a van.

The story was, indeed, all over the press some weeks later, but I'm afraid neither Constable Robinson nor the superintendent got their promotion. The case was thrown out of court on the grounds that the Truthful Phone was not a reliable witness.

In his summing up the judge said, 'Since Mrs Morris only purchased the phone that morning, it could not have been a witness to the events it described. It was simply spreading malicious gossip.'

As for Mrs Morris, she successfully sued the police for wrongful arrest and, with the £84 she received in compensation, she was able to buy a very nice telephone. It was red, and it said exactly what anyone who used it said and nothing else.

The Truthful Phone itself disappeared under mysterious circumstances. The police claimed it had escaped from custody when they proposed charging it under the defamation laws. But there were rumours circulating that the superintendent had paid one of his friends to tie it to a lump of concrete and drop it off Westminster Bridge.

Whatever happened to it, everyone agreed that they were well rid of such an evil contraption.

But all the same, Mrs Morris felt she'd been lucky; as she said to her friend Mabel, 'Goodness knows what would have happened if that switch had been pointing to "True"!'

Brian McConnachie

Yardwork

I want to make this clear from the start:
I do NOT object to mowing other people's lawns.

What I object to is this growing notion that somehow they don't have to pay me — that crossing my palm with a little silver would be demeaning to all concerned, because I am a neighbor who lives in a house that is, as often as not, larger than theirs.

In the beginning, I did go a bit overboard with the "nobility of labor" business. Especially that time during cocktails at the Williams', with them pulling me back on the porch for another gin and tonic but me managing to slip out again to the garage and their power mower which, by the way, has that checkerboard attachment they have at all ball parks. Then with all of us awkwardly waving to each other as I crisscrossed their lawn, I became convinced I was getting more out of this than they were. They were drinking; I was working. Labor is noble!

Maybe it was my conscientiously maintained upbeat attitude combined with my absence from the commuter train that first gave rise to the erroneous notion that through some unannounced cleverness I had managed to retire comfortably from my job and could remain at home indulging some penitent need to toil about on other's people's property. Yes, I know I should have declared it from the start: *I want money for this. The fee is such and such; take it or leave it.* This is how the high school kids do it, and they don't deliver a job half as good as mine.

But I didn't spell it out — I didn't feel I needed to. These are accomplished people living in a pretty swanky ZIP code and know quality work when they see it. I shouldn't have to ask! And if cash is a problem, they could do me a favor then, or give something I could exchange for cash.

Floor lamps come to mind, or a picture frame.

Bad timing's been part of the problem. As I was finishing the Orlandos' lawn, I pictured myself climbing the steps of his new deck, breathing heavily, dripping sweat on all that new pressurized wood, staring him in the eye. And not leaving till I got something. And something *real*, not a handshake and a micro-brewed beer. But when I had actually finished, somewhere around 6:30, the Orlandos, all six or seven of them, were inside behind a firmly shut door eating dinner.

I have always had a strong suspicion that the Orlandos, like all close families, use their evening mealtime to savor and examine their collective joy with their good fortune. Or they could be chasing each other around the table with their new croquet set. I really don't know. But either way, I was unable to walk in on them. As I wandered off with my resolve in a puddle, I knew the job I did would be quickly forgotten. It's been raining a lot. The grass has been growing like mad.

I was direct with Jerry Hodgson when he came trotting over to me one Saturday morning. He couldn't believe I had cut his whole lawn.

"Give me one of your five irons." I said, not really wanting it but knowing he had three of them and thus establishing exchange. Well, this must have been one of the looniest things anyone had ever said to him. Maybe it was the way I said it but he laughed, slapped my back and swore up and down that I was the wildest card in the deck.

"Then give me a box of golf balls, for God's sake. No, forget the golf balls...make it that big, ugly floor lamp on the porch!" I yelled after him as he staggered off towards his silver BMW and 9 o'clock tee time.

Maybe I should have made it more clear that I've been out of work for five months now. It doesn't have to be the focus of all conversation but it really should be acknowledged. I just can't believe I have to spell it out. *Somebody* must be aware that (a) I'm around the house all day and (b) when they get home, their lawns are cut and their shrubs are trimmed. And it's done a damn sight better than the Burns kid ever did it and he has the nerve to charge $20 an hour (in some cases even $30) and thinks he's taking my daughter to the Columbia Fair in the new Isuzu Trooper I heard he paid cash for.

I'm very near the point of coming right out and demanding the money and even asking for half up front just in case they don't think I'm serious. This is something I have to do myself. It was a mistake to send Max, my seven-year-old, to negotiate with Mrs. Everts. But we rehearsed the line: "My Daddy cut your lawn — why don't you pay him?" again and again.

That's all he had to say but when he got there, something went wrong. She got him off of the subject. Maybe she offered him cookies. I don't know. But the next time I saw Mrs. Everts at the Stop 'n' Shop, she was very clear in telling me that she loaned Max $20 and she expected me to pay it back by the weekend.

"Or it's going to be twenty-*five*," she added with a menacing leer which I guess was meant as sort of a Mafia "vig" joke.

Joe Driscole (his is the house bigger than mine, with three acres of lawn — a lot of it in steep forty-five degree terraces) knows damn well that I am out of work. He has some important job with Murdoch's News Corp corporation, and I am certain he could find me something there if he tried. I am quite qualified. I graduated in the top third of my class at Princeton which is a damn sight better than he did at some junior college off in the Dakota Badlands that no one can seem to remember. I can pay attention in meetings and look thoughtfully at spread sheets and have my people get back to their people and email with the best of them.

Still and all, I'm realistic: I'm not looking for a corner office with an Asian secretary with an English accent. I recognize I've been out of touch for a bit. I'll gladly take a few steps back knowing whatever the job, it's got to beat mowing lawns for nothing. And I've always been decent to Joe, in spite of the fact he is totally literal, annoyingly slow and basically morose. I have even at times gone out of my way to politely inquire into his big, dull life and ask for his hollow opinions. I have invited him into my home, put exotic foods in his belly and fine wines down his throat. In short, I have been more than nice to this overpaid, boorish ass who wont say boo about whatever the hell he's in charge of at the Murdoch News Corp operation.

But you have to set personalities aside in this business. When you lawn, you put on those blinders and concentrate on that strip of grass in front of you. And you think about your mower. You read that warning sticker with the severed hand and the red line through it, over and over. I was about to attack Driscole's steep slopes when I began to realized the safety features on lawn mowers make it pretty impossible to hurt yourself with the blade. With the possible exception of steep inclines where you and your mower could suddenly go tumbling down the hill together. But as soon as you let go of that bar that is squeezed toward the handle, the engine cuts off and the blade stops and then it's just you and the mower banging into each other on the big roll down.

It would be hard to commit suicide with a power mower because of that bar. That is to say, if you had the strength, which I don't, to hoist the mower into the air and lower it onto your head, you wouldn't be able to keep the safety bar depressed. Actually, you could tape the bar to the handle. But then there's still the matter of lifting and lowering it. You could probably put the mower on its side, tape the bar and run at the mower, head first.

That might work but most likely, at the last second, the not-in-the-face instinct would kick in and up would come your hands. But if your hands were taped to your sides, you couldn't throw then up and that's what sent me looking around in Driscole's garage for some duct tape. Just to see if it could be done.

I found some, started the engine again, taped the bar and put the mower on its side. I peeled off a strip and held it in my hand and put the spool down a shaft of a rake, wedged the rake and turned around and around until I had used up all of the tape. Then I walked back outside to the mower.

I should again add that I was merely curious. The propeller was a blur. I began to doubt that a person could run and dive at it with any accuracy. Without the use of your hands, running balance would be off. You could crawl at it and just jam your head in there. That would be the most direct. And I was in that position, kneeling by the over turned mower, all duct taped up when good old Joe rounded the bend and in his own slow, tiresome way became gravely puzzled by this sight.

I knew no explanation I could offer would penetrate so I left it to him to question me and waited for the one that would most directly deliver him some enlightenment. Mind you, his concern wasn't: Oh my God! You dear man. Here, let me get you out of this; are you all right? But close to the top of his questions was: "Did someone do this to you?"

I blamed it on the Burns's kid. However, I told Joe he was not to interfere; this was between me and the kid and I'd settle the score in my own time and my own way. I'm not sure if he believed me.

He took out his Swiss Army knife that has the dinky scissors and, as he carefully snipped away at the tape, told me he didn't want me cutting his lawn anymore because he didn't think he had the right kind of insurance. But before he escorted me off his property, Joe did surprise me. He gave me a hundred dollars cash, "for my trouble."

The more I think about it though, this may have put the skids under me for that possible Murdock News Corp position. It certainly didn't do the Burns kid any harm: Couple of weeks after that, he was offered a job in the city (I've successfully remained ignorant of the employer's identity).

On the other hand, a hundred dollars is a hundred dollars. And from Big Cheap Joe Driscole to boot! Which has lately set me to wondering what I might do in front of all those happy Orlandos to get them to crack open their happy checkbook. Something outside their dining room window perhaps...Right around dinner time... 🌼

"Gloria couldn't boil an egg when we first got married, could you Gloria? Have another one."

*It seemed Jack's longtime fear of Virginia Woolf
had been justified after all.*

Mike Sacks

Josh Alan Friedman

"I once saw a young man sucking on a stripper's breast, while she gently patted his hair. It was sad, funny, and kind of pathetic. Very much like Times Square, itself."

MIKE SACKS: When I first asked if you were willing to be interviewed, you said that you "find nothing funny about anything, anyone, anywhere, at any time."

JOSH ALAN FRIEDMAN: That might have been off-the-cuff, but there's a kernel of truth in there. Most of the time, what strikes me as funny doesn't strike others as funny. And vice versa.

MIKE SACKS: When did you publish your first cartoon with your brother Drew? What year was this?

FRIEDMAN: It was in 1978, but we had been recording reel-to-reel audio sketches and doing comic strips for ourselves over the years. I would kind of write and produce, Drew did voices and illustrations. We never thought about publishing or releasing them.

Drew began to draw constantly. He would draw his teachers naked on school desks. When I went to visit him during his freshman year at Boston University, the public walls of the entire dormitory floor were densely illustrated. Maybe I imagined this, but I seem to remember finding him upside down, like Michaelangelo laboring under the chapel. He spent months doing this, and although the frat boys loved it, Drew hadn't been to class in months. So I wanted to focus the poor boy's talent on something, and I began writing heavily researched, detailed comix scripts.

SACKS: What was that first published comic called?

FRIEDMAN: "The Andy Griffith Show." It ran in *Raw Magazine*. Drew illustrated the entire script very quickly. I loved how it looked. I said, "This is an amazing piece of work you've just done here," and he told me he could do better. He ripped up that first version and then redrew it—that's the version that now exists. When I saw how startling the strip looked after the second pass, I knew we were onto something exciting.

SACKS: To this day, the "Andy Griffith Show" comic strip remains slightly shocking. It features a black man wandering into Mayberry, North Carolina, and getting lynched by Sheriff Taylor and some other locals. This was not your typical misty-eyed look back at small-town life in the 1960s.

FRIEDMAN: That cartoon has since been reprinted many times—and we caught a lot of flak at first. Certain people accused us of being racists.

SACKS: If anything, you were mocking the nostalgia that surrounds a time and place that was anything but happy and perfect—at least for many people.

FRIEDMAN: Yes, of course. I wanted to provoke the heady sensation of fear, and also get some laughs. That, to me, was—and still is—a potent combination. The so-called comic nightmare. It's like mixing whiskey with barbiturates. It becomes more than the sum of its parts.

Over the years readers have told me that they can't remember whether they actually read some of our cartoons or dreamed them. People have asked, "I might have been dreaming, but did you once work on a comic strip about such and such?"

SACKS: You were writing about television shows and celebrities that no one else seemed to care about in the late '70s, early '80s.

FRIEDMAN: I'll confess that during childhood I never realized *I Love Lucy* was supposed to be a situation comedy. I thought it was a drama about the misadventures of this poor New York City housewife, which happened to have a surreal laugh track that made no sense. Years later, I was stunned to learn it was considered comedy.

I was always riveted by the lower depths of show business and sub-celebrities, maybe as an alternative to the dumbing down of American culture. The common man had higher standards in, say, the 1940s. And Drew's fascination went even deeper, as he depicted fantasies of Rondo Hatton, the acromegaly-cursed actor who starred in several freak horror flicks in the '30s and '40s. And, of course, Tor Johnson, the giant wrestler turned actor, from Ed Wood's *Plan 9 from Outer Space* [1959], who practically became Drew's alter ego.

There was something about The Three Stooges, after their stock had taken a dive in the '70s, that became more compelling than ever—even deeper than when

◆

Mike Sacks' probing chats with funny folk have made him the Studs Terkel of comedy. This talk with Josh Alan Friedman (*Warts and All, Tales of Times Square, Now Dig This*) was intended for Sacks' 2014 collection, *Poking a Dead Frog.*

Josh Friedman on 42nd Street, 1979. When you could find ecstasy for 25 cents. Photo by Vince McGarry.

we were children. Three short, ugly, but really beautiful, middle-aged Jews who slept in the same bed together, refused to separate, yet beat and maimed each other senselessly without end. It almost ceased being comedy, but you couldn't stop watching.

SACKS: What fascinated you about sub-celebrities at the nadir of their careers?

FRIEDMAN: If I were to speculate, I would say that worship of America's celebrity culture was becoming a mental illness without a name. It was the sickness of celebrity. It's only gotten worse: the false icons, the obsession with celebrity over substance. It demeans all of humanity. It's terribly unhealthy. So why not take it a quantum step lower—to its natural resolution—and worship Ed Wood, Joe Franklin, Wayne Newton, or Joey Heatherton, a Rat Pack–era actress in the '60s? Or serial killers posing with celebrities?

When Drew and I were doing this in the late '70s and '80s, there was no Internet. Information about old shows and movies and celebrities were difficult to come by back then. Now there are hundreds of websites devoted to The Three Stooges or "The Andy Griffith Show" or Rondo Hatton. You can now look up [the actress and model] Joey Heatherton's name and immediately find that her first husband, the football player Lance Rentzel, was arrested in 1970 for exposing himself to a child. Or that Wayne Newton once threatened to beat the shit out of Johnny Carson for telling jokes about Wayne being effeminate.

You had to search out arcane clippings' files in local libraries or newspaper morgues back then. For years, I kept accumulating photos and news clips on numerous subjects like Newton, Joey Heatherton or Frank Sinatra, Jr.

SACKS: Do you think that if your comics had come out during the Internet era they would have become a lot more popular and widely read?

FRIEDMAN: Well, the audience then was *National Lampoon, High Times, Heavy Metal, Raw*. I don't know if there is an online equivalent. Our strips attracted surprising attention at the time. Kurt Vonnegut was a fan, and wrote an intro to *Warts and All*. Recently, I read that Frank Zappa kept both of our books on his night table. I also heard that Kurt Cobain loved the strips and wrote a song ["Floyd the Barber," *Bleach*, 1989] based

on our Andy Griffith strip. But pimps, hookers, con men, heroin addicts, psychiatrists, jazz musicians, communists, and demented young starlets—those were our natural audience back in the day.

SACKS: You once mentioned that you suffered from suicidal depression. Do you think this affected your writing in any sense? Made it more melancholy?

FRIEDMAN: Personally, for me, depression is a killer of everything. Work is the saving grace. You're immersed in and possessed by a task that you are duty-bound to complete—and it often takes months or years. You feel this is what you were put on earth to do, and you're doing it. At those times, life feels right. When you are prevented from performing by outside forces, you start to self-destruct.

I fight to stay at sea level, but something must give in. I've gotten better at managing it. When I was a teenager and depression would swoop down like brutal punishment, I had no idea what was going on. I didn't know it could be quantified or there was a name for it. I went from extrovert to introvert. As a consequence, perhaps, I started to witness and interpret the world different than others.

SACKS: The dichotomy in your early life is interesting. On the one hand, you had this middle-class upbringing on Long Island, and then in Manhattan. On the other hand, you were surrounded by the uppercrust of show business and Hollywood. Your father, Bruce Jay Friedman, was a famous writer who was friends with many writers, including Vonnegut, Mario Puzo, Joseph Heller, Terry Southern, and Woody Allen.

FRIEDMAN: Right. There were movie stars, actors and writers all throughout my childhood. Joe Heller helped get me into NYU, after which I dropped out during the first semester. In the '60s and '70s, my father got around everywhere. He was received like a king in New York. He was on the cover of many publications, and I believe there was still a deep cultural respect for serious writers—which is no longer the case in the U.S.A. Unlike, say, Norman Mailer, Gore Vidal or Truman Capote, he refused to do TV. He felt it was demeaning for writers. By today's balls-to-the-wall marketing standards, that would seem insane.

My father did cast a shadow over me. It was like living with a giant. To this

day, when I dream about him, I am still a little boy and he is a big strong man. He still has quite a presence.

SACKS: According to your father, you once lit Woody Allen's hair on fire in the early 1970s. How and why did that come about?

FRIEDMAN: We were eating at Elaine's [*restaurant, on the Upper East Side in New York*]. Woody was eating next to us with a group of friends, and I lit an amaretto cookie wrapper which then floated into the air and landed on his head.

SACKS: That must have endeared you to him.

FRIEDMAN: He wasn't thrilled, if I remember correctly.

SACKS: Did you ever feel that your father's presence was too strong to escape?

FRIEDMAN: Yes, for a long time I felt I could never be as good as him. That's no longer the case, though.

SACKS: What did you learn from your father from a writer's standpoint?

FRIEDMAN: Absolutely everything. He always led by example. He taught me how to make every word count. He never believed that a longer book, like a novel, was better than a short story. Most Quality Lit readers seem to think a great book must be fat, but that's not how he felt. He always took the attitude that it is much more difficult to achieve something small and perfect than long and imperfect. Like [Voltaire's 18th century, 144-page satire] *Candide*. He writes stories that have a short burst of energy, with a big payoff.

His greatest skill is as a short story writer. He's written a few hundred, and every time he does so, there's something he needs to get off his chest. The fact that the story ends up funny is just an afterthought. Others may find these stories funny, but they are quite serious.

SACKS: Looking back, do you feel that your comic-strips broke new ground? *Playboy* described them this way: "Wicked realism and freakish horror typify the Friedman style, producing some of the slickest and funniest comics of our time."

FRIEDMAN: I suppose the non-sequitur style caught on with comic-strip writers and on *SCTV*. Some of our strips did not have endings. We didn't feel there had to be a joke or resolution at the end. When there's no clear ending, it leaves someone hanging uncomfortably, and is perhaps not fair to the reader.

Drew worked with pointillism in those years—thousands of little pinpoints that create a whole. He spent eight hours on each panel. The strips would come out hyper-realistic. I would provide what was almost a movie script—the conception of an idea, the narration, dialogue balloons and description of each panel. Then I'd drive him like a workhorse, which he was. In the name of sanity, he finally put a stop to it. Human beings can only withstand so much labor.

SACKS: What year did you start writing for *Screw* magazine?

FRIEDMAN: In 1976. My mother threw me out of our Manhattan apartment just before Thanksgiving—the one time in my life I was ever kicked out. I was 20. Reeling with self-pity, I trekked down to Times Square. I booked into a fleabag joint called the Sherman Hotel, which was located at 47th and Eighth Avenue, and I thought, This is where I belong!

There were toenail clippings stuck in the old, seedy carpet, and there was a rotary-dial phone from the 1940s. Nothing joyous ever took place in that room. A window faced out over an air shaft, a little bit of moonlight coming through. I heard old men—probably elevator men—moaning, crying, hacking phlegm all through the night. There was nothing remotely romantic about this scene.

At the time, *Screw* made me laugh more than any other magazine. It was truly anarchistic—*Mad* magazine with a cock. It outsold *Life*, *Playboy*, *Newsweek*, and *Time* on Manhattan newsstands. Many great cartoonists and art directors broke in by way of *Screw*. And let me say this about *Screw*: it was the only magazine where I freelanced—and I freelanced for a lot—where the editors dealt straight and paid on time.

There was a section in *Screw* called "My Scene," left over from the hippie days. Reader-submitted short stories, 40 bucks on acceptance. I had submitted one months before, about pressing up against a beautiful, big-assed Puerto Rican woman on the New York subway. Total bullshit. But the first night staying at this horrific hotel, I walked to a newsstand near Orange Julius and copped an issue of *Screw*—and there it was. I've published maybe 250 to 300 pieces since then, but this has remained the most exhilarating experience. I felt 10 feet tall that first time I saw my name in print. And I've been chasing that feeling like a heroin addict ever since.

SACKS: Why did you run toward Times Square to escape? What was it about this world that you found so interesting?

FRIEDMAN: I've always felt a magnetic pull toward bad neighborhoods—beginning with the ghetto school I attended, as the only white kid, from first through fourth grades. Whenever I visit a new city, I say "Take me to your slums." I've always felt a mystical connection with Times Square. I'm probably reincarnated from a 1920s song-and-dance man or gangster.

For a 20-year-old in the 1970s, there was a tremendous sense of liberation. This was an upside-down world, the golden age of pornography—when sex was dirty. Like a carny fun house. Once I entered, I didn't want to leave. It was like when I was a kid and my father would have to run in and fetch me out of fun houses on Coney Island. It felt more sane in there than in the outside world. Times Square was a shanty town of massage parlors and strip joints with plywood doors, with names like the Purple Onion or Topless Shoeshines, side by side with Broadway theaters. There were 1,200 prostitutes on the streets—some of them quite beautiful, though they didn't know it. Nothing like the crack addicts that came later.

SACKS: *You're almost making it sound like a fantasyland. To me, it sounds more like a scene from a Brueghel painting.*

FRIEDMAN: Listen, it was also a total hellhole. The gates of hell opened into Times Square. It was the dumping ground and end of the road for thousands of crusty old cadavers, flatback girls, midnight cowboys, old-time vaudevillians, brain-damaged evangelists, freaks, addicts, zombies—what's not to love? It was intoxicating and dangerous. Something forbidden or enticing was behind every door. When I began to write for *Screw*, my press pass got me behind all those doors. They wouldn't have let the *Daily News* in, but for *Screw*, the doors opened. Down the rabbit hole I went, where I learned all the secrets.

Where others saw depravity, I saw beauty. The electrical voltage and lights of Times Square felt sanctified to me. Maybe it was in my blood. My father's Aunt Essie worked in the box office at one of the grand Broadway theaters in the 1920s. And my grandfather on my father's side moonlighted playing piano for silent films. So there was something ancestral about Times Square for me, almost like an elephant happening upon an elephant graveyard and sensing a connection to its past.

SACKS: How many writers at this time—the late '70s and '80s—were also covering Times Square full time?

FRIEDMAN: Nobody. Not a soul—other than the occasional reporter who would write an indignant editorial of the "we need to clean this up" mold. No one was writing about Times Square from the inside. That was baffling. Here was a city with more writers than anywhere else on Earth. Thousands chasing after the very same subjects. I would think, You mean to say this amazing terrain is all mine?

SACKS: Why didn't other writers feel the same way?

FRIEDMAN: They were scared, embarrassed, or considered it beneath them. I was plagiarized often, even by stupid sex magazines like *Stag* and *Chic*. They wouldn't even venture into Times Square to cover stories—just lifted straight from *Screw*. A lot of editors—even if they were from other sex magazines—felt that they could steal whatever they wanted, because I wasn't writing "high art."

SACKS: *One would think there would have been a Damon Runyon type or Joseph Mitchell wannabe who would have loved to cover this area.*

FRIEDMAN: Great American novelist Nelson Algren wrote a few chapters about Times Square in his very last book, *The Devil's Stocking* [Arbor House, 1983]. Algren hung out at a massage parlor called Lucky Lady for a few weeks. He said in an interview before he died, in 1981, and I never forgot this, "If I were a young man, starting my writing career, I cannot imagine going to any other place than Times Square." I was emboldened by that.

SACKS: Your articles for *Screw* remind me of your cartooning work with Drew. There's that same comic-nightmare element to these pieces, and yet you also manage to capture the vulnerability and sadness of the characters.

FRIEDMAN: I always tried to treat my subjects respectfully. Sometimes this backfired. When someone whose whole life has been a silent scream puts their trust in you, spills their guts only to you, you're obliged to tread carefully. I may have overstepped my bounds, but I had

Al Goldstein in Times Square, circa 1995. Image by Danny Hellman, Screw's *in-house Bruegel.*

"wiseguy compassion," as film critic Michael H. Price described my intent.

Maybe like Diane Arbus, I was never really a part of those worlds. I was a nightly visitor. I always got to return to my apartment with clean sheets. I would often think, "Am I slumming here? Am I just a rich kid coming down for kicks?"—like tourists did in the Five Points section of Manhattan in the early 20th century?

I decided that I was not slumming—unlike others who would come in disguise to sleaze out. I saw soap-opera stars, Philharmonic conductors, city hall and church officials. But for me it was a much more personal, nightly connection. I very much cared for the environment. I wanted to preserve something. I am not sure what needed to be preserved exactly, but it was something unique—an urban ecosystem. A lot of citizens, including myself, seemed to need this world.

SACKS: These real-life characters you met were hilarious and fascinating personalities. For instance, Uncle Lou Amber, featured in your 1982 *Screw* article "Uncle Lou's Scrapbook."

FRIEDMAN: Uncle Lou remained my top mole on 42nd Street. He would call even after I moved to Dallas. I'd say, "Lou, I left the beat years ago." But he didn't hear me. He just phoned in what was going on backstage at the Triple Treat Theatre.

For years, he worked as a limousine driver for a company, but during his off hours, he would deliver strippers from various airports to their gigs—at Show World or the Melody Burlesk. He would do this for free. Hence the name, "Uncle" Lou. He's still alive. At 75, Lou is no different than when he was 50. A true old Broadway soul.

SACKS: Tell me about Pee Wee, the doorman. You wrote about him for *Screw* in an article titled "Pee Wee is Not a Happy Man."

FRIEDMAN: Pee Wee Marquette was the street-level greeter for Hawaii Kai, a tropical-themed tourist restaurant in Times Square. He was a short-tempered midget, maybe around four-feet high. He'd pace back and forth in a military-type uniform, carrying a metal cane. He would say: "First I hit 'em in their legs and when they bend down, their stomach and then their head." He worked at Hawaii Kai from 1960 into the early '80s.

In the 1940s, he was the master of ceremonies at Birdland on 52nd Street, introducing Charlie Parker, Miles Davis, and Teddy Wilson. Most of the characters I wrote about are long gone.

SACKS: How about Long Jeanne Silver, the one-legged porn star you wrote about in a Screw article titled "Season's Greetings from Long Jeanne Silver"?

FRIEDMAN: The gorgeous peg-legged stripper and second-story cat burglar? I have not heard from her in many years. Hopefully, she is married to some stockbroker, somewhere in the Midwest. I hope she's alive and doing well.

SACKS: And Eric Edwards, the only porn star to hold the distinction of being in sex movies in the '60s, '70s, '80s, and '90s?

FRIEDMAN: Eric would collect mannequins from department stores, dress them up like a film crew, and place them around his own bed.

SACKS: How deeply were you immersed in the seediness of this world?

FRIEDMAN: I never dropped trou during public events. I kept a separation of church and state. I remember when [porn actress and stripper] Seka first headlined the Melody Burlesk. The line went down the stairs out to the street. Seka sat spread-eagled onstage, and men would line up to give her a lick for one dollar. I remember thinking, "This would be great if you were first on line."

But, see, that's the thing: How would I have written about this world if I were immersed in it? As a writer, you have to be on the sidelines, impressed and amazed. I constantly asked myself, "How can these people possibly do that"?

SACKS: You say that, and yet, in the late '70s, you got into the act yourself by performing a breaststroke in a Jacuzzi at Plato's Retreat sex club in Manhattan. You wrote about it in your *Screw* article "Queen of the Gang-Bang."

FRIEDMAN: True, but that was with my long johns on.

SACKS: I wouldn't have gotten into that Jacuzzi if I happened to be wearing a full-length biohazard suit.

FRIEDMAN: The management claimed they abided by health codes and used chlorine in the water. But I don't remember sensing any chlorine, like a public pool, and was nervous after I accidentally gulped some down. I suppose I could have chased it with a shot of Olde Country, which was Plato's Retreat brand of mouthwash.

SACKS: Besides that, what was the saddest thing you ever experienced in Times Square?

FRIEDMAN: I sometimes saw old men in the open-window peeps, paying 10 bucks a kiss. Every 30 seconds, they'd hand over another ten spot for the only love they'd ever receive. Kissing, of course, was something most street-prostitutes wouldn't do for any amount.

I once saw a young man sucking on a stripper's breast, while she gently patted his hair. It was sad, funny, and kind of pathetic. Very much like Times Square, itself.

SACKS: Did you ever feel that you should have been writing for a different publication than *Screw*? I know your father was once quoted as saying that he would have preferred you to be writing for *The New Yorker*.

FRIEDMAN: Yes, but he said that tongue-in-cheek—I think. People were always telling me, "You should be in *The New Yorker*." I actually submitted an article idea to *The New Yorker* when I was 21, and—my father almost fainted—I received a personal letter from the then editor [from 1951 to 1987], William Shawn. It was an idea for an article on my favorite guitarist, Jeff Beck. I was told that Mr. Shawn had very rarely written a personal letter to anybody in his more than 30 years at *The New Yorker*, so I was very happy. He was passing on the Jeff Beck idea, but he invited me to send in more ideas—I never did.

SACKS: Did Mr. Shawn write to you because your father was Bruce Jay Friedman?

FRIEDMAN: No, this submission was plucked from the slush-pile. I kick myself now, because I should have jumped at the chance—and I never got the chance again.

SACKS: Is it true that Philip Roth once paid a visit to the *Screw* offices?

FRIEDMAN: He spent three days at our offices, because he was basing a character on *Screw*'s founder, Al Goldstein, for his novel, *The Anatomy Lesson* [Farrar, Straus and Giroux, 1983]. Roth's hero, Nathan Zuckerman, impersonates the Goldstein persona as an example of a conservative Jew's worst nightmare.

SACKS: And how well did Mr. Roth capture Mr. Goldstein?

FRIEDMAN: I would say slightly above average.

SACKS: It must have been interesting to have Al Goldstein as your boss. To say the least, he was a bit colorful.

FRIEDMAN: I wrote Al's autobiography, *I, Goldstein: My Screwed Life* [Thunder's Mouth Press, 2006]. I think we made the best case possible for the positive aspects of his career—that of democratizing pornography, fighting for the little man, going to jail so that others could view full-frontal nudity, and frequenting hookers.

SACKS: One of my all-time favorite photo-captions is in your Goldstein book. In the photo, young Al is posing with his parents in front of a large table of food. The caption reads: "I would later wear this bar mitzvah suit for my first hooker."

FRIEDMAN: He was a lower-middle-class, stuttering, bed-wetting Jew from Brooklyn—who absolutely changed sex in America, probably for the better. In his prime, he was much funnier than Lenny Bruce, and he withstood more prosecution than any other publisher. Your grandmother can buy her dildo at the local Walgreen's because of this man. Al went to jail for that. Jimmy Breslin wrote that Al was one of the four major defenders of the First Amendment in the last half of the 20th century. The other three were Goldstein imitator Larry Flynt, Lenny Bruce, and [publisher] Ralph Ginzburg [who went to prison for the 1962 sex periodical *Eros*]. Al faced down 60 years in prison during his federal obscenity trial in Kansas—and won. He paid the price more than anyone for sexual—and satiric—freedom. Whether that's for better or worse remains to be seen.

Goldstein was arrested more than any other publisher in American history. He would have been a martyr, like Lenny Bruce, if he was assassinated or died in jail as a sexual freedom and First Amendment fighter. He assumed something like that would happen. But it didn't. Instead, he self-destructed, lost his money, his marbles and destroyed his friendships. Nevertheless, at one time, he was the litmus test for freedom of speech like nobody before him. I'm not so sure he strengthened the First Amendment, but he proved it meant business.

He never did make it easy on himself, though. He once ran a centerfold in *Screw* of Nixon's two "daughters"—in reality, porn stars—performing oral sex on each other. And he ran a story in the early '70s that asked: "Is J. Edgar Hoover a Fag?" This was when Hoover was still alive, mind you.

Al loved to get arrested. He loved the attention, and he was fearless. He spat at authority that needed to be spat at. But he paid the price.

People forget how popular *Screw* was

for awhile. The magazine's circulation, at its peak in the early '70s, edged upwards of 100,000 copies a week.

Quite a few celebrities sat down for a Screw interview: Sammy Davis, Jr., Timothy Leary, Joe Namath, Jack Nicholson. The Internet ruined *Screw* and a lot of other sex publications. Al never saw it coming.

But it was the best fucking job in the world. For starters, you're twenty-two years old with access to demented young starlets around the clock. They haven't yet invented AIDS, and it's the final years of the great sexual revolution. I quit smoking there, made all my contacts in the underworld of Times Square, and met my wife at a residence for young Southern women attending college in New York, run by the Salvation Army. I learned how to write under deadline, and my pieces got reprinted throughout the men's magazine market. So for me, at least, it was a great job. It's still paying dividends.

SACKS: *Any truth to the rumors that you left New York because the Mob was after you?*

FRIEDMAN: I received a few nerve-racking threats from low-level Mob guys when I edited the "Naked City" section of *Screw*, the listings that rated two hundred sex establishments in New York. Likewise, there was grumbling from a couple of mob guys who thought I had revealed too much about their business in *Tales of Times Square*. But unlike in Russia or Latin America, the old criminal underworld in New York had "respect" for writers. They figured if they broke a writer's legs, dozens of reporters and newspapers, including Jimmy Breslin and Pete Hamill, would jump to the writer's defense. Also, I knew that a real threat never came with advance warning.

I moved to Dallas with my wife in 1987—she's originally from Texas.

SACKS: *Do you ever re-read your own work?*

FRIEDMAN: I'll admit that I love re-reading my books. I'm proud of every moment. I've had friends say they wish they could have written something more along the lines of what I did. They are not proud of their work. I hope that doesn't sound conceited.

So now, after years of being a daddy-o, I'm just plain daddy, with a young daugh-

Elevator Conversations

River Clegg

"Boy, some weather out there."
"I don't understand your comment."

—

"Nothing like that first sip of coffee, eh?"
"Coffee is very important to me."
"You said it."
"Coffee is all I have."

—

"How was your weekend?"
"Pretty good. My friend had a house-warming party in Greenpoint."
"Cool! How was it?"
"Okay. I guessed where the trash was on my second try."
"Nice! What were you throwing away?"
"Paper napkin."
"Sweet."

—

"Six people. The perfect amount for an elevator ride."
"If a seventh gets on, I'll get off."
"No! There's got to be some other way."
"Don't cry. There is no other way."

—

"Big plans tonight?"
"Nah, I'll probably just watch some *Frasier*."
"That sounds great -- I love relaxing at home."
"The Frasier character is hiding something."

—

"Whoa, I almost wore that same shirt today!"
"Ha, how about that?"
"It's a great shirt."
"Let me be clear. The red gingham

shirt is my thing. Mine. I've worked here twelve years. I've paid my dues. If I ever see you wearing that shirt in this office, I will beat you where you stand."

—

"This seems like a good elevator."

—

"Any plans coming up?"
"Yep, going to Philadelphia next week."
"Neat! Why Philadelphia?"
"Well, Bruce Springsteen wrote all those songs about it. I want to see what all the fuss is about."
"I think you mean New Jersey."
"No way. The Chief always sang about Philly."
"You mean the Boss?"
"I don't think so."

—

"How's the wedding planning coming?"
"Not bad. We finally settled on a DJ last night! It's crazy how the costs pile up, though."
"Yeah, it's nuts. I remember when I got married, I couldn't believe how expensive things were. It actually got to the point —"
"This is my floor. I want to hear what you were going to say, though."
"Oh. Don't worry about it."
"No, what was it?"
"I'll tell you later."
"No. *Now*."

—

"When they were filming *Jaws*, the shark's nickname was Bruce."
"Stop telling me that." ♟

ter. I have a gorgeous wife of 30 years. We hit New York every other month, and I feel like Nick and Nora Charles, of the Thin Man series. My wife directs high-fashion photo shoots, while I have Uncle Lou, retired cops, and assorted lowlifes visiting our fancy hotel room.

My daughter sits on my shoulders

when we visit Toys 'R' Us, the Hello Kitty Store, and The Lion King in Times Square. We stand outside and peek in. She doesn't mourn the loss of Show World or the Melody Burlesk. But what I see in the windows' reflection is far more shocking. ♟

Sloane Tanen and Stefan Hagen

Goodnight Moon, Hello Martini

Goodnight moon, hello martini.

ANASTASIA
was through making out with Ian. He was never going to change.

YEARS AGO, *Marion's shrink told her she needed to come up with a version of her childhood she could live with. She thought he said "aversion," and promptly took hold of a hideous tale of woe she particularly liked. It was thousands of dollars later that she finally sorted out the distinction.*

PAIGE DIDN'T CARE. *She knew she had the right of way.*

BORIS THE BOY GENIUS
was stumped.

I DON'T KNOW,
the last thing he said was
something about
being king of the world,
and then I may
have accidentally
pushed him."

SAMANTHA

looked around the playground in amazement. Her mother had been right. She really was the smartest and the prettiest.

MARY KATHERINE

blamed it on Mary Margaret and Mary Margaret said it was Mary Josephine. All Sister Agnes knew was that one of the girls was going down.

Roz Chast

POST-LIFE SURVEY

1. Overall, how satisfied were you with your life on Earth?

- ☐ Very satisfied
- ☐ Satisfied
- ☐ Somewhat satisfied
- ☐ Neither satisfied nor dissatisfied
- ☐ Somewhat dissatisfied
- ☐ Dissatisfied
- ☐ Very dissatisfied

2. Please rate the extent to which you agree with the following statements:

Completely Disagree
Disagree
Somewhat Disagree
Neither Agree nor Disagree
Somewhat Agree
Agree
Completely Agree

A. The fruits were mostly delicious........... ☐☐☐☐☐☐☐

B. Horses are too big..... ☐☐☐☐☐☐☐

C. Two legs was exactly the right number...... ☐☐☐☐☐☐☐

D. Trees should be able to talk.......... ☐☐☐☐☐☐☐

E. Blue is a nice sky color........... ☐☐☐☐☐☐☐

3. Overall, please rate this incarnation compared to previous ones:

- ☐ Much better
- ☐ Better
- ☐ Somewhat better
- ☐ About the same
- ☐ Somewhat worse
- ☐ Worse
- ☐ Much worse

4. How much money did you lose to Bernie Madoff?

- ☐ $29,999 or less
- ☐ $30,000 to 39,999
- ☐ $40,000 to 49,999
- ☐ $50,000 to 59,999
- ☐ $60,000 to 79,999
- ☐ $80,000 to 99,999
- ☐ $100,000 to 149,999
- ☐ $150,000 or more

5. Based on your experience to date and given the opportunity, would you ever want to be reincarnated?

Definitely Would Not
Most Likely Would Not
Might Not
Unsure
Might
Most Likely Would
Definitely Would

☐☐☐☐☐☐☐

6. Did you feel pressure from anyone to answer this survey in a specific way? (e.g., I felt I had to give positive answers).

Yes ☐   No ☐

Back of the Bus

*In December 1955, **The Honeymooners** was the toast of television.
But when the show got political, the sponsors said "no."
Here is that infamous lost episode.*

<u>ACT ONE</u>
INT. KRAMDEN APARTMENT – NIGHT
Alice is fixing dinner. An unhappy Ralph enters in his bus driver's uniform.

(APPLAUSE, CHEERS)

RALPH
Not a word. Not a word. Just gimme my dinner and I'm going straight to bed.

ALICE
But Ralph, you know the Nortons were coming over tonight to play hearts.

RALPH
Hearts, Alice? Hearts?! With the day I had, the only thing I'll be playing tonight is "Twinkle, Twinkle, Little Star."

ALICE
Okay, Liberace, I'll bite. Just what happened today that's so terrible the Nortons can't come over?

RALPH
All right. The bus was crowded see? And this one passenger, you know, from downtown see? Wouldn't go to the back of the bus. Miss Rosa Parks. A blabbermouth, Alice. A real blabbermouth!

NORTON enters, flashing a deck of cards.

(APPLAUSE, CHEERS)

NORTON
What's the good word, Ralphie boy?

RALPH
I got no time for shenanigans Norton. Because of my passenger there's a boycott against the Montgomery Bus line. A boycott! Mr. Marshall's gonna kill me!

NORTON
Passenger huh? What did they do?

RALPH
Wouldn't move to the back of the bus.

NORTON
That's odd.

RALPH
What's odd?

NORTON
With someone as fat as you driving, I thought everyone rode in the back of the bus!

RALPH
Out Out Out!!!

A flustered Norton drops his cards. There is a knock on the door.

ALICE
I'll get it. My mother's here to join us for dinner.

RALPH
(anguished moan)
A perfect night gets even worse.

Alice opens the door. Her mother sees Ralph moping.

ALICE'S MOTHER
So, what did Mr. Wonderful do now?

ALICE
He made a passenger go to the back of the bus and now there's a boycott.

ALICE'S MOTHER
Well, Alice, it's not my business but…

Over Ralph's increasingly angered face we hear —

ALICE'S MOTHER
(CONT'D)
You could've married Sherwood Thurlby. He's a lawyer now. Earns a good living. Makes his money in a racist system while still being a gentleman. I hear he's about to buy a line of segregated chicken shacks. I'm sure Ralph knows his share about chickens. No doubt he's eaten every one in the coop.

RALPH
That's it!!! You're a blabbermouth! Rosa Parks is a blabbermouth! You're all blabbermouths! Out! Out! Out!!!!

Norton and Alice's mother flee the room. We push in on a dejected Ralph's face as we hear a SOUR HORN.

INT. KRAMDEN KITCHEN – DAY
No one can be seen. There is a knock, then Norton enters. Seeing he is alone, he takes a turkey drumstick from the icebox. He hears Ralph from the bedroom.

.... ◆ ....

Al Jean (@AlJean) *is pleased to return to his print roots after 25 years of heaven at **The Simpsons**.
Al is hoping that this article finally lands him a staff job on **Saturday Night Live**.*

LOUISA BERTMAN

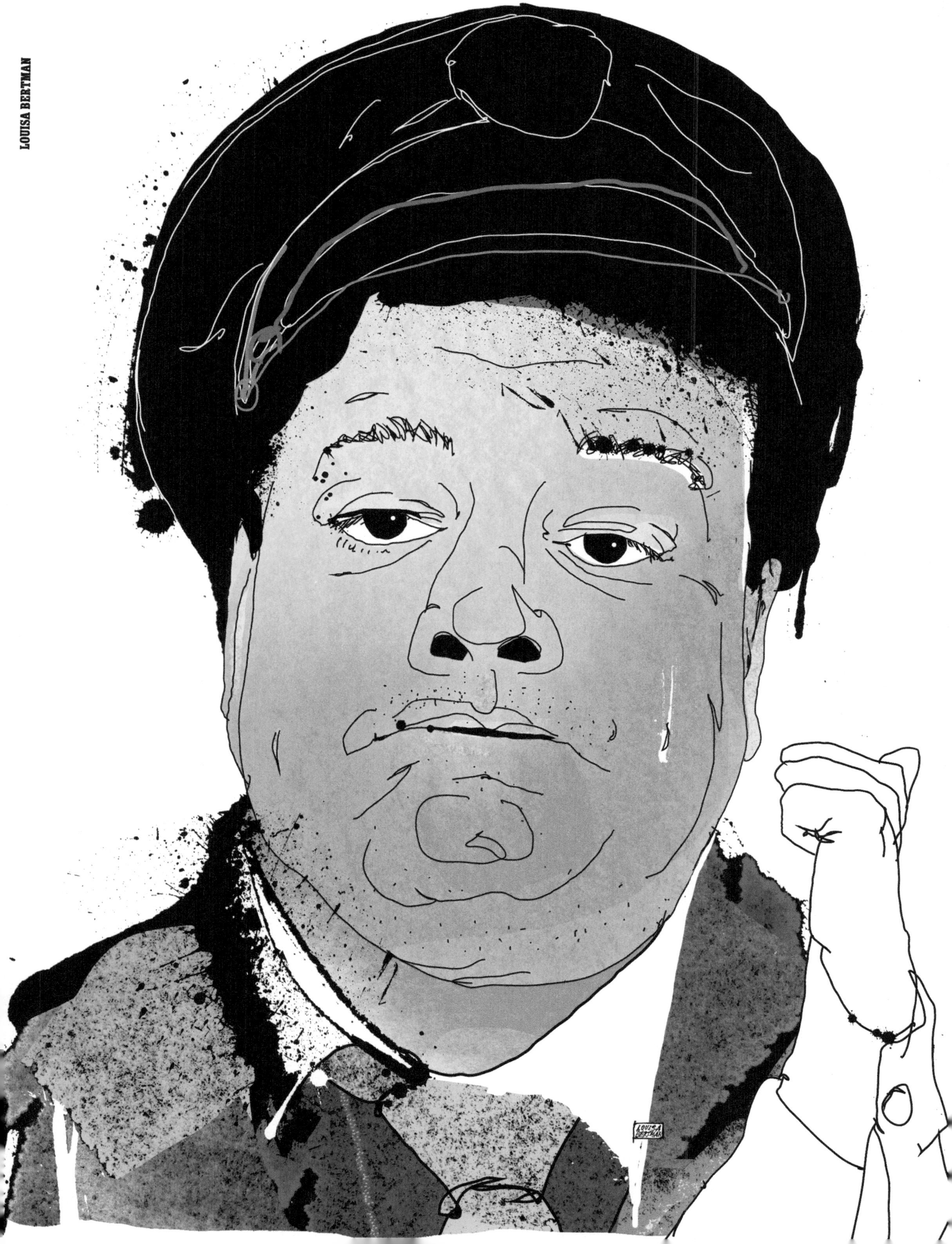

RALPH (O.S.)
Norton, is that you?

NORTON
(mouth full)
Uh-huh.

RALPH (O.S.)
Well, I got some good news. I was feelin' down, you know, over this boycott and everything, then I got a fan letter. Some hoity-toity big-shots want me to join their club. They even sent over a uniform.

Ralph emerges from the bedroom dressed head-to-toe in a KKK outfit. Norton's turkey leg remains stuck in his mouth.

RALPH
Well, how about it? Whadya think?

NORTON
(takes turkey leg from mouth)
You remind me of something...I got it — the blizzard of '38!

RALPH
(pulls off hood)
Knock it off! These guys like me. They said someday I might even be the Grand Dragon.

NORTON
That's odd.

RALPH
What's odd?

NORTON
I figured you more as the Great White Whale!

RALPH
Out. Out! Out!!!!

Norton leaves. Ralph sits at the table rubbing his face as we hear a SOUR HORN.

END OF ACT ONE

(COMMERCIAL – SLOT FOR LI'L COW-POKE CHEWING TOBACCO.)

ACT TWO
INT. KRAMDEN KITCHEN – DAY
A group of men, including Ralph and Norton, stand drinking beers. THE LEADER approaches.

KLEAGLE
Candidate Kramden, you have struck a mighty, mighty blow. It's a pleasure to welcome you into our brotherhood.

RALPH
Thank you, sir. The only thing we

ever joined before is the Raccoon lodge.

KLEAGLE
(catches self)
Oh, *rac*-coons.

RALPH
(misunderstanding)
Only the highest class of people, sir. Fatso Fogerty, Crazy Guggenheim, Nuthouse McGhee...

KLEAGLE
Maybe we should just begin the meeting. If you could please put on your sacred raiments, gentlemen.

All including Ralph and Norton put on their white sheets and pillowcases.

KLEAGLE
(CONT'D)
Now before we swear our oath to Liberty and White Supremacy, let us dance to our solemn hymn.

He puts on a phonograph playing "Dixie." The members start dancing. Ralph in his outfit stands out with an exuberant Jackie Gleason dance. He begins waltzing with Norton. Just then the door opens. Alice enters. The music screeches to a halt.

ALICE
What in the world? Ralph Kramden, are you in this Halloween parade?

RALPH
(terrified)
Homina homina homina...

Ralph pulls off his pillowcase.

RALPH
(CONT'D)
What are you doing here? I thought you were meetin' someone for lunch!

ALICE
I was, Ralph. Miss Rosa Parks.

Rosa Parks enters.
(AUDIENCE "UH OH!")

RALPH
(terrified)
Posa Narks. I mean, Nosa Barks. I mean *ay yi yi*...

ROSA
Mr. Kramden, I want to ask you something. Who wrote "all men are created equal?"

RALPH
Uh...Leon Trotsky?

ROSA
Thomas Jefferson.

NORTON
(laughs and points at Ralph)
Look, an elephant with a lousy memory.

ALICE
Ed Norton, does Trixie know you cut up her good pillowcase?

NORTON
(pulls off hood)
I'm doomed.

Alice turns to the Kleagle.

ALICE
Sir, are you aware that both of these prize recruits of yours are Catholics?

KLAN MEMBERS gasp, mutter unhappily.

NORTON
Now, now Alice that ain't exactly true. Ralph here is one-eighth Jewish. And an eighth of him is plenty!

RALPH
What's Gramma Kramowitz got to do with anything?!

KLEAGLE
I'm afraid, sir, that's got *everything* to do with everything...Candidates Kramden and Norton, we no longer want you in our ancient, sacred organization that dates back to 1915. Let's go, gentlemen.

Led by their haughty Kleagle, the Klan members stiffly file out.

NORTON
Well, let me tell you guys something. I think you stink...and I spend all day in the sewer!

Ralph hugs Alice.

RALPH
Once again you've saved me from a BIIIIIG mistake. Baby, you're the greatest.

Norton stands beside Rosa Parks.

NORTON
I've heard of black and white TV but this is ridiculous!

Rosa slaps his arm at the joke, over --

APPLAUSE
AND OUT.

STEP ASIDE, POPS

KATE BEATON

FROM THE AUTHOR OF

HARK! A VAGRANT — KATE BEATON

Ayn Rand Helping the Poor

Edward Sorel

Ellis Weiner

ATLAS SLUGGED AGAIN

ANNYN RANT'S LONG-LOST "SECRET SEQUEL" TO ATLAS SLUGGED

Editor's Introduction

1. The Work

A subject of speculation and rumor for decades, *Atlas Slugged AGAIN* (ASA) is the so-called "secret sequel" to the monumental *Atlas Slugged* (AS), by Annyn (rhymes with "hannyn") Rant.

ASA has acquired an almost Grail-like status among the devotees of Rant's work, the phrase "Where is *Atlas Slugged AGAIN*?" having become metonymic shorthand for an expression of futility or eternally-deferred salvation. The following exchange, recently encountered on a Rantian website, is typical:

HRORK22: *When will society ever be free of the parasides that steal our Freedom and pallute everything for us producers?*
DOMINIQUEFRANK1: *LOL. Where is Atlas Slugged AGAIN?*

It is to such readers that news of the publication of this work will be particularly welcome.

But why "secret sequel"? For two reasons: "Sequel," because AS revisits the characters and situations first explored in *Atlas Slugged*, published in 1957 by Fandom House. But "secret," not only because Fandom declined to publish *Atlas Slugged AGAIN*, but because word of its very existence has been suppressed and denied from the moment its editor first perused the manuscript—a decision supported (albeit reluctantly) by the book's author.

How the manuscript—the only one extant, as far as I know—came into my possession is worth a brief recounting. In fact, it was delivered to my door by the mailman, in an ordinary manila envelope addressed to me. Inside I found what appeared to be an indisputably authentic document: a sheaf of pages, not printed with a computer's uniformity and precision, but hand-typed on a manual typewriter, bound by two crossed rubber-bands, the title page of which bore the publisher's official stamp noting the date of receipt (November 24, 1968). Attached by paper clip was a computer-printed letter reading:

"Mr. Ellis Weiner:

I saw your review of Atlas Slugged *on Amazon and decided that you should be the one to take custody of this, which has been in my possession since 1968. At the time, I worked as an editorial assistant to Annyn Rant's editor at Fandom House. My boss had been the original editor of* Atlas Slugged. *When a messenger delivered this sequel, my boss (who had not been expecting any such thing) said, "Hot dog!," told me to hold all calls, and shut himself in his office. When he emerged two hours later, his face was white as a sheet. He handed me the manuscript and said, "Burn this. And let us speak no more of it." I laughed and said something like, "Well, I don't know about 'burn.' But I'll dispose of it." I took the ms. but curiosity got the best of me. I hid it in a drawer until I could smuggle it home that evening.*

The days that followed were full of crisis. My boss contacted both Ms. Rant and her agent and told them that publishing ASA would be "career suicide—for all of us." His principal objection—supported by Fandom House's legal counsel—was that one character in particular was so clearly modeled on an actual, living person, that that individual would have "a damn good" case to bring suit against the publisher, the author, "and any poor bastards in the immediate vicinity." The upshot of such a suit would, he felt certain, not only result in substantial monetary damages, but in a complete recall and pulping of all extant copies of the book. Not only would Fandom House suffer, but so would Rant's reputation, and probably Rant's personal life as well.

Ms. Rant—who as you know was a highly intelligent and determined woman—at first insisted the work be published. But after several days,

---

Ellis Weiner *is the only person, living or dead, who has published in the* **National Lampoon, Spy,** *and (still)* **The New Yorker.** *His novels about the Templeton Twins, for kids 9-12, are hilarious.*

she, too, began to think the better of it.

In the end, she agreed with my boss, and sent a formal letter withdrawing the ms. When I read it at home I was saddened to think about its suppression, as it seemed to me to be a perfect sequel to Atlas Slugged. As for the "new" character, I was not at the time as familiar as I came to be, with the man on whom he was (so clearly) based. At the time I simply took it on faith that my boss and our lawyers knew what they were talking about. And so I held onto the manuscript but never mentioned it to anyone. In fact, I actually forgot about its existence until recently when, packing for a move to a retirement in Arizona, I came across it again.

I do not know if Ms. Rant kept her carbon, and if so, who has it now. So this may be the only copy left.

I leave it to you—a proven fan of her work—to decide whether to destroy it, turn it over to her estate, or arrange for its publication yourself. I apologize if this places an unfair burden on you, but as I said, your review of Atlas Slugged on Amazon

was so positive and insightful, I decided this poor orphaned work could have no better guardian. Thank you for your attention to this matter."

So touching was this letter, and so intriguing an opportunity did it present, that I couldn't find it in my heart to inform the writer of it that in fact I had never reviewed Atlas Slugged on Amazon. But a brief glance at that web site confirmed that "Ellis Weiner" had given the book five stars, and had reviewed it thus:

"THIS BOOK IS GREAT!! IT IS MY FAVORITE BOOK. THE PHILSOSOPHY (sic) IN THIS BOOK WAS VERY INTERESTING. IT SHOWS THAT BECAUSE THE UNIVERSE EXISTS YOU SHOULD USE YOUR MIND AND BE INTELLIGENT AND NOT LISTEN TO STUPID PEOPLE! NO ONE SHOULD DO ANYTHING FOR ANYONE ELSE UNLESS THEY GET SOMETHING IN RETURN BECAUSE THAT IS THE ONLY THING THAT MAKES SENSE."

After several hours of Googling and other detective work I discovered that the Ellis Weiner who had written this re-

view was a ten-year old boy from Sherman Oaks, California. (It was merely one more strange facet of this tale, that there should be anywhere on earth another person named "Ellis Weiner.") As I had, for decades, been published as an author and co-author of various books, as well as a writer for many magazines and a national blog, I could hardly blame the person who had sent me Atlas Slugged AGAIN for assuming that its Amazon review had been written by me, and not a fourth grader fond of his Caps Lock key.

So I decided to return the manuscript (after reading it) to the person who had sent it. But I discovered that the envelope had no return address, and the signature at the end of the letter was indecipherable. I made a token effort to research who, in 1968, had been Annyn Rant's editor, and who had been his assistant, but both inquiries yielded nothing.

I could, of course, have delivered the manuscript to the Annyn Rant Society, or to a university, or to Fandom House. But, frankly, I didn't want to. I was one of the few people I knew who had actually read the entirety of Atlas Slugged, and I found the possibility of being associated with its legendary sequel to be too tantalizing to relinquish.

So I arranged to have Atlas Slugged AGAIN published. The present text is a complete rendition of the manuscript as I received it. Apart from the routine correction of typos, nothing has been edited, excised, or added.

Before proceeding, however, it might be helpful to place the characters and events covered in ASA in context.

2. The Precursor: Atlas Slugged

Atlas Slugged was Annyn Rant's second major novel. (Her first, The Figurehead, dealt with the theme of personal genius, set in the cutthroat world of tall ship design.) At the center of AS are five principal protagonists:

Dragnie Tagbord—Beautiful, brilliant, stylish, bold, fit, flirty 'n' fabulous. She inherited Tagbord Rail from her grandfather, Old Man Pop Gramps "Professor" Zayde Poppa Tagbord, who built the transcontinental railroad empire single-handedly, with his bare hands, in the snow.

John Glatt—Handsome, brilliant, enigmatic, a genius engineer who becomes disgusted with society and goes into hiding, thus acquiring the stature of a messianic leader.

Hunk Rawbone—Handsome, brilliant, founder and sole owner and operator of Rawbone Metal. Rawbone invents Rawbonium, a miracle metal that "will save the entire U.S. economy." Turn-ons: watching "heats" and "pours" of steel. Turn-offs: mean people, nice people, poor people, rich people, and his wife.

Sanfrancisco Nabisco Alcoa D'Lightful D'Lovely De Soto—Handsome, brilliant, a childhood chum of Dragnie while the two were growing up in different hemispheres. Heir to the Desoto Talc Mines in Chile, "World Capital of The Powder of Babies." Spends all his time pursuing empty hedonism as a feckless playboy, which is the worst kind.

Regnad Daghammarskjold—Handsome, beautiful, attractive, brilliant, drop-dead gorgeous, tall and tan and young and lovely, a (naturally) blond Swedish pirate.

The plot of *Atlas Slugged* is lengthy and convoluted, but can be summarized thus: The U.S.—which is not exactly the U.S., as its government seems to have no Executive, Legislative, or Judicial branches—is run by "Mr. Thomas," who has no first name. He is surrounded by a coterie of spineless bureaucrats, self-seeking careerists, hypocritical moralists, and contemptible weaklings. These men share a secret knowledge: that, all over the country, persons of achievement (businessmen, entrepreneurs, tycoons, moguls, big shots, etc.) are "disappearing."

One day they simply stop coming to work and utterly vanish, sending the national economy into a tailspin.

Meanwhile, every other country in the world (except, by the end, Goa) has succumbed to the urge to collectivize, and declared itself a "People's State of the People."

Throughout it all, Dragnie and Hunk Rawbone struggle to run their businesses, Desoto displays a seemingly callous indifference to the talc industry, Daghammarskjold rampages all over the bounding main…and everyone wonders aloud, "Who is John Glatt?"

Eventually it is revealed that Glatt

"Chinese, Kemo-sabe! Billions *of them!"*

has been constructing, in a secret valley in Wyoming, a hideaway for tycoons. Dubbed "Glatt's Gorge," it is there that the "disappearing" moguls have gone—a Meritocratic Retirement Community™ where rich men pursue their hobbies, artists-in-residence live for free and explore their vision, and the cares and vexations of the outside world (society, history, politics, poverty, children, race, disease, natural calamity, competition for resources, crime, corruption, pollution, hunger, terrorism, religious conflict, etc.) are forbidden by law.

Glatt's Gorge is a combination Shangri-La, Brigadoon, and Camelot, and all—from the gold coins the community mints as its private currency to the custom-made cigarettes stamped with the Glatt's Gorge symbol of the dollar sign and the exclamation mark—sustained in its concealment from the rest of the world by a sort of "lens" that projects a disguising image over its valley, to hide it from prying eyes. (Like another 1950's novelist-philosopher, L. Ron Hubbard, Annyn Rant was unafraid to make use of the crowd-pleasing genre conventions of science fiction.)

Glatt's scheme is to demonstrate to society what happens when its productive members, who philosophically object to labor unions and collective bargaining, decided to "go on strike," to withhold their abilities and talents until the "leeches," "moochers," and "parasites" that comprise most of American society (and essentially all of humanity) show sufficient

appreciation for the strikers. As the climax nears, the national economy deteriorates; Mr. Thomas and the fawning courtiers around him become increasingly desperate; and drastic measures are employed to persuade John Glatt to rescue the nation and demonstrate, to all mankind, the benefits of having a reclusive engineer control an entire nation's economy.

It is a vast, winner-take-all epic set against an immense, brawling tapestry about a wild, untamed continent as passionate and sweeping as turbulent America herself. But it is more than that. It is also a love story, one in which both Hunk Rawbone and John Glatt love, and therefore desire, and therefore despise, Dragnie. She, in turn, loves and despises them.

The entire saga reaches its thrilling climax in a speech given by John Glatt.

Commandeering a radio broadcast, Glatt (who has cannily concealed his true intent by behaving for most of the book like a monosyllabic, sulky child) expounds on his theory of existence, life, human nature, morality, creation, productivity, art, economics, virtue, ethics and the self. A masterpiece of high indignation and elevated rhetoric, Glatt's oration is a forthright attack on those who preach that "Man has no mind." He openly mocks those who would assert that "the Mind is impotent." He explicitly refutes those who believe that "the individual self is worthless."

The address is famous—or notorious—for its length. It has been estimated that, if read verbatim on an actual radio broadcast, Glatt's Speech would take three hours to deliver and, since almost all people who listen to radio do so while driving, would so thrill, inspire, terrify, bore, outrage, or baffle listeners as to result in two hundred and forty-five traffic accidents and at least thirty-seven fatalities during a non-rush-hour time period.

The novel ends in a thriller-like flurry of imprisonment, torture, rescue, escape, and triumph. That it was, from its original publication in 1957 up until today, a best seller, should surprise no one. Half again as long as Ulysses and second in influence only to the Bible, Atlas Slugged is a titanic, sprawling epic set in a politically-imaginary America surrounded by a world that never existed, replete with science fiction devices and impossible technology, and all in the service of a 643,000-word treatise on "reality." Small wonder tens of thousands of readers have, for more than fifty years, clamored for a sequel.

And yet it was not to be. Once written, *Atlas Slugged AGAIN* was blocked from publication, not only by its publisher, but by its author. As alluded to by my mysterious correspondent, the sequel's character of "Nathan A. Banden" was thought by many (including Fandom House's legal counsel) to be too clearly and obviously modeled on a real-life figure--a man with whom Annyn Rant engaged in an extramarital affair in the early 1960s, begun when she was age 50 and he (her protégé, acolyte, and business partner) was 25.

Conducted with the knowledge and consent of their respective spouses, the relationship ended four years later amid accusations of betrayal and disloyalty, and scenes of shouting, slapping, and banishment. Rant, who had dedicated AS both to her husband and to her young lover, removed the latter's name from subsequent editions and repudiated much of his work with her.

Thus, rescued from oblivion, *Atlas Slugged AGAIN* arrives with a dual identity: as a perhaps too-rash reply to a faithless lover from a woman scorned, and as the inspiring sequel to one of the most inspirational, if controversial, novels of all time.

—*Ellis Weiner*

PART I

That that is, is;
That that is not,

is not;
That that is is not
that that is not.
Is not that it?
It is.

• Chapter One •

Where Eagles Dare to Gather

"Who is John Glatt?" Dragnie Tagbord chuckled as the arms of the students before her shot with arrow-like directness and clean mechanical precision toward the ceiling. Among this group of third-graders, such a response--the lifting of hands and their display to the gaze of their instructor, each other, and to the distinguished woman visiting their school—was a proud and public announcement of knowledge. I know, proclaimed each raised hand. I know, with pure awareness in the consciousness of my mind, the answer to the question I have just been asked.

Their teacher, Miss Pigg, was a short, squat woman in a shapeless, baggy garment the color of desiccated oatmeal. Although constantly informed by politicians and television personalities of her value to society, in her outward, personal appearance she looked shabby and morose, as if harboring in some unconscious recess of her intelligence the shameful awareness of the fact that, like all those whose livelihoods involved servicing the needs of children, she produced nothing.

She pointed. "Yes, Johnny Timmons? Do you know?"

"I?" The boy, a ten-year-old unafraid to proclaim his love of truth, suppressed a smile tinged with amused mockery. "Yes, I know it. John Glatt is the smartest, bravest, most rational man in society," he replied. "It was he who, ten years ago, recruited our nation's true producers—the entrepreneurs and businessmen whose vision, courage, and energy wrest value from the mute, raw earth—and led them into a strategic retreat from the forces of theft, cowardice, and corruption that prevailed over men in that desperate time. It is to him...um..."

Dragnie whispered, "It is to him we owe—"

"It is to him we owe the Age of Production, which we enjoy—"

The rest of the class joined in. "—TO

THIS VERY DAY!"

A laugh escaped from Dragnie's lips. Exercising her free will, she recaptured it and restricted it to solitary confinement. She had chosen to spend this John Glatt Day touring one of the ten thousand Kindergarten-through-Grade-Twelve institutions, all of them independently owned and operated and all of them called The Glatt School, that had replaced the hidebound and notoriously inefficient public educational system. It would not do, she thought, to display levity in this, or any, environment.

Wordlessly, Dragnie turned and left the classroom. There was no need to thank the pupils. There was no need to thank their teacher. There was no need to wish them well. Her exit was itself a kind of lesson. Do not ask for praise, it said. Do not ask for acknowledgment or good wishes or pampering. Do not ask for "please" or "thank you" or "you're welcome" or "Gesundheit" or any of the other tokens of mental enslavement with which men have for centuries sought to limit the sacred freedom of the individual ten-year-old and draft him like a chump into the unconscious mob that men call "society." We have no time for nurturing. Our enemies are massing. We need you to be strong—not only when you become adults, but today.

We need strong third-graders, and second-graders, and first-graders. We need strong kindergarteners and nursery-schoolers and pre-schoolers and Mom-and-Me toddlers and babies and infants. We desperately need strong neonates, fetuses, and zygotes. For that matter, we need strong housepets. We need strong dogs and cats. We need strong hamsters. We need strong gerbils.

Dragnie's heels clicked with rhythmic percussiveness and her smart gray suit fell perfectly and shifted gently as she strode down the corridor. Two tiers of lockers lined the walls of the hallway, each locker with its own reinforced padlock built to withstand a blast equivalent to twenty pounds of TNT, to ensure the sacred privacy and protection every peanut butter-and-jelly sandwich, every Yum-Time juice box, every Super-Fun-Pak of Fat-Free Mockolate Chip cookies, from looters of the world.

A distinctive sound caught Dragnie's ear as she neared the main entrance lobby. It was the sound of a human voice, emanating from the school's auditorium. She felt

herself drawn involuntarily toward it, as if something in her unconscious were responding to something of which she was not conscious. Her slim legs and trim suit cast a gliding shadow across the lobby's travertine floor in the slanting afternoon sun. Opening the heavy, ornate oak door of the auditorium, she entered.

The theater was dark, its house lights turned off and therefore providing no illumination by which things might be seen. Chilly white fluorescent lights beamed down from over the stage, however, and by their efficient glow Dragnie could perceive, with her sense of vision, the presence of two persons. One was seated in the front row. She was an adult, obviously a teacher or administrator, whose slouching posture and indifferent air revealed her as someone for whom existence was a thing to be taken for granted. "Not so fast, Nathan," the woman called, smugly pleased with her authority and the sanction it provided for dispensing criticism of

the work of others. "Start over."

The target of her command was the young man onstage. He was an older student, probably a senior. Standing erect at a lectern, he wore the trademark dark slacks and sage-green shirt and tricolor necktie embossed with dollar signs of the Upper School boys. He received the woman's advice with an unruffled ease, as if already accustomed to being subjected to the glib, careless directions of the second-guessers and public-speaking-correctors and high-school-student-bossers-around of the world.

"Parents, teachers, Principal Slough-ninny, fellow students," he proclaimed. "We have come tonight to celebrate John Glatt, and I? Who am I, you ask? I am the senior who has been selected to represent the student body. I am the senior who has written this speech which I myself am giving to you now. I am the senior who is alive as himself and is the me that you see before you at this very moment."

Dragnie found herself stumbling into a seat as though in a daze as if in a hypnotic trance.

Her eyes never left his tall, erect, noble, commanding, confident figure even as her ears never left his astute, devastating words.

"You have said, 'How can an eighteen-year-old give a speech that will do justice to John Glatt?' I am doing so for you now. You have said, 'No school child is competent to offer adequate praise to the smartest, bravest, most rational man in society.' I am proving you wrong as I speak. You have said, 'The mind of a high school student is impotent and without value.' I am refuting that assertion in ways you have hitherto found unimaginable."

His voice was rich and well-modulated. His articulation was exact and flawless. Dragnie's conscious mind possessed the fullest awareness of the fact that he had composed this speech for an audience of students, teachers, and parents, to be pre-

"Hey, pal, people have to ride trains on those tracks."

sented that evening at the school's John Glatt Day celebration. Nonetheless she felt, with a sudden shudder and a flush of pleasure, that he had written it expressly for, and was now delivering it solely to, her, to be detected and processed by the auditory system functioning flawlessly within the living mind of her personal and inviolate head.

"Yes, we will praise John Glatt tonight. But I will do more than that. I will honor John Glatt by asserting my values. I will honor John Glatt, not by kowtowing to the bumming-out expectations you would lay on me, not by kneeling on bended knee to the bad trip of pious slogans that the so-called 'adults' deem okay for a ceremony of this kind. I will honor John Glatt by asking questions you would rather not be asked, which you fear being asked—but which must be asked, if in this school, and in every school, men are to be truly free."

"Wait a minute, Nathan—" the teacher began.

"Let him finish!" Dragnie cried.

The teacher turned with a start and peered back toward the rear of the auditorium, seeking to determine the source of the outburst. "Miss Tagbord?"

"Yes," Dragnie replied with icy veracity.

"Sorry. Continue, Nathan."

The boy peered deeply into the gloom of the unlit seats. He seemed then to catch Dragnie's eye and, with a small mocking smile of amusement and con-tempt, returned to his text. "It is I, then, who will now ask you, Principal Slough-ninny, and you, Vice Principal Flabb, the question which all seniors now ask—or should be asking, if their faculties of rea-son have not been so damaged by the no-where nature of this institution and their self-respect not sundered by what's going down in this school's freaked-out scene. The question is this: Why must the Senior Prom, the theme for which this year is 'Some Enchanted Evening,' be held in the gymnasium of this school, and why can it not be held, as everyone wants it to be, in the La Superba Room of Chez Elegance Caterers? The cost of renting the facility can be recouped by the sale of tickets, at a suggested rate of five dollars stag, eight dollars drag. True, admission to the Prom in the gym is free. But no student utiliz-ing his mind, no student exercising his reason, will balk at the patent justness of this nominal fee in exchange for a much cooler set-up.

"Furthermore, regarding the matter of chaperones, we who tremble on the brink of adulthood, we who'll by term's end be eligible to serve in the nation's armed forces, we who for two years now have possessed the legal right to drive a mo-torized vehicle and have had experience doing so—we insist: we will have no chap-erones. We reject their authority. We ask: By what right do they presume to monitor and inhibit our celebration of existence, our rejoicing in the impending milestone of graduation, our frankly erotic fooling around?"

The speech lasted an hour and twenty minutes, during which the young man, calmly and with exquisitely controlled passion, announced his defiance of hall monitors, presented unanswerably his critique of "the legislative sham that is our so-called 'Student Council,'" and de-livered a ringing challenge to the policy of requiring cheerleaders to wear tights both at practices and at interscholastic athletic competitions. By the time he ended with the traditional tracing, toward the audi-ence, of the dollar sign and the exclama-tion mark, Dragnie had slowly risen to her feet and, her chin held high in open admi-ration, begun a quiet but pointed round of applause.

The young man descended the three steps from the stage to the auditorium floor and joined her in the aisle. He was taller than she, gaunt and lean and erect in a body that hinted at hidden reserves of productive energy and rationally-man-aged ardor. His face belied his youth, and seemed to harbor a wisdom and experi-ence beyond his years. His gaze at her was direct and uncowed. "I'm glad you approve, Miss Tagbord."

They were interrupted by the appear-ance of another young man. He was dressed in an identical manner to that of the young man who had given the speech, as if the two of them, though distinct indi-viduals, attended the same school--which, as a matter of objective fact, was in fact the fact. "Nice speech, Nathan," said the other young man.

"Thank you, Eddie," said the speech maker. "Oh, Miss Tagbord? Allow me to introduce Eddie G. Willikers. He's on the stage crew here."

"Gosh," Eddie Willikers said. "Are you Dragnie Tagbord?"

"I am," Dragnie replied.

— STEVE YOUNG

"Not so fast, Eddie!" Nathan said with a hint of mockery. "I saw her first!"

"Yes, you did," Eddie replied. "Well, nice to have met you, Miss Tagbord. See you later around the school, Nathan." He walked away in a manner consistent with his own personal choice.

"Your name is Nathan, young man?" she asked.

"Yes, it is," he replied. "Nathan A. Banden. Will you be attending the commemoration tonight, Miss Tagbord?"

"No," Dragnie said, electing not to insult his intelligence with an apology, a condescending smile, or any other expression of regret. "I have other plans."

"That is regrettable."

"To you, perhaps."

"Yes…to me. Isn't that the only one who matters?"

"To you, perhaps."

"Yes, to me. But don't I matter to you, too, Miss Tagbord? If only a little?"

"No."

"Quite right. And yet…"

"Goodbye, Nathan. My compliments on an excellent speech."

The boy hesitated. Then he said, "Thank you, Miss Tagbord."

Almost against her will, Dragnie found herself saying, "You're welcome."

Looking at each other, they exchanged glances on an equal, voluntary basis. "Am I?" he asked.

"Yes, you're," she said. "You're welcome." And as she made her way up the slanted floor toward the lobby, she knew, as deeply and as confidently as she had known anything in her life, that it was true.

• Chapter Two •
Be a Do-er, Not a Viewer

The apartment occupied the penthouse of the Johnsonwood Building, the most indomitably proud and heroic skyscraper in New York, considered in the consensus of top experts to be the greatest building in the world and, therefore, in the universe. From its four immense windows Dragnie and her husband could, and with unfailing regularity, did, look out in all directions at once, in steely indifference and unchallengeable certainty.

Her husband was John Glatt.

That they were not legally married, had never been engaged, had never formally been lavaliered, or ever gone steady, was of no importance. He was her husband be-

D.WATSON

cause no one else was or possibly could be. And Glatt's understanding was identical to hers. Openly he professed in the privacy of his mind that she, to him, was his wife no less than he, to her, was her husband, and equally so was he her husband to him, just as she was wife to him to him no less than to her.

Consumed with hatred for her by his love for her, he never spoke of it, nor of anything else.

Yet Glatt demonstrated every day his approval of Dragnie: with every cold glance with which he acknowledged her existence each morning, every slit-eyed smirk with which disdained her over cocktails in the evening, every hand-written card he proffered on the anniversary of their first meeting ("I despise you more than ever, dearest."), and even that one time, when they had engaged in sexual intercourse, when he demonstrated his admiration and respect by brutally degrading her into a humiliated submission as he sneered his contempt and she laughed out loud in silent mockery.

They were husband and wife because they considered themselves to be so in their minds.

They now sat across from one another at the beautiful mahogany table in their elegantly appointed dining room as the sun slowly set, as it had done for billions of years all over the universe. Pierre, their footman, had just served the night's meal, a repast of gourmet food possessing the highest deliciousness, impeccably com-

plimented by an excellent wine that John Glatt had decanted, opened, chosen, unpacked, shipped, aged, bottled, fermented, stomped, picked, and planted himself with cool, swift precision.

Glatt's eyes skimmed the evening newspaper, affording him the opportunity to see the words printed on it and transferring the information they conveyed to his mind. Then his lean, sardonic face lifted from the page. He surveyed the platters of steaming, perfectly prepared meat, healthful garden vegetables, and taste-tempting side dishes arrayed before him. In a single silent act he shifted his gaze from them to Dragnie until their eyeballs silently beheld one another's. "You who claim to serve no one," he said. "You for whom the very idea of granting a favor is a metaphysical chimera, an imaginary creature possessing no reality; you whose sole allegiance is, not to some comforting but fictional construct called 'society' but, simply and utterly, to existence; you for whom life itself is rational and self-interested or it is nothing; you who, without shame or boasting, call 'self-reliance' what the mass of men call 'selfishness;' you who ask nothing of any man for which you will not, at once and without cavil, give some other thing of equal value; you, who know in the deepest recesses of your consciousness that to perform the slightest kindness to others, without the promise of reciprocity in a manner that is meaningful to you on your own terms, is to collude in the enslavement of both

ZEITGEIST

YOU ARE HERE
★

them and yourself; you, who ask nothing of the world apart from its consent to leave you to freely pursue your desires in a manner consistent with your own values and morality—will you, not so much in violation of these principles as from an unthreatened position of strength afforded by them, pass the brisket?"

"Yes, John, I will," Dragnie said. "But I will do so, not out of some received and, thus, limiting sense of obligation as imposed upon me by centuries of unconscious habit transmitted by a corrupt, anti-life, mind-fearing culture, but because I freely choose to do so. I will in full awareness of the fact that, as affirmed by laws of physics established over centuries in response to the sacred human desire to acquire knowledge, the brisket will not pass itself. I will, not because I think you incapable of either rising from your chair and transporting yourself to a position from which you would be able to obtain the brisket yourself, or of extending your arm across the table to take hold of the platter from your current position, but, paradoxically, because you can do these things. You, who're the apotheosis of heroic humanity, the completely free man, ask nothing from me and, for that

reason, deserve to have the brisket passed to you by me. While the mass of men demand something for nothing, you offer everything: your energy, your attention, your consciousness, your mind, your existence. You are the only man on Earth to whom I would pass the brisket willingly and in full awareness of the meaning of that act."

Taking hold of its elegant china platter, she passed him the brisket. Glatt used a pair of beautiful sterling silver tongs, a gift from a wealthy individual with excellent taste, to transfer several slices of the rich, delectable meat to his plate. He cut through the braised animal flesh and impaled it on the tines of a fork—efficiently, pitilessly. He tasted it, and a dark scowl formed on his face. He rang for the footman, who hurried in from the kitchen. "Pierre," Glatt said contemptuously, "the brisket has gone cold."

The footman took the platter and hurried off to the kitchen. Dispassionately eying a basket of dinner rolls, Glatt picked one up in his bare hands and began to eat it. "Oh, Dragnie, Dragnie," he said. "How was your day?"

"Mine?" Dragnie exclaimed. It was not like Glatt to express an interest in

her day; indeed, it was not like him to express an interest in any other person. His independence, his self-sufficiency, his supreme individuality were the character traits for which she most admired and despised him—and for which, she knew, she would willingly kill him and be his slave.

She became suddenly aware, with a deep certainty, that the pressures on Glatt, his responsibilities—not to others, for he had none, but to himself—were taking a toll, as they would on any man. Glatt not only functioned both as C.E.O. of Glatt Industries as well as its Top Breakthrough Inventor, but as Head Advisor of Governmental Bureaucracy Affairs for Economic Ideas for the federal government. The international situation had been deteriorating for some time; no wonder, Dragnie now thought, Glatt looked vexed. "My day was rather interesting," she said. "In fact, I met a most extraordinary young man at the Glatt School—"

The butler silently entered the room, stopped before Glatt, and said, "Excuse me, sir, but three gentlemen are down in the lobby and insist on meeting with you."

Glatt chuckled and made a gesture of impatience and mockery and contempt. "Who are they, Farnsworth?"

"Mr. Rawbone, Mr. De Soto, and Mr. Daghammarskjold."

Glatt and Dragnie exchanged a look, a look of significance and meaning and shared visual contact.

"Send them up," Glatt said.

Moments later, having ascended the 287 floors of the Johnsonwood Building in a streamlined supersonic elevator of Glatt's invention, the trio where ushered into the apartment.

"Hello, John," said Hunk Rawbone. "Hello, Dragnie."

Dragnie chuckled and Glatt chuckled. That Rawbone had once been Dragnie's lover was known to all present. Tall, handsome, with the muscular build of an athlete and the brilliant mind of a genius, Hunk Rawbone had founded Rawbone Metals and single-handedly invented the miracle metal Rawbonium. Stronger than steel, lighter than aluminum, cheaper than sand, one-hundred-percent gluten-free and packed with important vitamins and minerals, it had revolutionized the railroad industry, the aviation industry, and every other metal-using industry.

There had been a time, ten years before, when its manufacture, distribution, and sale had been strictly regulated by the second-raters and me-too-ers and so's-yer-old-man-ers of the national government, when the entire metals industry had been hobbled and bound and gagged by men like Francis Tinklepants, the Bureaucrat-in-Chief, and T.T. Mucklicker, director of the National Board of Caution.

That, however, had been before John Glatt had convinced various businessmen to hide out in Wyoming, and brought the entire world to its knees. Now Hunk Rawbone was both President of Rawbone Industries and Head Business Person of the Department of Business.

"Hello, Hunk," Dragnie said. She turned to their second visitor. "How are you, San?"

Sanfrancisco Nabisco Alcoa D'Lightful D'Lovely De Soto chuckled in a mischievous South American way, a way outwardly suggestive of lighthearted frivolity and consistent with his former but faked-up image as a feckless, womanizing and girlizing playboy but now openly proclaiming his absolute fidelity to a code of values that held that the mind was the supreme expression of man's intellect. "I?" De Soto chuckled. Like Dragnie, Sanfrancisco was a self-made man who had inherited an industrial empire.

Handsome, brilliant, dashing, and with a certain dangerous but appealing Latino flair, he had become director, upon his father's death, of the fabled De Soto Talc Mines. El Mino De Soto de Talco Incorporado was now the source of eighty-six percent of the world's baby powder, which was daily administered to more than seventy-one percent of the world's babies in both Natural and Springtime Fresh scents. "I am well, Dragnie," he said with an amused twinkle.

"Well, I am fine, too, in case anyone cares!" joked Regnad Daghammarskjold.

"And what if we don't?" chuckled De Soto.

"Well, then, you can go to hell!" rejoined the boisterous Swedish-American Swede to the chuckles of everyone else except the servants.

Dragnie pursed her lips in amusement as her eyes glittered with appreciation for his rascally personality. Handsome, blond, and attractively beautiful in a way that appealed to men as well as women, Regnad Daghammarskjold was a pirate. He spent most of his time aboard his ship, the Fjord Fusion, with his rollicking but deadly serious and often lethal band of beautiful blond fellow pirates, plundering

merchant ships from other countries and pillaging the state-owned vessels for loot, swag, and booty. When not haunting the shipping lanes of the bounding main and asserting the supremacy of private theft and entrepreneurial swashbuckling over state-run maritime mediocrities, Regnad lived in a modest two-bedroom co-op in Murray Hill with his wife, Grace Adams, the beautiful movie star.

"Would any of you like a drink?" Dragnie asked.

"I would like a beer," Regnad Daghammarskjold said. "Do you have any?"

"I don't know," Dragnie replied.

"You might," the pirate said. "Look around. Check your premises, Dragnie."

"Let me tell you something about beer," Sanfrancisco De Soto said, his eyes blazing.

Thirty-five minutes later, when he had concluded his discourse on the history, morality, and metaphysics of beer, Dragnie signaled for Pierre to bring three bottles. She handed them around.

Each of the visitors gave her a ten-dollar bill. There was no need for anyone to thank anyone for anything. "I won't insult you by offering you food," Glatt said. "You are all perfectly capable of obtaining your own sustenance."

"I know it," Regnad said.

The group settled in the living room and Hunk Rawbone opened the discussion. "I don't know if you've heard, John," he said. "But Goa has fallen."

"I didn't know it," Glatt said. "Goa be damned!"

"That's the last one," Sanfrancisco added. "Now every nation on earth has become a People's State of the People."

"Every nation—save one," Dragnie murmured. "The United States."

"Shall I tell you what the product safety boys are saying?" Rawbone asked out loud.

"They're saying that the People's States're complaining that our manufactured goods're dangerous. They're talking about an embargo."

"Then we must meet with Mr. Jenkins," Dragnie said. "We should also alert the boys in the Pentagon, our nation's most brilliant scientist boys, and our leading achiever-boys in industry, research, and engineering."

"This is serious, isn't it, John?" Regnad said with unflinching directness.

"Yes," Glatt replied.

The three visitors had gone, and Dragnie and Glatt were preparing for bed, when Glatt mentioned their earlier topic of conversation. Standing in their elegant bedroom, clad in the simplest of pajamas whose clean design, quiet sense of style, and always-tasteful pizzazz made a striking statement of individuality wherever he went, he said, "You were telling me about an extraordinary young man you met today."

Dragnie suppressed a smile of amuse-

"The time is now 7:42—and if you can hang on for half a sec, I'll switch you over to Phil with the weather."

ment. "It's of no importance," she said, and only afterwards, while falling asleep, did she ask herself if that were really true.

• Chapter Three •
The Veracity of Truth

Dragnie stood up from her austere, stoical desk, as if announcing to the world with a single decisive gesture that she had completed the work she had sat at it in order to accomplish. She allowed herself a brief chuckle of amusement at her achievement, followed by a contemptuous chuckle of mockery at the amused contemptuousness with which she regarded her own chuckling mockery, which was so amusing.

Tagbord Rail's Southwest Division was expanding to her satisfaction. The augmented schedule of the Chimichanga Line in Arizona, linking to the Tamale-Caliente Line in New Mexico, would take some of the pressure off the trunk lines of the Enchiladas Suizas Line in Texas. The entire region was doing well. The economy of the Southwest had shown steady growth in the past ten years, as if that area's system of production and trade among men had been a human being, eating right and staying fit and as a consequence becoming larger.

In fact, the economy of the entire U.S. had undergone a similar expansion over the same period, although not before what came to be called The Great Takeover. Until then, the government, controlled by Mr. Thomas and a small cadre of corrupt and physically-unattractive bureaucrats, had sought to maximize its power and safeguard its incompetence and mediocrity with laws mandating "fairness."

No one was allowed to produce anything new. No one was allowed to use anything old. No one was allowed to accept a new job or quit their current job. No one was allowed to be a genius. No one was allowed to have fun or have nice things or go anywhere or do anything or go out or see their friends or anything.

John Glatt's response to this state of affairs was to persuade society's achievers to withdraw from humanity and hide in a valley in Wyoming. As many as twenty important tycoons abandoned their companies. Some even destroyed their factories, refineries, and warehouses with dynamite and fire, miraculously without injury or loss of life to anyone of importance.

What had transpired then was what always happens when a corporation's founder retires or dies: the companies went out of business. All that remained of the country's economy ground to a halt.

Then Glatt hijacked the radio waves and made a three-hour speech about his view of the world, and the government—as governments invariably do, after being denounced in long, philosophical lectures—surrendered. The boys in Washington pleaded with Glatt to restore order.

Mr. Thomas, convening a formal committee including such cowardly lapdogs and obsequious pontificating high-ups as Jason Bellybutton, the supposed economist; Dr. Cyrus Pussyface, the prevaricating expert; Professor Jones, the world-renowned person; and Secretary of Union Greed Mumph Slimetrail, importuned Glatt to take the reins of the economy and rescue it from disaster.

Glatt refused. The government attempted to coerce him into cooperating but that, too, failed. Finally, it abdicated, and Glatt led his courageous, principled team of businessmen and classical music composers and actresses out of Glatt's Gorge and back into the world.

Their first actions were swift and decisive. They fired Mr. Thomas and replaced him with the impotent puppet Mr. Jenkins. They then nullified every undemocratically-imposed edict and authoritarian-enforced regulation of the past twenty years, and supplanted them with rules supporting individual achievement. They repealed the Everybody Be Nice Act and replaced it with the Leave Business Alone Directive. They cancelled the Nobody Gets to Have More Than Anybody Else Act and instituted the Finders Keepers Losers Weepers Ruling. They reversed the If You Don't Have Enough to Share With The Rest of the Class Then You Can Leave Those Cupcakes With Me And Collect Them At The End of The Day Edict and, in its place, promulgated the This Is My Fudgesicle Go Get Your Own Law.

The results were immediate and profound. Everywhere, in every industry, millionaires went back to work. Useless regulators and corrupt bureaucrats committed mass suicide, publicly begged for forgiveness, or found themselves simply shot on sight. Labor unions, openly acknowledging the superior wisdom and unfailing justice of the marketplace, voluntarily disbanded after first publishing, in newspapers throughout the land, full-page advertisements apologizing to management for any inconvenience they had caused for the past one hundred years. Reality, as properly defined, resumed.

But now, Dragnie mused to her own private self as she began to walk toward her office door, a new enemy of freedom loomed: the consolidation of the People's States of the People, whose cancerous collectivist malignancy had now spread to

MOTHER GOOSE SPOILERS

Peter locks his wife inside a pumpkin shell. He is never caught.

The mice lose their tails to the farmer's wife's knife.

HELP! HELP!! SOMEBODY HELP!!!

Humpty Dumpty passes away.

We did all we could. Poor guy.

every nation on earth—save one.

"Miss Tagbord? A delivery for you."

Miss Smith, her loyal and obedient secretary, stood in the doorway, an expression of open admiration obscured, on the face of her head, by an immense bouquet of vivid, luxuriant magenta orchids in a handsome cut-glass vase created by one of the city's top vase designers. Dragnie suppressed a small smile at the inadvertent double meaning of the secretary's announcement.

The notion that she would ever take part in "a delivery," and from the sacred and inviolable sanctity of her body's individuality, bring forth another human being whose helplessness and weakness would subject her—at least according to society's superstitious tribal standards—to years of unremunerated toil and slavish subservience, was literally inconceivable to the mentality of her mind.

A standard business card sat in a small clip amid the heavy, flesh-like blooms. She plucked it out and, as Miss Smith placed the vase on her desk in an attractive orientation, Dragnie read the meticulously hand-written message:

"Dear Miss Tagbord:

Kindly permit me to express the gratitude of which I felt on the occasion yesterday of your extremely neat visit to our School. It was an affirmation of my love of my own self and the life that it lives to see you in the audience as I rehearsed my speech. And yet I do not express here the typically obsequious homage of a nobody to a celebrity. My theory is that celebrity feeds off of fame, which is its bread and butter and meat and potatoes and mother's milk and just dessert.

And what is fame, but the afterglow of men's discussion of an individual providing value for the admiration of the mob? A visitor can be no more distinguished than the place to which he visits.

Therefore I will not speak of being honored by your presence. The mass of lesser men seek elevation of their self-respect in the proximity of their selves to the heightened significance of the lauded one. But to the individual of true mind such turnons are irrelevant, because they find their value in the accomplishment of their own achievement. Do you dismiss my assertion as being merely

"It's the circus...they say it was all a big misunderstanding...they want you to come back!"

that of a student? Then you do so at your peril. A society indifferent to its students, and to their ability to determine without obstruction the site of their senior prom, is a society that is doomed. It is a society ruled by cowards for the benefit of weaklings, squares, and numb-nuts. That is no society in which I deem it worth living my one life, which is all one can live, and be alive. I hope you like the flowers.

Yours truly,
Nathan A. Banden."

Dragnie threw her head back in a gesture of defiance. Informing Miss Smith that she would return to the office tomorrow, she left.

On the train to Washington Dragnie read the card five more times. Something in the boy's words touched her deeply. She found herself compelled by his unflinching willingness to address even the most trivial of topics in terms of heightened philosophical discourse. The tone of the card bespoke a sensibility almost frighteningly in sympathetic harmony with her own. She wondered if his parents were aware of the boy's potential for greatness.

The porter, a dignified man named Ben Dover, wearing the official dark blue Tagbord Rail uniform, stopped on his way up the aisle and bent in professional deference. He had been serving the needs of passengers of the Executive Car since the earliest days, when Old Man Pop Gramps "Professor" Zayde Poppa "The Guv'nor" Tagbord had created the line, and had watched Dragnie grow from infancy. He was now ninety-seven years old, blind in one eye and functionally deaf, and yet he still worked, willingly and with the highest competence, for such was his dedication to his job and its ability to protect and safeguard his individuality from the effects of undeserved cost-of-living wage increases, unnecessary health care, and employer-funded pensions that enslaved workers on other, still-vaguely-unionized rail lines.

He now demonstrated his undiminished ability to transport, with one hand under a tray, a martini from the galley car without spilling a drop. "Is something wrong, Miss Dragnie?" he inquired in his wise and aged manner. "You look to be the subject of vexations."

Dragnie forced a reassuring smile. "It's nothing, Uncle Ben," she murmured. "I'm just worried, I suppose—worried about the future of the entire world."

The old man chuckled. "Well, I don't know nothing about that," he said. "All's I know is, we're out of chicken salad."

Dragnie smiled. The courageous train rushed on to its once-dignified but now shamefaced destination.

The conference took place at the White Home, in a secret room unknown about by men not informed of its existence. As Dragnie entered she saw that John Glatt had already arrived, as had Sanfrancisco De Soto, Hunk Rawbone, and Regnad Daghammarskjold. The four men sat along one side of a table set with pitchers of water and glasses, both of the highest transparency, and legal pads and pens. Opposite them sat three representatives of the nominal government in whispered colloquy with its loathsome head, Mr. Jenkins. A sweat-soaked, fat man with repulsive male breasts, he gave a weak, contemptible smile as she moved toward her seat. "Ah. Miss Tagbord. Splendid. We're all here." He glanced at the hate-worthy bureaucrats flanking him and then gestured to Glatt and his companions. "So let's get started." The repellent chief executive composed the features of his ugly face into a stern and grim arrangement. "The word from the People's States of the

People is what we'd been fearing," he said in a voice soaked in terror and self-pity. He shifted, his chair emitting squeals of protest as if in violent objection to being sat on by such an inferior individual. "They're imposing a comprehensive embargo on all products made in the U.S. That's not good. That's not good at all!"

"But, why?" Dragnie said, her voice low.

"They say our products are too dangerous," Mr. Jenkins replied.

"But, why?" Dragnie asked, her voice low.

"Our toys are covered with lead-based paint. Our cars explode when the odometer reaches three hundred. Our broccoli, kale, and Romaine lettuce harbor dangerous impurities such as salmonella, E. coli, and other pathogens. Our kitchen appliances burst into flame the first time you plug them in. Our telephones generate X-rays that cause brain cancer." Mr. Jenkins gulped convulsively and wiped sweat from his forehead with a disgusting handkerchief. "The common man doesn't want brain cancer. The common man doesn't want brain cancer at all, I tell you!"

"The market will decide that," Hunk Rawbone murmured coolly. A thousand words screamed in his mind but he did not permit himself to give them voice. Instead, he mentally recommended that they shut up. "We manufacture our products as cheaply as possible in order to maximize profit. Perhaps that's something they don't understand any more in the People's States of the People of France or England or Germany or Spain or Portugal or Greece or China or Australia."

"Or Goa," added Regnad Daghammarskjold, deliberately speaking with his voice.

"Look, Hunk," Mr. Jenkins whined in the manner of a child seeking to escape blame for everything all the time. "I know that, and you know that. But the boys in the People's States of the People don't see it that way. They have objections to their kids being poisoned and their mixmasters blowing up. And now, with this embargo, we have no place to sell our exports."

"We'll sell them domestically," Dragnie said, her voice low.

"To whom, Miss Tagbord?"

The question came from the man seated languidly to the right of Mr. Jenkins. He was Phillip Sissyberger, the Minister of Equality, a thin, meticulous aesthete in a

custom-made, purple silk suit and a florid green bow tie. He sported a pencil-thin moustache and affected the airy, condescending manner of an individual for whom the supreme achievement of life was to be a big know-it-all. "The vast majority of our population can't afford much more than food, clothing, and shelter. True, we boast an upper class the income of which may comfortably rival that of any aristocracy anywhere in the world— if there still are any aristocracies left, in our benighted age. But those people—one might call them 'the achievers' or 'the successes' or 'the good people'—comprise less than one tenth of one percent of our populace, and in any case they scarcely have need of the cheap consumer goods our factories produce. They purchase their appliances and automobiles from the prestigious manufacturers in the People's States of the People of England, Germany, Italy, and Sweden. No, my friends. We may all applaud the free-market revolution led by you four gentlemen and Miss Tagbord ten years ago. You may congratulate yourselves on the complete removal of all government regulation and oversight of industry. You may likewise take pride in the realization of your primary goal, which is and always has been the elimination and, indeed, delegitimization of the very idea of taxation, and for the complete subjugation of the public sphere to the interests of private enterprise. In this you have succeeded admirably. The popularity of Grand Canyon Fun Park, the lines at the District of ColumbiaLand ticket booths that surround this nation's capital, the conversion of the Great Lakes into water hazards for the world's largest miniature golf course—all of these attest to your achievement. But the equality characterizing our nation now consists in a near-universal state of lower-class subsistence. The American people can no more afford to buy their own products

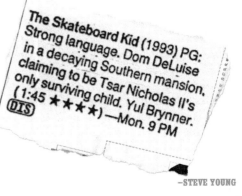

—STEVE YOUNG

Akiko **STEHRENBERGER**

than they can afford to catch the flu or purchase loin lamb chops to feed a family of four."

"The American people, sir, have one thing denied to the richest person in any other country on Earth." Sanfrancisco De Soto leaned forward, his boyish charm apparent in his twinkly-eyed playfulness and faintly mocking smile. "It is something far more precious than German eggbeaters or English sports cars. Or, I might add, lamb chops. Perhaps you have heard of it. It is called 'freedom.' And it is with this freedom that each person is free—for that is why it is called 'freedom'—to succeed or fail according to their own abilities. Each person is free to start his own steel mill, unburdened by government meddling. Each person is free to create a railroad and to do his damndest in competition against Miss Tagbord here. Each person is free to inherit a talc mine that has been in his family for generations, and to run it as he sees fit."

"Yes, yes, freedom is wonderful," Mr. Jenkins said hastily. "But we all have a country to run. I'm merely head of the

Federal government. You five are calling the shots. What are we to do?"

Everyone, as everyone always did, turned toward John Glatt.

Once again Dragnie found herself marveling at the face and the appearance of the man whom she had, in essence, married. It was a face so comfortable with itself that it seemed to fall asleep on itself, yet simultaneously a face so hardened by a life not merely lived, but consciously experienced, that it betrayed no sign of having aged or, in the end, existed. His mouth was pure, a mouth that, if it could speak, would announce to the world what a mouth should and must be, for all men, throughout time. His eyes, existing as a matched pair as if they were diamond cufflinks or precious earrings fashioned by one of the top jewelry designers in the world, conveyed a dual nature. They were at once both proud and shy, sensitively concerned and cruelly indifferent, alert to danger and blankly oblivious of the actual meaning of the words "danger" or "alert" or "to." His hair was as wise as his eyebrows were intelligent, while his ears

had the hard, sculpted purity and radiant tensile strength of a bridge that spanned chasms, announcing to all who saw it that no challenge was beyond the ability of man's mind to meet, solve, and then forget about utterly and forever.

"John?" she said, unaware that she was speaking, unaware that she was breathing, unaware of anything and everything of which men can be aware. "Do you have an idea?"

"Yes," Glatt said.

"What is it, John?" asked Hunk Rawbone, silently vibrating with a desire to obtain an answer to his query.

"Good."

"It's a good idea, John?" inquired Regnad Daghammarskjold, falling silent after he had finished speaking.

"Yes."

"Care to let us in on it, old pal?" Sanfrancisco said.

"No."

"We'll just have to take your word for it?" Mr. Jenkins cried. "Is that what you're saying, Glatt? Is that what you would have us believe? Is that what you're communicating to us? Is that the idea?"

"Yes."

"Well, that's fine for you," Mr. Jenkins cried. "But when word gets out that none of our overseas customers're going to be buying our products, there'll be mass panic. Everyone'll be afraid of losing their jobs. What if they look to the government for help? That's not what I signed up for. That's not what I signed up for at all! But I'm the nominal Head Person of the United States of America and I'll have to say something." He pressed a button on the intercom in front of him. "Miss Davis? Call the press boys. Tell them in a week I'll be making a speech about the international economic situation to the general public boys. Then call the speechwriter boys and have them come up with something. Then call my wife and have her tell the in-law boys that I'll have to work over the weekend and won't be able to attend the drama festival, and to convey my regrets to the Boys From Syracuse boys, the Three Sisters boys, and the Guys 'n' Dolls boys." Mr. Jenkins turned to the others. "You people had better think of something," he cried. "It doesn't remove any skin off of my nose if this country's population all becomes unemployed. I've got a job. But that job is to tell everybody else that nothing's wrong when everybody knows that everything's wrong."

The person to Mr. Jenkins's right, a puling and whiny person of no substance, cried, "This is a terrible crisis and I'm afraid!"

"Yes!" yelled Mr. Jenkins. "We're all frightened of what might happen to us!"

"Are you afraid, John?" Dragnie asked.

"No," John Glatt said.

• Chapter Four •
The Selves of Men

You still despise me, don't you, John?" Dragnie and Glatt were back in their home, in the proud penthouse of the dignified but good-natured Johnsonwood Building. It was night, and all daylight had disappeared, as if the sun had gotten tired and gone to bed. Glatt sat pitilessly at his desk, his attention focused with unswerving intensity upon the notebook in which he had been writing since their return on the train earlier that afternoon. Now, as then, his implacable posture announced his absolute immersion in his task. Now, as then, his confident, strong, clean hand responded to his will, grasping the pen

and moving it in specific, controlled, clean gestures to inscribe letters on the clean, college-ruled, white paper, the letters in their turn forming words, from which, when reading it back, his consciousness would derive meaning.

Glatt did not look up when responding to Dragnie's question. His eyes squinted slightly with amused contempt. "Yes," he said.

"And you know that I despise you?"

"Yes."

A faint smile played about Dragnie's mouth. She left Glatt's office and went to the bedroom. There was no need for either of them to say goodnight. There was no need for either of them to exchange physical gestures of affection. There was no need for either of them to engage in sexual activity with the other, nor had they done so in ten years. Sex, Dragnie knew, was the body's way of externalizing the ego in all of its desires, fears, fantasies, and requirements. Most people needed to have sex multiple times in order to assuage the needs of a self that had been irreparably damaged by the cowardly, life-hating mediocrities that controlled society—the looters, who simply stole what others had created or achieved; the leeches, who sucked wealth and reputation from those who had their true claim; the moochers, who sought for free what others had paid for in thought and labor; the koochie-koo-ers, who begged for care and support in exchange for their winning cuteness; the hootchie-kootchers, who demanded acclaim and reward simply because they could dance in a provocative manner. But Dragnie and Glatt were immune to this need, because, as supremely rational beings, their selves—and this they knew with the absolute certainty of purest certitude—were perfect. It had therefore only been necessary for them to engage in sex once. That had taken place ten years earlier in a mutually brutalizing act of seduction, rape, triumphalism, surrender, gloating, name-calling, bullying, shaming, taunting, objectivizing, sneering-and-leering, self-glorification, and self-loathing.

Their "marriage," their partnership, their union, had been undistracted and undiminished by sex, or conversation, ever since.

Dragnie turned out the light as, in his study, Glatt continued to work on his achievement.

• • •

"Prepare for landing."

Regnad Daghammarskjold's voice echoed throughout the spaceship as, below, the mottled and dusty surface of their destination drew nearer. "Coordinate the rockets. Get ready to turn off the engines."

All around him, the crew flawlessly operated switches and, with cool efficiency, checked important readings preparatory to the craft's touchdown.

"I hope this baby works properly!" Sanfrancisco De Soto chuckled in roguish humor.

"It will," Dragnie murmured. She spoke, not out of hope, but conviction. The ship had been designed over the course of three days by John Glatt, its materials supplied by Hunk Rawbone's mills, and fabricated under her personal supervision in Tagbord Rail's most experienced factory.

Now, under the command of the breathtakingly attractive Swedish pirate, its maiden voyage was on the verge of a successful completion.

"Stabilize the gyroscopes," Regnad ordered. "Adjust the controls and line up the necessary components properly."

Finally the craft touched down on the surface. "Confirm that everything is pressurized," the pirate said. "Turn off the motors and turn on the lights. Assure that the cabin pressure is correct for human habitation."

"How much time do we have?" Sanfrancisco asked.

Dragnie glanced at her watch, an expensive timepiece she proudly wore in unashamed pride.

Beautifully enhanced with precious jewels and waterproof to thirty atmospheres, it was built with the utmost precision and expressed her own personal style. "Fifteen minutes."

"Ready, John?"

John Glatt unbuckled his seat belt in a single clean, decisive, confident motion. It was a motion that had the cleanliness

—STEVE YOUNG

and the decisiveness and the confidence of a certainty that, unlike the certainty of other men who, however much they had felt a similar certainty about other things, had been proven wrong, was right. "Yes."

On Earth, in the country of the United States, in a state called Nebraska, a family sat in its living room, preparing to watch an address delivered by the Head Person of the United States government. They had been told to anticipate this event for a week, and had obediently gathered before their television to hear their leader's words of wisdom. "Be sure to watch Mr. Jenkins!" the television ads had cried. "Mr. Jenkins will have something important to say!" read the billboards on signs and buses. "Listen to Mr. Jenkins because he is smart!" ran the ads on the radio. This family, whose members had been instructed from birth to believe whatever certain authorities told them, whether the authorities were the church, the government, or the education system, consisted of a father, who was a contemptible weakling, his wife, who was hatefully stupid, and their two children, each more repulsively "idealistic" than the other.

"Mr. Jenkins cares about us," the mother said reassuringly. "He will be able to help us."

"Mr. Jenkins is not one of those heartless, selfish capitalists," the father said, believing himself to have expressed an opinion of wisdom. "He is able to empathize with the ordinary man."

"I love Mr. Jenkins!" cried the daughter in a voice indistinguishable from that with which she squealed her adoration of the latest pop star.

"Mr. Jenkins is my favorite person. When I grow up, I want the government to give me everything," announced the son, believing himself to be a mature and thoughtful human being.

Suddenly a voice announced Mr. Jenkins, and a face appeared on the television, and the family fell silent and paid attention to it. "Ladies and gentlemen, my fellow Americans, boys and girls, and people all over the world," said Mr. Jenkins. "I come before you tonight with a grave announcement." He spoke in the dull monotone of a man who did not love life. There were pouches below his eyes, as if reality had hung there twin bags of ethical compromise, while the lines of his face formed the latitude and longitude demarcations of a map of moral corruption that no cosmetologist's pancake makeup

D. WATSON

could conceal. "The People's States of the People of all the states and nations and people of the world have determined that they can no longer engage in trade with the United States of America. They say our products are too dangerous. They say that when we removed all regulatory oversight from the private sector, ended corporate taxation, outlawed unions, and eliminated the minimum wage, our work force degenerated into a pool of depressed and angry wage-slaves for whom quality no longer mattered. And so…" He paused to lick his thin, terrified lips. "And so they are issuing a blanket embargo on…on…" Suddenly Mr. Jenkins lurched up from his seat and toward the camera, as though desperately seeking the attention and sympathy of a skeptical onlooker. "This isn't my fault!" he cried, sweating visibly. "You can't blame this on me! I can't help it! I just do what I'm told by John Glatt and that wife of his, and that Frisco fellow and that, that pirate! You've got to believe me—"

And then the picture went black. The channel seemed to have ceased transmission.

"Attention, the ears of men. This is John Glatt speaking."

Before the family a new face had appeared, a face only vaguely familiar to the adults and almost entirely unknown to the children, and yet a face which each of them—man, wife, son, daughter—sensed belonged to a man that could be trusted. It was a face not only at perfect peace with itself, but at perfect peace with life and with man and with existence. "You are now receiving me on every channel on every television and on every station on every radio on Earth," Glatt said in a tone of supreme confidence. "It is useless to try to change the station or the channel. We are controlling transmission. We control the horizontal. We control the vertical.

"How is it that we are able to dominate the airwaves in this fashion, you ask? We are able to do so for one reason: I am speaking to you from the Moon.

"I have come here, in a craft of my own design and constructed at my own expense, to issue a reply to the people of the People's States of the People. I address them as follows: You have, with the fall of Goa, consolidated your grip on all the nations on earth--except ours. You have elected to embargo all of our private sector products, claiming that it is our governmental responsibility that some of them are dangerous, unwholesome, or lethal. We have sought, in good faith, to avoid that responsibility. We have made the logically irrefutable case that, for every shipment of arsenic-tainted minty-fresh toothpaste or dioxin-laced lo-fat yogurt or spontaneously-combusting strawberry-scented bowling balls or carcinogenic E-Z-Fit sweat pants we sell, there is another shipment of the same product that poses no danger to its users. But, rather than allow the market to sort out the dangerous commodities from the safe ones—rather than allowing some consumers to die or sustain injuries so that others may enjoy the safe versions of those products—you now choose to impose a global ban, denying your citizens access to these products and unfairly victimizing both us and them, but mainly us, in the process.

"We have protested, we have argued, and we have petitioned, but all to no avail. You continue to reject our products—and, in so doing, our very society. You continue to reject our values. You continue to live differently than we do—and, thus, to contradict us. It is for this reason that we hate you. We have arrived at our values, and our society, through the use of mind. We are the men of mind, and the women of mind, and the kids of mind. That is how we know we are right. To your attacks and criticisms we have ample reply. You say that your economies are growing and ours is stagnant. We say: economies are like hair, and too much growth can result in unmanageability and a fly-away society. You say your unemployment rates are at an all-time low while ours are skyrocketing. We say: when everyone is employed, there is an insufficient labor pool for the starting of new businesses; then innovation dies and everything gets old and depressing. You say that your governments are able to assure a modern, efficient infrastructure and a pleasant array of public amenities such as highways, parks and libraries, via the taxation of the individuals and corporations who make use of them. We say: taxes are the people who make so little that they need not pay them anyway, while the others, the successful, should not be taxed, so they will have an incentive to make more money, whereas if they were taxed, and therefore had less money, they would have no incentive to make more. You say that you have created a decent safety net to assure every one of your citizens a minimally civilized existence from infancy through old age, while we have abandoned our poor and infirm and aged to lives of degradation and poverty. We say that safety nets are for amateur tightrope walkers, while the tightrope walkers that men truly admire, and pay good money to watch, are the professionals, who work without a net. You say your defense budgets are sensible and targeted to actual enemies, while ours is larger than the rest of the world's put together and targeted at enemies that no longer exist. We say: the bigger one's defense budget, the stronger one feels.

"You say that your literacy rates are higher than ours. We say: a nation filled with people reading is a nation filled with people not doing other worthwhile activities, such as writing a stirring symphony, painting a breathtaking new masterpiece, or delivering an unforgettable cinematic performance of astounding depth and sensitivity. You say your life expectancy is higher than ours. We say: No one can accurately guess how long they will live, so why try to? You say that your percentage of population per capita in prison is lower than ours. We say: a high rate of imprisonment attests to both a society's ample temptations to criminal behavior, and to the existence of an efficient and effective criminal justice system. You say your infant mortality rate is lower than ours. We say: that our supply of babies is so large and excellent that we can afford to have more of them die. You say your average costs of medical procedures and prescription drugs are lower than ours. We say: men place the highest value on what costs them the most, and that when health comes with a high price tag, men cherish their lives all the more. You say your rates of medical bankruptcies are zero while ours are astronomical. We say: if life is not worth going bankrupt to prolong, then one shouldn't be alive in the first place. You say you have lower rates of venereal disease, teenage pregnancies, and abortions per capita than we do.

"We say: the more syphilis and gonorrhea and unwanted pregnancies a nation has, the sexier its population has proven itself to be. You say that polls indicate that your populations are consistently happier and less frightened of the future than ours are. We say that happiness without fear is like rice pudding without cinnamon, that fear makes you conscious, and that consciousness is what differentiates man from the non-conscious entities of the universe, such as rice pudding.

"All of these characteristics—the American mortality rate, American life expectancy, American bankruptcies, American venereal disease statistics, American defense budget, American absence of a safety net, and so on—are components of one essential fact that has defined America from its very birth: American exceptionalism. America is the only country in history that not only believes itself to be exceptional among all the nations of all time, but that really is exceptional among all the nations of all time. America is the only nation in history founded on the American idea—the idea of universal liberty and self-government for all white men owning property. It is this American Exceptionalism that has made the United States the envy of the world, the exemplar of hope, and the dream destination of the poor, the oppressed, and the dispossessed, until only fairly recently.

"But you have treated us badly. So it is this very American Exceptionalism that we now propose to deny you.

"You have always looked to the United States as an example of a free society? Henceforth and until further notice we will restrict our own freedoms to deny you their example. You have always desired to immigrate to our shores in search of religious liberty and material prosperity? We hereby announce our intention to encourage religious intolerance and impoverish our population. You have long considered America a beacon of freedom and a force for good? Effective immediately we will deny freedom to ourselves and become a force for bad—for indifference, if not outright evil, in the world.

"In a word, we are going on strike. Do not look for our participation in the world of international affairs, because we are withdrawing our involvement in the doings of men. Do not anticipate the export of our Hollywood productions of films and television shows that promote the values of liberty, opportunity, and justice, because we shall now make them for and distribute them solely among ourselves, and they shall be about servitude, hopelessness, and things like that. Do not expect foreign aid for your populations or the arrival of Peace Corps volunteers

BEATON/MEANS

to help with your latest efforts to build a school or inoculate your village against polio, because you have done us ill and hurt our feelings. If you change your mind, we will be where we have always been, in the northern hemisphere, between Mexico and Canada. If you decide to behave differently, and can provide convincing evidence to that effect, we will be only too happy to review it. Until then, however, we wish not to be contacted, and we'd appreciate it if you would take our name off any international communications, telexes, mail postings, diplomatic cables, and broadcasts. Thank you, and good night."

• Chapter Five •
On the Being of Existence

A muffled roar could be heard as Regnad switched off the rocket engines once the ship was safely back on its launch pad on Earth. He looked around, an expression of baffled amusement flitting over his unutterably lovely Swedish piratical features, while attending with cool precision and clean, flawless skill every task required of him.

"What's that noise?" he asked Sanfrancisco, who had spent the entire flight back lounging in the co-pilot's chair, outwardly reading a motorcycle magazine while, at the edge of his mind and part-way in toward the interior of it, marshalling his intelligence to address a vexing problem concerning the dispersal coefficients of aerosolized powder. "I thought I told you to turn off the ventilation system."

"I did," Sanfrancisco replied with flippant unconcern. "I guess John's design for the exhaust fan was flawed."

From her seat beside a window, Dragnie looked out onto the area around the launch pad, her expression of purest calm unaltered by the stunned amazement, or anything else, that she felt.

"That's not the sound of the exhaust fan," she murmured, then tilted her chin toward the vista outside the glass. "It's them."

In a single uninterrupted motion, Hunk Rawbone transported his body to the main hatch and worked its mechanism. The moment it swung open a deafening roar flooded into the control room. "John?" he said. "Look."

John Glatt, responding instinctively to the mention of his own name, joined Rawbone at the hatch. The rest of the

crew gathered behind them. Outside a tumultuous crowd had gathered.

As one, when they saw the hatch open and the ship's crew step out, the multitude cheered. They cheered as crowds have cheered for millennia the return of conquering armies, the arrival of admired kings, the celebration of praised heroes waving from convertible automobiles as they are paraded down Main Street. Many of them held aloft signs they had created by their own hand, signs which read "WE LOV YOU JON GLAT" and "DOWN WITH MR JENKINS!" and "JHON GLATT IS OUR LEADER." Making their way through the throng, Dragnie and the others were applauded, their backs were slapped, they were waved at and hugged and kissed.

Mothers held babies aloft to burn into their infantile awareness the significance of the occasion.

An old woman in a threadbare shawl had tears in her eyes. A man who looked like a factory worker held out the collo-quial American gesture of a thumb's up. Another man, who looked like a white collar worker, made the A-OK sign with his thumb and index finger. A man who looked like he might be a farmer chewed on a piece of straw and, his weathered face firmly affixed to his graying head, nodded wisely. A woman who looked like a mother of two clasped her hands in gratitude. An elderly couple, who looked like they had one son who was a dermatologist in Sarasota, Florida, married to an Italian girl and with a boy toddler who was allergic to pistachio nuts, and a daughter named Corinne doing graduate studies in anthropology at UCLA while working part-time waiting tables in an exclusive restaurant, smiled.

Suddenly Dragnie saw a familiar face. It was the face of a young man who, when her eye caught his, looked away, as though to deny the contact, and then returned the look, as if announcing his mastery of an instinctual shyness and his ability to use his will to overcome fear and advance his interests. With an expression of amused contempt he threaded his way through the crowd until he was standing beside her and smiling with contemptuous amusement.

"Hello, Miss Tagbord," Nathan A. Banden said.

Something in his insolent attitude made Dragnie recoil. And yet a part of her responded in a different manner.

"Hello, Nathan," she said. "We've just returned from the Moon."

"I know it."

"John made a speech."

"I know it."

"By the way, thank you for the flowers. You were quite eloquent in your note."

The young man chuckled mockingly. "I?" he said. "Eloquent? Quite? Was? I merely wrote words—words that needed to be read by you, silently, to yourself, in order to receive my meaning."

"Not everyone would see it that way."

"I know it. But not everyone is me."

"I know it. Only you are you."

"Are you certain of that, Miss...Dragnie?"

They stood there, saying nothing wordlessly and looking at each other, like the last man and woman on earth, surrounded only by several thousand other men and women. Dragnie felt something stir deep within herself. His face was youthful, unlined by a lifetime's struggle to discover his values. His cool blue eyes seemed to look directly at her. He was taller than she, and so in conversation with him she acquired that characteristic that is among the most feminine qualities it is possible for a woman to display: that of being short. But her femininity transcended mere physical diminutiveness, attaining its apotheosis in a tableau attesting to her subjugation to him. After her long, half-million-mile trip, she was unkempt, whereas he had obviously showered and shaved that morning, to the extent that he needed to shave at all. She was thus hygienically his inferior as well. It was a thought that gave her pleasure. She was on the verge of saying something. She did not know what it was. She did not know why she was about to say it. She did not know why she did not know these things. She only knew that she was about to say something, when Sanfrancisco appeared beside her, grasping her arm and drawing her away, saying, "Dragnie, John needs you."

She allowed herself to be guided to where John Glatt stood, watching the journalists ask fawning questions of Hunk Rawbone. The reporters, supposedly of a professional class concerned with discovering and communicating the truth, had long ago ceased to pursue such matters. Their only concern now was the unearthing of scandal and the publication of innuendo, gossip, and triviality. All of them hated their profession and, therefore, hated its allied professions as well. They hated their editors. They despised their art directors. They loathed their circulation staffs, advertising departments, and press operators. The crowd surrounding the journalists, conscious of the moral bankruptcy of their profession, hated them.

"Hunk seems to be holding his own with the jackals of the press," Sanfrancisco said.

Glatt's reply hinted at a vast reservoir of emotions held in check by his will. "Yes."

"John," Dragnie said. She spoke with her eyes on the crowd. It was not necessary to look at her husband, as she had just addressed him by name. "I've been thinking. Once our strike against the rest of the world begins, I'd like to travel around the country on a fact-finding mission, to monitor how it progresses."

"All right."

"Of course, I'll need an assistant to help me take notes and compile my findings. I think that boy I told you about, at the Glatt School, who made the speech—I think he'd make a fine assistant."

"Very well."

"Of course I'll have to consult with his parents, but that shouldn't be a problem—"

The rest of her words were drowned out as the crowd began several rhythmic chants at once.

"LET'S MURDER ALL THE OTHER COUNTRIES," went one, while another announced, "HURRAY FOR US BECAUSE WE'RE THE BEST!" Across the tarmac, Dragnie saw Nathan A. Banden watching her. A sleek limousine slowly crept through the crowd and stopped. Its door opened. Dragnie climbed in and was followed by the others. As the car pulled out, the mob cheered and waved.

• • •

"You wish to take Nathan with you on a trip around the country, Miss Tagbord? How odd a request."

The person speaking, Nathan A. Banden's mother, was one of those individuals who believe that a woman's most exalted purpose in life is to adorn a husband and give birth to his children. She consequently regarded Dragnie with a combination of personal suspicion and moral disapproval.

"Yes," Dragnie replied. "For about a month."

Mrs. Banden was a slim, tightly-coiffed woman with a showily blasé attitude, the kind of person for whom appearance was reality and reality was an illusion. She regarded Dragnie from a complacent divan, on which she lounged in a lazy caftan crafted of haughty material. "But do please be seated, Miss Tagbord," she said, indicating an antique wing chair of unquestionable confidence. The Banden home, a large Tudor-style dwelling in a suburb of New York City, occupied several acres whose gardens and landscaping were designed to celebrate man's dominance over Nature and over his fellow man. "Don't you agree that the idea is somewhat unusual?"

"Not particularly, no."

"Well, I must say, I do. Of course, Nathan is about to graduate high school, and will have to find something to do before starting college in the fall. Does one say 'graduate high school' or 'graduate from high school'? No, don't bother trying to answer. I wouldn't expect you to know matters of proper grammar and syntax. You work on a railroad, after all. I wonder, Miss Tagbord, do you work 'all the livelong day'? Or is that merely a misconception propagated by the familiar folk tune?"

"I work during the day and often at night."

"Yes, I believe you do. For what else is a woman without children to do? In any case, you are a grown woman, Miss Tagbord. Indeed, if one is to credit the news reports, you are married—to none other than John Glatt, the man who, we're led to believe, single-handedly saved the economy and our country ten years ago. Do you deny it?"

"I do not deny it, although we are not married."

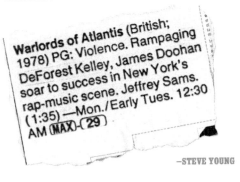

—STEVE YOUNG

"Nathan is, of course, a teenager, and teenage boys are notoriously immature. Although of course all men are. All men are at bottom children, don't you think so?"

"'I do not."

"You must not know very many men, then. I assure you, I do know many men. Mind you, I'm not saying I've had sexual relations with all of them, although you are of course free to infer such a thing and, in fact, I'm not saying I haven't. You will find it interesting, perhaps, to learn that my husband and I happen to be married to each other. And yet I will tell you that he, like the other men I know, is an overgrown boy. Well, then, in that sense, I suppose there's no harm in allowing Nathan to accompany you on your journey."

Dragnie nodded her head slightly, in acknowledgment of the woman's consent and in full awareness that such a gesture meant "yes" to men. "I would like him to move in with me and Mr. Glatt in preparation for our trip, if you don't mind," she said.

Mrs. Banden laughed gaily with a sort of carefree cynicism, as though implicitly confessing the depravity of her values.

"Oh, you'll have to ask Nathan if he is willing. As for me, Miss Tagbord, it can hardly come as a shock to you to hear that I don't mind a whit. Nathan's absence will afford me increased opportunities to pursue my customary activities, such as shopping, attending luncheons and cocktail parties, participating in high-stakes auctions for cultural artifacts deemed important and valuable by noted experts, and arranging charity events featuring famous entertainers and attended by individuals whose great wealth has been obtained, not via the messy and arduous invention of a new process, material, or device, or, as indeed you yourself do, by attending to the affairs of an industry, but by intelligently manipulating the financial instruments that all corporations and individuals require to pursue their business in our modern economic system. I speak, of course, of investment bankers, currency speculators, financial planners and advisers, and the other experts in the vital field of finance. That is my social set, Miss Tagbord, and although it may seem somewhat pallid and bloodless to a woman whose daily labor concerns the movement of massive and filthy railroad cars and their cargo, I assure you it is as essential a service to society as that pro-

"Is the baby sideways?"

vided by you or, indeed, your renowned boyfriend. In that sense, I suppose it would be interesting to Nathan to spend some time with you, to observe how other people live—people who care about such things as railroad ties, and lengths of track, and roundhouses and switches and the sundry other equipment that plays so important a role in your life as a childless executive."

"Thank you."

"You will find Nathan in his room."

Following his mother's instructions, Dragnie discovered Nathan upstairs, reclining on his bed, reading. His room was the embodiment of order and precision, and Dragnie was unable to resist the thought that this clean tidiness, this exact and meticulous arrangement of his personal effects, was merely the outward manifestation of the clarity of his mind.

He did not look up from his book. "Hello, Miss Tagbord. Did you enjoy meeting Mother?"

Dragnie felt provoked by his rude insolence. A grown man would have had no business lounging in bed when an adult woman entered the room; far less did an eighteen-year-old teen.

She felt compelled to correct him, yet she found herself speaking in defense of a person whom she found detestable, and a part of her consciousness wondered how this callow youth had the power to un-

settle her. "Your mother is a remarkable woman," she said.

"She? Remarkable?" he laughed bitterly. "Has she fooled you, too, then?"

She was suddenly aware of not knowing what he meant, and succumbed to an inner urge to question him accordingly. "What do you mean?" she asked.

He turned a page with casual ruthlessness. "Nothing. Only that she is a self-centered, hypocritical, loathsome harpy and I detest her with every fiber of my being."

She found herself surprised at his precocious eloquence—surprised and, in some distant point of her awareness at the center of her being, strangely aroused. He spoke urgently, as though words mattered. He spoke concisely, as though opinions mattered. He spoke offhandedly, as though nothing mattered.

"Then you may be interested in why I've come here," Dragnie said. She explained her purpose: the proposed inspection tour of the country to determine the effects of the Strike against the People's States of the People, her need of an assistant, and her suggestion that he might find the position interesting. Banden listened impassively, his expression unreadable save for the mockery visible in his blue eyes and the contempt implicit in his hair.

Finally he smiled coolly. "It sounds rather tedious. When would we start?"

To her astonishment she reacted to his

skepticism with something verging on panic. It suddenly seemed very important that he be persuaded to agree to her proposition. "In a month. But I would like you to move in with me and Mr. Glatt as soon as possible, to prepare for it."

All trace of amusement vanished from his face. "I accept, Miss Tagbord."

She smiled lightly and hoped her reaction did not make visible the flood of relief she felt within her emotions. "Please. Call me Dragnie."

•   •   •

They began that afternoon. Nathan quickly packed several bags, bade his mother good bye, and told her to explain everything to his father, who was out of town attending an important meeting with some of the nation's top meeting-attenders. A moment later they were in Dragnie's limousine, cruising toward the city. They did not speak. Nathan gazed out the window and affected an attitude of nonchalance, as though the entire event were of no consequence. Dragnie busied herself with documents pertaining to Tagbord Rail but, from time to time, cast glances his way, partly in casual curiosity about her young charge and his comfort during the trip, but partly for some more obscure reason. It was as though in order to see him she was compelled to look at him. She wondered what that meant and, whenever she did so, she quickly dismissed the matter from her mind after first asking herself, with ruthless introspection, what she was doing and why she was asking, and why.

By the time they reached the city, and the Johnsonwood Building, and Nathan had unpacked and settled in, it was early evening. New York stretched out across the vista visible from the dining room's great windows like a model train diorama of a city, with distant lights twinkling in remote windows and cars creeping along serpentine expressways with astonishing realism. Glatt was late; Dragnie and Nathan were chatting over dinner when he arrived. Dragnie introduced him to the young man.

"It's an honor, sir," Nathan said.

"Hello," Glatt said. He ate quickly, with the quiet ferocity and intense focus of a jungle animal, as if still responsive to instincts born ten million years earlier, when competition for food was fierce, and an individual's chances of survival depended on making the most of an ability to take advantage of eating as many orders of eggplant rollstini as possible.

"I'm very excited about what Dragnie's told me about our project."

"Good."

"Making the American way of life seem undesirable is the only way to show the world how desirable it is and how much it would miss us if we weren't here."

"Exactly." Glatt, finished, placed his utensils on his plate with a deliberate gesture, as if obedient to an impulse requiring him to signal to the world: I have completed the eating of my meal. "Now, if you'll excuse me, I have work to do."

Glatt left the dining room. Dragnie felt Banden's eyes on her as she watched him leave. "It must be difficult for you," the young man said. "To have a husband to whom you are not married, and who is so busy."

Dragnie's head jerked back in surprise. The accuracy of his statement came as both a gift and an intrusion. She did not know whether to praise his powers of observation or slap him for his presumptuousness, or perhaps both, or perhaps half of one and half of the other, a response she considered weak and conciliatory and which she despised in herself even as she adored that part of her that found the other part so despicable. "Difficult? Why?"

The young man shrugged. "A wife likes to spend time with her husband." He laughed bitterly. "Or so I assume. It's not as though I've learned that from my parents' example. They seem to detest one another."

"I'm sorry."

"Why? It's not your fault. And I assume each of them finds…other people to take up the slack." Banden sat back and leveled his gaze at hers. "As, indeed, you might."

"Why, you—" she began. But then her words seem to catch in her throat, and she found it difficult to breathe, and her mouth hung half-open as she stood up and sent her chair falling to the floor behind her. Then Banden, too, stood up, assigning to his chair a similar fate, and a moment later he was there, beside her, looking down into her eyes from his masculinely superior height. She groped for something to say, some pretext to decline or forbid what she knew was about to happen, what she wanted to happen, what she knew he knew was about to happen, but none appeared in the consciousness of her mind's awareness. And then he had with violence and a proprietary sense of ownership pressed his mouth to hers, and she, raised to the exalted height of femi-

ninity both by her shortness and by virtue of having been transformed into an object for his casual use, could do nothing other than respond in like manner. They fell to the floor, tearing off their own and each other's clothes until, to her surprise, he, then and there, without further preamble, instituted the ultimate act of possession, destroying in a moment every category that had differentiated them, including age, personal interests, yearly income, gender, and medical history, until a moment later he succumbed to a soaring triumph that left her gasping with amazement. Then they rested, lying on the rug half-under the dining table and half-surrounded by chairs, trusting in the discretion of the footman who had served their dinner not to interrupt them. Suddenly, after what seemed at most ten minutes, she was shocked to witness him rousing himself and taking her again, as they re-enacted that earlier drama, and she noted with interest and a faint, dawning hope that, while his ardor was undiminished from its first expression, his endurance was improved, and Dragnie felt herself approaching that state of inexpressible pleasure which derived from the assuaging of the ultimate greed but which, as again he sought and obtained the supreme release, she was once more doomed to fail to attain.

She stood up, entirely naked, and took his hand and drew him to his feet. He, too, was entirely naked. "Come with me," she said.

He let her lead him down the hall to a lighted room where John Glatt sat a desk, poring over documents and jotting notes. Glatt looked up. His face, gaunt and sharp-planed in the light of the desk lamp, betrayed no emotion other than a contemptuously amused contempt.

"John," Dragnie said. "Nathan and I are going to have a sexual relationship. I know you will have no objection to such an arrangement. He can be no compe-

The Big Sombrero (1949) NR; Strong language. In 1962, a widowed mother of six (Kathy Bates) supplies the voice of a magic 500-lb. dolphin. Courtney Cox. (1:30 ★★)—Sat. 1 PM, Mon. 9 AM, 6:30 PM (HBO)

—STEVE YOUNG

tition, let alone a threat, to you as my lover, or as my friend, or as the husband to whom I am not married. You know my feelings for you are inviolate and cannot be usurped by a youth twenty-five years my junior. Indeed, it is this very disparity in our ages that makes such a liaison desirable for each of us and recommends its indulgence and consent on your part. Nathan shall benefit from the experience and wisdom I am able to impart to him as a (so-called) 'older woman,' and also conceivably enjoy a frisson of Oedipal conquest and satisfaction in engaging in the sexual act with a woman symbolically old enough to be his mother. (Although I mention this strictly for the sake of completeness and without any real endorsement of the concept, since neither you nor I, as fully rational beings, ascribe any reality to the notion of the unconscious, and reject out of hand its ability to affect conscious human cognition, perception, thought, action, volition, feeling, or belief.) I, for my part, will enjoy not only the vigor and

enthusiasm he brings to the physical act of love by virtue of his youth, but will greatly appreciate the access it will afford me to his viewpoints, opinions, and values, offering a first-hand encounter with what 'the kids' are 'into' these days. Moreover, let me point out that this is not betrayal but its opposite—the betrayal would consist in keeping our affair a secret, in treating you, not like the rational adult you are, but like an authority figure to be feared and, therefore, deceived. It goes without saying that this setup will have no effect on the sexual relations between you and me. Don't you agree, dearest?"

Glatt shifted his gaze over each of them. "All right," he said.

• Chapter Six •
The Strike

The train, dubbed by the press boys "The Tagbord Special," raced through the evening twilight past lonely farms and smug towns and stoic road crossings like

a living thing intent on attaining the destination that would fulfill its highest purpose. Its passenger manifest contained only two names: Miss Dragnie Tagbord, and Mr. Nathan A. Banden.

Its destination this night was Chicago, where Dragnie was scheduled the next day to attend a meeting of the openly racist National Association for the Abolition of Colored People in the morning and, that evening, a rally for the Student Violent Coordinating Committee. Each organization was barely two weeks old. Each was the consequence of a new ruling passed summarily into law by John Glatt's Strike Committee. "To deny the world the America of its dreams," he had proclaimed, "We will pull off a switchback and undo America." The first new law, known as the Pro-Be Nasty to People You Don't Like Act, made it a crime to prevent, inhibit, or protest expressions of disapproval or enmity about any racial or religious group or organization. "The very word 'tolerance' is patronizing and insulting,' an-

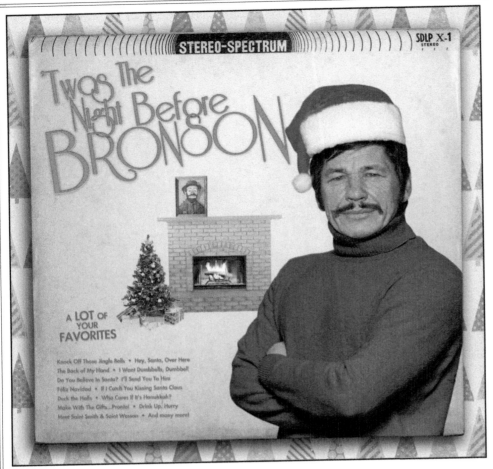

nounced Communique No. 2 as issued by the Strike Committee. "If Americans cannot be free to hate whomever they want, then they cannot be free in anything." The result was an immediate proliferation of openly racist and religiously bigoted op-ed columns, hate groups, publications, tracts, speeches, pageants, parades, Off-Broadway musicals, and halftime shows. This drew the predictable criticisms from individuals and groups for whom "brotherly love" was the highest form of man's achievement—the same groups, many noted, whose sympathies lay more with the empty abstraction of "humanity" than with the actual American people. "With this ruling encouraging bigotry and hate, America has betrayed her proud heritage and taken a large step back toward the Dark Ages," announced the Prime Minister of the People's State of the People of Great Britain, a short, sweaty man with perennially unkempt fingernails. It was noticed, however, that applications for immigration to the U.S. from Muslim, Latin American, African, and Asian countries dropped by 68%.

Dragnie was seated in the office car, putting the finishing touches on her speech, when Banden entered. "We're pulling into Centerville to take on water," he said. "Care to stretch your legs?"

She smiled with a hint of a smile. She did not mention the familiarity he had acquired with her legs. She did not feel it necessary to remind him that they would be sharing her executive car that night, as they had every night since the journey began. "Yes," she said.

They walked across the platform, her practiced eye noting with satisfaction its state of decay and disrepair. Her reaction was the same to the ill-lit, trash-strewn terminal. Outside its doors, the main street of Centerville gave similar evidence of neglect and lack of upkeep. Potholes in the street, vandalized signs, garbage festering in alleys and clogging sewer drains all offered proof that, in the ten years since the elimination of state and local taxes, what some intellectuals attempted to glorify as "the public sphere" had, in accordance with John Glatt's Fifteen Year Plan, been allowed to rot into a nutrient-rich mulch to be used to fertilize the private sector.

Private property, embodiments of the highest achievement of civilization, flourished: store fronts, office buildings, and private residences all looked new, and all displayed the logo of a corporation called Centervillecorp.

"You...you're Dragnie Tagbord, aren't you?"

The question, which carried with it an undertone of surprised pleasure, had come from a bum loitering nearby. His greasy coat was shabby and threadbare; he had not shaved in weeks.

The weathered, soiled state of his face made his age unreadable. He could have been twenty-five or three times that. Banden gently grasped Dragnie's arm as though to guide her away from what he perceived as possible danger, but she met the bum's gaze and said, "Yes."

"Well, ma'am, I just want to thank you."

Dragnie chuckled with a chuckle. "Thank me? For what?"

The bum gestured broadly, indicating the entire main street. "For this. I was against it, at first. You see, Miss Tagbord, I used to be a professor of political science. Oh, my name is of no importance. What matters is that I used to feel that society had an obligation to attend to the public, social aspect of man's nature. I used to think that that's what society was, a way to reconcile private desires and needs with public needs and amenities. And so when John Glatt and his colleagues took over the country ten years ago, I feared the worst. I thought their radical form of individualism would do nothing more than serve a narrow constituency of private interests at the expense of the vast majority of the American people, that a philosophy lionizing 'producers' was merely a self-serving bit of cant to advance the interests of the wealthy. But over ten years of such policies I've realized my error. As every public institution, from the federal government down to the local street-cleaning crew, was denied funding or eliminated altogether, I realized how fragile and weak a creature government is. Government can be hobbled or eviscerated by the actions of any ignorant mob. All that's required is for the stupid, the frightened, the resentful, the credulous, and the desperate to vote in candidates whose interest in working in government consists in wanting to cripple it. Government is therefore like a servant, who must do what his master tells him, and if his master is a fool, so much the worse for him. Whereas corporations are like heroes! Or, really, superheroes, such as those adolescents read about in lurid comic book periodicals. The powers and resources of superheroes dwarf those of mere men. Why, then, would a society wish to be ruled by individuals elected by idiots, when it could be guided by experts and demigods? Granted, we have filthy streets. The state university I worked for has gone out of business. Our local privatized fire department has just raised its rates again. A flu shot costs an average week's wages. Criminal gangs of disaffected youth, led by unscrupulous professional crime lords, rule the night. But in exchange for that, we have our individual freedoms guarded by a Superman, who grows more powerful and invincible each day. As you can see, Centervillecorp has taken over every business in town, including nail salons and the ice cream shop. Imagine its power, its scale, its scope! And now, with the new anti-anti-trust laws being promulgated by your husband, it will be capable of even more!

Business will at long last be free of the lingering restrictions and inhibitions still left over from the old we-know-best, eat-your-peas, play-fair-or-go-to-your-room nanny state. Successful companies will at last be free to acquire less successful companies, with the large subsuming the small until each industry will be free to be dominated by one or two hyper-efficient behemoths.

The resulting layoffs will not only tarnish the image of the U.S. in the eyes of the rest of the world, but will also free millions of American citizens, who were previously employed by pre-existing companies, to start their own corporations—to compete with the giants, to be swallowed up by them, and so make them even mightier and more magnificent. So thanks, Miss Tagbord, both to you and to your visionary, heroic husband."

"We're not married."

"Boyfriend, then."

"You're welcome," Dragnie said.

"One question, fellow," Banden said. "What do you live on?"

The bum shrugged. "Bottle deposits, petty crime, and restaurant refuse."

"That's terrible!" Banden cried.

"I get by," the bum said.

Later, lying together in Dragnie's executive car on a full-sized bed made expressly for rail travel by a top bedmaker, Banden grew reflective. "When I said, 'that's terrible' to that man, I was serious."

"I know it," Dragnie replied.

"How, in this day and age, can there still be such a thing as bottle deposits?"

Dragnie smiled in amused amusement. She turned toward him, the dim light playing fleetingly over his strong, youthful body and her admittedly twenty-five-years older but no less toned, attractive torso. "We're working on it," she murmured, and reached for him, and he reached for her, and after several forays into the realm of highest desire, in which her body was able to communicate to her her own deepest values even while his exertions vouchsafed promises of physical consciousness that were not kept, they voluntarily submitted themselves to a self-extinguishing of consciousness and the thorough obliteration of their awareness and love of existence, and slept.

The appearances in Chicago went well, as Dragnie gathered data on the public's widespread endorsement of the Strike. The next morning the Tagbord Special set off north, to Milwaukee, and from there northwest, toward Minneapolis. En route, gazing from the clear bubble dome of the observation car, Dragnie and Banden beheld a tableau of American freedom, as motorists stranded for lack of money for gas, and farmers on stubble-strewn fields following behind plows drawn by patient, aged horses, and shopkeepers undisturbed by deliveries of goods or by customers to demand them, all glanced up as the train hurtled by, and raised their hands in triumphant celebration of their shared national resolve. This, Dragnie thought, is proof of what men are capable of.

It took three days, traveling northwest, to reach Spokane, Washington. En route the Special made sporadic stops in small villages and hamlets, where occasionally a welcoming committee met it at the station, and men in their one decent suit offered handfuls of cash if only they could board the silver train and ride it to any destination that wasn't the present town, and shy little girls in party dresses were pushed forward by their noble, clear-eyed mothers to hand to Dragnie a plate of cookies or a jar of lemonade, along with a note asking for one thing or another—a job; money; or simply that Dragnie adopt the child and raise her as her own daughter. In each instance the gift was received gratefully and its receipt logged by Nathan A. Banden, except for the offered children, which were politely declined. When Banden asked the assembled wellwishers how they felt about the Strike, no one, other than rotters or bums, replied with anything but praise. "Well, sir, I don't rightly know much about inter-whatchamacallit politics," mused a former grain dealer, squinting into the distance and divulging meaning from his consciousness. "But the way I figure it, anything that gets the rest of the world to buy our yams, that's what I'm for."

On the third week of their tour, word came via telegraph that John Glatt and the Strike Committee had succeeded in establishing its most visionary law to date: the privatization of everything once

"Take his wallet."

managed by the Federal government. The armed forces had years before been replaced by private security contractors, but the new law, dubbed The Mind Your Own Business Act, continued in that rational, efficient tradition. Environmental protection, highway maintenance, air traffic control, the minting of currency: all sloughed off their old, diseased governmental skin and were born anew under private, for-profit exploitation. "Let the word go forth," John Glatt announced. "From this day forward, the United States is a gated community. Visitors must announce themselves at the guard station, and trespassers will be prosecuted."

The consequences of these new policies were quickly forthcoming. In a small town in Italy, a cobbler whose lifelong dream had been to emigrate to the U.S. decided to remain in his hometown and pursue his cobbling there. In a large city in Algeria, a family of four who had saved for years to emigrate to the U.S. concluded that, with no more public amenities, services, entitlement payouts, emergency room medical care, or food stamps available in America, they'd be better off moving to Spain. An Indonesian grocer, disheartened at the news that America was no longer a place where the weak, the mediocre, the lazy, or the incompetent might thrive on the wealth extracted from the industrious and the successful, killed himself.

But a young man in Senegal, either in ignorance of the new laws or in defiance of them, went forward with his plan to move to America. When word of his arrival at JFK reached the citizens of Queens, N.Y., they covertly formed a "Citizens' Strike Support Committee" and, by cover of night, burned down the airport. All that remained on the smoking site was a note reading, "We're taking back this land and returning it to its original state." Within a week of this event, ports, airports, and cross-border highway checkpoints all over the continental U.S. were ravaged by fire, explosives, or the concerted efforts of massed demonstrators. The instigators of these actions became folk heroes overnight. One broadcast on a shortwave radio frequency, "If they don't get the message when we deny them the America of their dreams, they'll get it when we deny them a way to enter our shores." When airport or maritime unions protested these acts, John Glatt and the Strike Committee issued Communique No. 12,

which outlawed collective bargaining in all corporations employing more than three persons. This, Dragnie thought, was the apotheosis of the highest American values: The rejection of collective action as being repugnant to the American ideal of self-sufficiency, and the defense of each corporation's right to deal honestly and straightforwardly with each employee on an individual basis. This, she concluded as the Tagbord Special pulled into Sacramento, was the very essence and enactment of moral significance.

• Chapter Seven •
The Scum of the Earth of the World

The meeting took place in a squalid, filthy room in the basement of the White Home in the nation's capital. Formerly used as an office for the social secretary of the Head Person of the Government of the U.S., it had fallen into neglect over the past ten years as that office, once highly admired by men, was seen to be an empty shell devoid of meaning and significance, and important people from industry, agriculture, the arts, and the sciences no longer wished to be seen associating with its occupant. The nauseatingly mint green institutional paint was peeling from its unhappy walls. Several bulbs were missing from its harsh overhead array of disingenuous fluorescent lights, presenting the appearance of a series of dark gray bruises amid the glare. There were no windows. A scent of mold, dead things, and moral exhaustion permeated the air.

Present at the meeting were Mr. Jenkins, the Head Person of the U.S., and his usual coterie of experts and advisers: Philip Sissyburger, the effeminate and complacent Minister of Equality; Dr. Francis Tinklepants, the Chief Diplomat to Foreign Places, who was incapable of offering a direct answer to any question put to him; Professor Davis, the Secretary of Wisdom, who insisted that his conception of reality was superior to all others; and T.T. Mucklicker, who was an authority on what was known as Public Relations. They had assumed their seats along one side of the conference table and now watched as, under conditions of the highest security, four other men arrived: M. Jacques Beaucoup, of The People's State Of The People Of France; Sir Lord Derek Blimey, of The People's State Of The People Of Great Britain; Dr. Ivan Lubyanka,

of The People's State Of The People Of Russia; and Signore Giuseppe Tortellini, of The People's State Of The People Of Italy.

The conference, which was to be held under conditions of absolute secrecy, began with an exchange of banalities, preliminary small-talk, and a shared sardonic admission that the clandestine nature of the event gave ample proof that its participants were moral weaklings and deserved the contempt of good, clean, rational men everywhere. Then the agenda was called.

Mr. Jenkins began. "Everyone has been briefed, so you know our major concern. It's this damn Strike. I don't like it, I tell you! I don't like it at all!"

"If I may, Monsieur Jenkins," said M. Beaucoup. "It is liked by none of us. Having deceptively and self-servingly foisted collectivization upon our people, we are now discovering that, without a fantasy of one day escaping to a free America full of tolerance and opportunity, they have begun to believe that they should overthrow the People's State and institute actual Capitalism! *Sacre bleu*, as we French say!"

"Quite so," said Sir Lord Blimey. "It's the same with us Brits in Britain. As career government workers, we found it in our narrow interest to expand the public sector as much as possible, resulting in a People's State of the People which, as some wags have commented in their witty and ironic British manner, should more properly be called the People's State of the Bureaucrats. We are happy to endure their sarcasm, and consider it a small price to pay for our large salaries, guaranteed job security, lavish expense accounts, and handsome pensions. In addition, we enjoy the kind of prestige among our fellow human beings that would be unknown to us were we to somehow find employment commensurate with our abilities in the private sector. But now that the U.S. has removed itself from the imagination of our people, there is widespread discontent and talk of re-instituting private enterprise! It is appalling, simply appalling."

"Is John Glatt," sneered Ivan Lubyanka. "He is crafty adversary. And wife. Also Mr. Hunk Rawbone and the Chilean talc merchant, De Soto. And Swedish pirate. Why you do not lock them up and throw away key?"

"Don't blame me!" Mr. Jenkins cried. "I'm just the Head Person! I can't help it! I have to do what I'm told. Moreover, I'm a weakling! I can't assert even my own modest powers! I lack the inner strength that comes from consciously having integrity!"

"Be peaceful, my friend," said Signor Tortellini. "We all want the same thing, in truth."

"And what is that, gentlemen?" All conversation ceased as Professor Davis slowly removed the pipe from his mouth, puffed on it, filled it, and surveyed the men at whom he was looking.

He was a repulsive fat slob with a shiny suit and a stain on his tie, the pattern of which was no longer in fashion. "Shall I tell you what it is that we all want? It is stability, security, and respect."

"In our societies, do you mean?" asked M. Bonjour. "But of course."

"Don't cause me to laugh. I mean in our jobs. We want to protect our careers. Mr. Jenkins here, and the rest of us, are mere figureheads. The actual decisions in the U.S. have, for the last ten years, been made by John Glatt and those around him. This is so, not only because the people demanded it, but because we ourselves demanded it. We had no choice but to beg Glatt to rescue us with his community of businessmen, and to accede to his demands. We eliminated taxes. We amended what was left of our Constitution to protect production and trade. We removed all restrictions on manufacturing and scuttled all product safety requirements and food and drug purity laws. We did it in the name of freedom."

"One is aware of this," Signore Tortellini said coolly. "What now?"

"What now? I will tell you, my friend. This Strike has shown the American people that they can feel proud and alive, that they can love existence, just as much when government provides no social services, as when it provides many. They are discovering that such things as poverty, anxiety, fear, starvation, misery, and despair, endured in the context of physical squalor and societal turmoil, are nothing compared to the exhilaration experienced in the presence of true freedom. It is only a matter of time, then, until they conclude—with, no doubt, Glatt's assistance—that they need no government at all."

The room was silent, as if the individuals in it did not permit themselves to speak or possessed no will to do so.

"But see here, Professor old chap," Sir Lord Blimey objected. "Surely one needs a government for national defense."

"Maybe it will help if you take the hat off.'

"One does not, sir," Professor Davis said, lighting his pipe and filling it and puffing on it wisely. "One needs only an army—or, as in our case, private security contractors." The professor rapped the ash from his pipe into an ashtray with a decisive series of taps. "No, gentlemen, the truth is this: all of us, if we are to retain our jobs, must stop John Glatt."

"Is question how," Ivan Lubyanka muttered.

"Just so," said Dr. Francis Tinklepants. "But we've come up with a plan. At least—" he added in his haste to avoid saying something definite, "I think it's a plan, and I think we've come up with it. As an articulate spokesman who is essentially a coward, I could be wrong."

"All right, Frank, all right," Mr. Jenkins said, clearly uncomfortable with this meeting, and with existence. "Here's the idea. You boys—" He gestured toward the heads of the People's States. "—declare war on us."

There was an explosion of befuddlement, outrage, and indignation. M. Bonjour called the idea "extreme." Sir Lord Blimey asked, "What will that accomplish, exactly?" Signore Tortellini dismissed the idea with "Bah. Ridiculo," and a rude, typically Italian gesture. Ivan Lubyanka looked cautiously intrigued.

"Okay, settle down," T.T. Mucklicker yelled. "Now just hold on to your horses. Think about it. You declare war on us. We announce a wartime footing and maybe introduce a bit of martial law. Then we proclaim Glatt and his pals as the cause of all this, and we take them into custody for questioning. We let them out in maybe a hundred years or maybe never. We bring back the laws that once made America

synonymous with edible broccoli, you end the embargo, and everybody goes back to work. Especially us."

There was a minute's silence as all in the room contemplated the idea. Finally Ivan Lubyanka said, "Could work."

"But on what basis will we declare war?" Sir Lord Blimey asked. "We're already applying an embargo. If anything, it's you who should declare war on us."

"We thought of that," Mr. Jenkins bleated. "But in order to rally the whole nation behind us, we need the country to feel like it's being unfairly victimized. It works better if you attack us than if we attack you."

"You realize, gentlemen," Sr. Tortellini said. "That when you are talking about the rest of us, you are referring to the entire world—every nation on earth except your own. If there really were a state of war between you and all of us, we probably could defeat you."

"Slim to none chance," T.T. Mucklicker said. "You forget, Giuseppe—your people love us. They're rising up against you because they miss us."

"Look, everyone," Mr. Jenkins yelled. "There isn't going to be any real war. Nobody is going to mobilize their army or kill anyone. It's all just to give us a pretext for seizing John Glatt and his friends. Agreed?"

Seven heads nodded silently as everyone said, "Agreed."

• Chapter Eight •
Anti-Maim

The Tagbord Special hurtled through the night, traversing farmland and undeveloped rural tracts, past cozy encampments of families clustered around blazing campfires, the men rising to their feet at the approach of the roaring train to lift an arm in hearty greeting, the women's faces illuminated by the ruddy orange light of the fire and smiling softly as their children gazed in wide-eyed wonder and sucked on fresh carrots pulled from the living earth not five minutes earlier.

Occasionally Dragnie would hear a muffled thud from the rear of the executive car, as an ambitious vagabond would attempt to clamber aboard the car's entry steps but, finding his way blocked by her security men, would leap or be helped off a moment later. Over the four weeks they had been conducting this tour, Dragnie and Banden had become used to the sight of three or four stowaways who, having clung to the rear of the last car for hundreds of miles, ducking low to avoid detection and enduring weather ranging from northwest downpour to southwest desert heat, leaped off at the next station when the train stopped to take on water. They would then scramble away over the weed-choked sidings or through the dilapidated terminal building and into the town, in their endless quest for economic opportunity and the realization of their deepest values.

She thought about what one such man had said to her in her own office car as the train barreled across the verdant, moist bottomland between Pensacola and Tallahassee on its gleaming rails of light, strong, vitamin-enriched Rawbonium. "You're Glatt's wife, aren't ya," he said, combining insolence and respect. He was young, in his twenties, with a week's worth of beard and wearing dungarees and a blousy shirt, and looked like a handsome movie star who, once seen, could never be forgotten. She could tell he found her physically attractive but was even more attracted to and intimidated by her mind. "You tell your husband something from me," he said with virile directness. "You tell him that we ain't got nothing. No job, no food, no home, nothing. When a man can't sell his crops, and he can't sell his manufactured goods, and he can't sell what the smart boys call durable goods, well then he ain't got no business. But we do got one thing, ma'am. We got our freedom. We're free to look for work until we find it. And then we're free to not find it. And then we're free to slap our wives around if they give us any sass, and we're free to say things about the black man and the Chinaman and the Jew and the faggot if we want to, because that's what freedom means. And that's what's important. God bless you and your husband, ma'am." Dragnie had just enough time to thank him before her security men escorted him off the train as it raced on into the night.

The Special pulled into Charleston, South Carolina, at ten o'clock that evening. Nathan A. Banden had announced his intention of strolling the city's streets in an effort to find sources of entertainment and amusement, but Dragnie had uncharacteristically declined his invitation. She did not feel well. Dinner that evening had left her nauseated, its aroma, normally enticing and pleasurable, a torment. She was also unusually fatigued and wished only to lie down and not smell anything. But she was unable to specify the source of her discomfort, as if a symptom of a disease were a saboteur of the factory of her body, and had infiltrated its defenses to inflict damage covertly, without possessing the honor and decency to do so to her face.

She remained in the office car as Banden left for his nighttime meandering. It was while coordinating a rolling order to purchase stock with a purchase order for rolling stock that a thought occurred to her awareness unbidden, as if a messenger had arrived unannounced from another country and forced entry into her home and shouted something at her in a language she realized that she understood. The idea roiled her consciousness. It was as monstrous in its implications as it was distressing in its meaning.

Then, suddenly, her concentration was interrupted by a knock on the executive car door.

"Miss Tagbord?" a youthful voice queried.

Dragnie looked up. Young Billy Stevens, the coach boy, stood there holding a sheet of paper. "Yes, Billy?" she said.

He approached nervously. He looked distraught, as if something bad had happened and it was his task to bring it to the attention of Dragnie's awareness. "This, uh, came in on the wire just now. Gosh, Miss Tagbord. What does it mean?" He handed her the teletyped message.

As Dragnie read, something within her seemed to collapse. They've gone and done it, the fools, some inner voice within her screamed. "It's bad news, Billy," she murmured. She read it again to make sure she understood its content and its meaning. It said:

"A Public Communication From the People's States of the People of the World: We, who don't care about the individual; we, who believe that the group is superior to the one; we, who believe that all men should live for society rather than vice-versa; we, who despise existence whether or not it actually exists; we, who feel bad when many men are embarrassed or made envious by the success of one man; we, who resent excellence; we, who insist

"They say that in America the streets are paved with blood."

that man has no mind because he has no brain, and cannot think because he cannot know anything; we, who find inherent value in mediocrity precisely because we are ourselves men of mediocrity; we, who proudly equate desire with greed, ability with pull, talent with luck, and genius with being a big show-off, do hereby ordain and establish this Declaration of War against the United States of America. We do this because we hate you, so help us God."

There was a noise outside. Nathan A. Banden burst in. "Dragnie!" he cried. "Darling! Have you heard?" Dragnie held up the teletype and wordlessly nodded her head to signify "yes" to his intellect.

"This just arrived. It was sent by John." She handed him the sheet and he forced himself to read it without once removing his gaze from the paper. Finally he lowered it and stared at her. "What do we do now?"

"Billy," she said to the wide-eyed boy. "Tell Conductor Mills that we're leaving for New York. Tonight. Now."

"You bet, Miss Tagbord!" the boy cried, and dashed out.

Banden rushed up to her and took her in his arms. "This has been wonderful," he breathed.

"Hasn't it?"

She smiled. It was the smile of a woman in complete awareness of her capacity to communicate ideas to another human being, of a woman for whom agreement with her lover was neither an obligation nor a gift, but a mutuality of perception, of assessment, of values, freely dispensed and presented without expectation of reward, of a woman for whom being a woman was a condition of her gender and for whom smiling was an expression of her emotions. "Yes," she said, and in the flurry of packing and preparation for return that followed, she made a mental note to conduct a vital telephone call the moment they arrived.

• • •

"Dragnie? Are you listening?"

The question was asked by Sanfrancisco De Soto, but upon its asking Hunk Rawbone chuckled as Regnad Daghammarskjold shook his handsome blonde head and chuckled. John Glatt, sitting near a blackboard at the head of the table around which this meeting was being held, glanced quickly at his girlfriend and invisibly, inaudibly chuckled.

Dragnie smiled and said, "I'm listening, San."

"Because you have this faraway look in

your eye," De Soto explained. "Ever since you got back two days ago from that national tour with our friend Nathan here, you haven't been yourself."

Dragnie traded a wry look with Banden, who hovered off to the side, taking notes. He did not permit himself to blush in unspoken acknowledgment of their passionate weeks together.

"I'm just tired, I guess," she said. "I haven't been sleeping well lately."

"Can we resume?" Rawbone said, and, as all faces again turned toward him, he continued.

"So far the declaration of war seems more rhetorical than actual. Our private military and security contractors report no mobilization in any of the People's States of the People anywhere in the world."

"They could be doing it clandestinely," the pirate said.

The steel magnate frowned, an expression of skepticism rather than of sadness, in this case.

"Marshalling troops? Moving men and materiel? Mobilizing navies and air forces? Those are things you can't do in secret, Regnad."

"Maybe it's all a feint," Sanfrancisco De Soto said. "Maybe they have a super weapon we don't know about, and they're just waiting to unleash it on us."

A rap was heard on the door, and an aide from an outer office leaned into the conference room. "Miss Tagbord? You have a call on line two. They say it's somewhat urgent."

Dragnie excused herself and left the conference room as five sets of male eyes

followed her exit. Finding an empty office, she entered and shut the door. Then she sat, pressed the blinking button on the telephone, picked up the receiver, and said, "This is Dragnie Tagbord" because it was, as she knew, her name. She listened carefully to the voice that spoke to her. It was a male voice, calm and confident, secure in its owner's awareness of his ability to perform his job with competence and skill. Finally, after asking a question and receiving an answer, she said, "Thank you, Doctor," hung up, and returned to the conference room.

The conversation ebbed as she entered. "Who was that?" Sanfrancisco asked. "One of the military-industrial complex boys?"

She smiled. "My office. A question about tunnel maintenance." Dragnie resumed her seat, then turned to look over her shoulder a Nathan A. Banden, who returned her glance with one of his own. She tore a piece of scrap paper off a steno pad and scribbled a brief note on it, then folded it in half and handed it to the young man. He glanced at it, and it was only through the exertion of an iron discipline and self-control unknown to his less impressive peers that he was able to resist leaping up and shouting, although whether for joy or in dismay even he did not know.

"I'm pregnant," it said.

PART II

I am he as you are me

• Chapter One •
A Horse is a Horse, Of Course, Of Course

Is it…is it true?"

They were in Dragnie's office in the apartment. Rawbone, De Soto, and Daghammarskjold had left. John Glatt was in his own office, drafting a response to the declaration of war. Nathan A. Banden stood before her desk as Dragnie sat back limply in her chair, physically but not morally or philosophically exhausted. "Yes," she said.

Banden's eyes grew wide, his manner animated. "Really?" He kept his voice pitched at an urgent whisper, somehow sensing that Dragnie had not yet informed Glatt and that, for the moment, she preferred he not know. "Does John know?"

"No."

"Wow." He nodded, not looking at her. It gave the appearance of a young man nodding to himself, as if he were two persons at once, both the nodder and the noddee, a paradox for which, had he been asked, he would have been unable to offer an explanation. "I'm going to be a father! The father of your child!"

"No."

He laughed as he chuckled. "I know. It's sheer madness. I can't believe it either. But this is perfect! Look, I didn't want to go to college anyway. The idea of spending four years at some ideologically-corrupt institution, where the pampered children of the middle class are lectured to by cosseted intellectuals one moment—so-called scholars, who spend half their time mocking and disdaining the elements of society who actually create the wealth that goes into their tenured paychecks, and the other half soliciting alumni donations from those selfsame industrialists and entrepreneurs in order to keep the university solvent so that they may continue to deride men of business—and then massing in the quads to protest the policies of the very institution that affords them the luxury of living the so-called life of the mind, while abler and stronger men are actually out in the real world, creating and producing things from which all men benefit, is disgusting! This way, I'll stay at home with the baby, you'll go to work, John'll go to work, and we'll be one big happy family!"

"Will we?"

"Why…why sure we will. Oh, I know—

you don't look forward to nine months of incapacitation and then being laid up a couple weeks after delivering. You'll have to curtail your work schedule and possibly delegate some responsibility to your underlings. But you have good people working for you. They can pick up the slack."

"Really?"

"Sure! And the first eight months or so you'll be able to work anyway. I mean, I think.

What do women do, who get pregnant when they have jobs?"

"They quit their jobs."

"But you don't have to do that. Oh, to be sure, that's what ordinary women do. But you're no ordinary woman, Dragnie."

"Thank you."

"You're extraordinary! That's why I'm so excited. Just think of it: Dragnie Tagbord is going to be the mother of my child!"

"No. I'm not."

The youth looked baffled, as though he had been slapped during a moment when he had not been expecting such a thing. "What do you mean? I thought you were pregnant."

"I am pregnant."

"Then what do you mean, you're not going be the mother of my child?" He pondered this matter in confusion and puzzlement for a moment. Then, suddenly, it was as though a light went on in the room that was his mind. His eyes went wide. "You mean… I'm not the father?" He forced a bitter laugh. "Of course. I've been such a fool. I just naturally assumed…But then, you do have a live-in boyfriend, as I of all people should be eminently aware."

"No, the baby is yours."

His face once again lit up with dawning joy. "But, then, what's the problem? I want you to have my baby! And by the way, I'm not just any common Joe who's fantasizing about the great Dragnie Tagbord giving birth to his spawn. I've had plenty of women after me to sire their offspring. Women my own age and, if you must know, older, including some of my mother's friends. Are you shocked? I didn't think so. To be an adult in the world of men is to become familiar with such matters. In any case, it is of no consequence. The important thing is, you are pregnant, and we're going to be parents. Now: do you want a girl or a boy? I have my own reasons for either, but I think— and this may surprise you—I think I

want…a girl!"

He fell silent and stood there beaming, as though having just presented Dragnie with a precious gift the value of which he knew she appreciated and for which he assumed she would be grateful. Several seconds passed in which both of them, wordlessly, said nothing, as if his extended monologue and its excited tone had burned up the air in the room and they must wait until it was replenished. Dragnie looked away and fretted. She did not permit herself to cry although she felt the urge to do so. She did not permit herself to shake her head and say, "Oh, Nathan, you fool," although somewhere, at the far edge of her mind, she knew that his name was Nathan, and that he was a fool. Finally she drew herself up in her chair and permitted herself to address him directly.

"I do not wish to give birth--to your child or to any child. I do not wish to be a mother," she said.

He looked stunned and perplexed. "But…darling! You don't know what you're saying! Every woman does. Motherhood represents the apotheosis of womanhood."

"According to whom?"

"Why, according to a wide range of authorities. Not just the spiritual experts who promote the ideas and values of what middle-brow organs of news and opinion call 'the world's great religions' (ideas and values of which I suspect you are as skeptical and dismissive as I), but according to eminent female writers of both fiction and non-fiction and to the received wisdom of society at large!"

"That is their opinion. It is not mine."

He spread his hands, at a loss. "But… then…what do you intend to do?"

"I intend to terminate the pregnancy."

His mouth fell open in shock. "But… you can't."

"I can."

"But I don't want you to."

"It is not your decision to make."

"But I'm the father."

"That is less significant than the fact that I am the mother."

"But…what if I forbid it?"

"You have no authority to forbid it."

"But by what right can you do such a thing?"

"By what right can you prevent it?"

"But that's our little son or daughter in there! It's a person, damn it!"

"No. It is not. It is not a person. It is less than a lizard. It has no volitional consciousness. It has no awareness. It lacks the one thing that elevates man above the rest of the living world, the one sacred characteristic that differentiates man from every other entity in existence: a mind. Without a mind, it cannot possess a code to guide its actions, and without such a code, it is not human. Ask a fetus what is its code of existence and you will get a nullity for an answer. Question it as regards to it values, and you will obtain an evasive silence. Inquire of it how it is able to survive in the absence of these things, and you will hear nothing—but you will discern that it manages to remain alive, not by the conscious pursuit of its values, but by the passive, unthinking, and unreflective absorption of nutrients from another human being.

"You have heard men condemn slavery. Yet even the slave produces something of value, and is given something of value in return—food, clothing, shelter, and the harmonicas with which he creates his distinctive music. What is objectionable about slavery is not the fact that the slave must work—for all men must work—but, rather, that his freedom is curtailed by means of force. What is shameful about slavery is not that the slave is prevented from receiving or sharing in the profits derived from his labor—for no man may receive or share in the profits of any man's labor unless he owns the company for whom others labor—but, rather, that he is unable to quit his job if he so chooses. End slavery, forbid that application of force, and the slave is able to exercise his freedom, pursue his values, and live a human life by laboring for the owners of companies under conditions he is free to quit whenever he so chooses.

"How much worse is the enslavement of the mother by the fetus! For what force is applied by the fetus to the mother, to ensure and coerce her support of the parasite that literally feeds off her? The worst kind of force there is: the force of public opinion. Women who become pregnant must carry the baby to term and give birth to it, or they are condemned and shunned by so-called polite society. Worse, the fetus does no meaningful work. It creates nothing. It transforms nothing. It grows, manufactures, refines, harvests, or assists in, nothing. It creates no immortal works of art that inspire countless thousands over the centuries. And then, not content merely to enslave the adult female woman human individual-type person whom it holds in this unspeakable bondage, it

provides its slave with neither food, nor clothing, nor shelter, nor harmonicas. Indeed, it insists the mother provide it with food, create its 'clothing,' and provide her body as its actual shelter. In so doing it robs the mother of nutrients, deforms her body, stimulates in her all manner of distasteful reactions and excretions, distorts her appetite, subjects her to exhaustion, transforms her into a quasi-public plaything whose belly may be groped and caressed by strangers on demand, and in the end dooms her to a prolonged exposure to excruciating pain and possibly mortal danger, prior to its termination of her enslavement—after which commences a new kind of enslavement, as the infant uses its absolute helplessness to control her every action, emotion, and thought, and to require increasing amounts of the mother's income in order to survive.

"Acceding to this kind of physical, emotional, and moral subjugation may be appealing to men for whom society's approval and the sentimental contemplation of cultural stereotypes is appealing. But I am not one of those. And so I will terminate this pregnancy and retain my human freedom."

Nathan A. Banden took this all in with an outwardly stoic calm. Finally he said, "Then where will you have this procedure done? May I accompany you to it, at least?"

"No," she said. "You may not."

"Oh, Dragnie, Dragnie, Dr—"

"You may not because there is only one physician I trust with this kind of procedure, and he practices in a place where you may not go."

Banden did not chuckle. He did not chuckle because he laughed. It was the laugh of an anxious man uncertain of what another human being had said to him but fearing its content would reveal itself to be objectionable. "Where does he work? In a prison?"

"In Glatt's Gorge."

The young man, unafraid to reveal the limitations of his education and disclose his inability to understand what had just been said to him, replied, "Huh?"

"You've never heard of Glatt's Gorge?"

"Of course I've heard of it. But I thought it was a…you know, a mythical place. Like the Garden of Eden or Shangri-La."

Dragnie permitted herself a slight smile. Then she withdrew the permission and

the smile vanished. "It is quite real. I have been there. And that is where Doc Hastings still resides. I would not trust anyone else with this matter."

"But why can't I go with you?"

"Because," Dragnie said in a tone of wistful nostalgia. "No one except a very privileged few is allowed there. It was the perfect society. There you would find wealthy people, and the people who love them or work for them, creating a self-sufficient community of gentlemen farmers, hobbyist craftsmen, amateur civil engineers, and artists-in-residence. There you would find a world-renowned philosopher running a chicken-and-waffle diner while expatiating on 'truth,' or a brilliant composer writing an opera about Marcus Aurelius for a full orchestra and a cast of thirty, to be performed by three people playing ukeleles. There you would discover a society in which everything, from obtaining electrical power to asking someone what time it is, was mediated by money, which was minted right there in the Gorge by an internationally acknowledged metaphysician whose hobby was the minting of money. It was a place where a lecture on the irreducible value of currency and of its unregulated use in the valuation and conduct of all human affairs could be attended for a token fee of twenty-five cents. It was an entirely self-sufficient place because it was a place entirely underwritten by private wealth. In short, it was Paradise."

"You keep saying 'was.' What is it now?"

"Exactly the way it was ten years ago."

"It sounds wonderful, darling," Banden sighed. "But can't you vouch for me and get me in?"

She shook her head regretfully, because it was her head, and it was full of regret. "It's just not possible."

The change in Banden was sudden and volcanic. Whatever effort he had made at a sympathetic hearing of Dragnie's explanations and a courteous response to them were now invalid. Anger rose within him like a fever; his normally pale white skin grew pink with agitation and ire. "Oh really?" he cried. "Then what you're telling me is, you refuse to have my baby, and you refuse to even allow me to be present at its termination. And why? Because I'm not a millionaire?"

"No," Dragnie said rationally. "It's because—"

"Never mind," he cried. "I can see now what I've meant to you this past month— not a boyfriend, not even a lover, but a plaything, to amuse you for the few weeks you'd be away from home and your world-famous, other, long-term, 'steady,' boyfriend."

"Nathan, don't be silly—"

"And now I'm 'silly.' Very well." He made a visible effort to regain his composure, drawing himself up to his full height and extending himself out to his complete width. "I thought we had something special, Dragnie. I see now I was wrong. I won't trouble you with my presence any further. If you change your mind, and wish me to accompany you to your tycoon's paradise, I shall be at home, living with my parents."

He turned and strode from the room.

• Chapter Two •
A Chair is Not a House

Dragnie checked her coordinates and glanced out the window of the small plane that responded to her will as with unerring precision she flew it through the air of the atmosphere. A faint smile played about her lips. Visible below her was precisely the forbidding series of mountain crags she expected to see, identical to those she had seen ten years previous when, in pursuit of another plane, she had unknowingly penetrated the optical illusion shielding this valley from the eyes of the world and had crash-landed in Glatt's Gorge. With a clean turn of the rudder and a firm, clean adjustment of the flaps, she began her descent toward the small airstrip that she knew, in her mind, would reveal itself as she began her skillful, controlled, clean descent.

A car was waiting for her when she got out of the plane. It was an old Humpmaster, one of the costliest models of its year, now scrupulously maintained in accordance with the modern-day object and purpose of Glatt's Gorge. Standing beside it, grinning happily, was a young man.

"Miss Tagbord? It's a pleasure to meet you. I'm 'Dirk Biceps.'" He smiled. "Not really, of course. My real name is Claude Bawlz. But as far as you're concerned I'm Dirk Biceps. The pet food magnate."

Dragnie extended her hand and grasped his in a firm, clean handshake of hands.

"The pleasure is mine, 'Dirk.'"

"They're waiting for you in town. Shall we go?"

He put Dragnie's suitcase in the car's trunk and they set off down the unpaved mountain road. Dragnie gazed at the foothills to either side, and at the undisturbed meadow over which the road ran, and decided that none of this had changed in ten years, exactly as she knew it would and, more importantly, wouldn't.

"How long have you been here, 'Dirk'?" she asked the driver in order to obtain information.

"About six months," he said with casual accuracy. "Mr. Glatt came and visited me in my office in February, and by mid-April I had shut down the factory, dissolved the corporation, dynamited the warehouse, murdered my wife and children, cancelled my subscriptions to *Dog Food Age* and *Modern Gerbil*, and ended up here."

She knew he was talking about the actual history of the real Dirk Biceps, and responded in kind. "Was it a good decision?"

He took his eyes off the road for one moment and directed them to look at Dragnie's, which they did with the certitude of human visual organs obeying their owner. "The best you'll ever make," he said.

It was exactly what she expected him to say and hearing it filled her with triumph. This was a place founded on an idea; and, as ideas never change provided they are shielded from the world, Glatt's Gorge had not changed, and never would.

She saw familiar landmarks that she remembered from her week's stay a decade earlier, when the real Dirk Biceps, the real John Glatt, and all the other tycoons, entrepreneurs, and industrialists, plus a philosopher and a composer and a beautiful movie star, had removed themselves from the outside world and repaired here, to mount their strike against society.

Nestled in a knoll against the hillside was Douglas Sinew's Fabric, Trim, and Notions-o-Rama, its sign, with Sinew's trademark emblem of a smiling abacus, testimony to Sinew's previous profession as an actuary. He had, during his time at Glatt's Gorge, discovered an entirely new method of being an actuary, one that sped up actuarial calculations tenfold, provided three times the predictive accuracy, and at a cost of mere pennies a day. Like everyone else at the Gorge, however, he refused to take it into the outside world, either to exploit it commercially or to present it to his fellow professionals.

Across the field stood Kent Wallbricker's distillery, the source of what was considered by experts to be the best pine cone liqueur in five counties, an achievement made all the more impressive considering Wallbricker's job back in the corrupt world, where he had been a professional

tap dancer and performed on television network variety shows for the entertainment of cowards, weaklings, and other members of the cannibal class. During his time at the Gorge he had invented a revolutionary new method of tap dancing, one that enabled him to tap five times as fast, with double the time accuracy and one-tenth the fatigue. He, too, refused to share it with the world. Kent Wallbricker's "dynamic tap technique" died with him two years earlier.

"'Mr. Fasnacht' is waiting for you at the hotel," Dragnie's driver said.

She nodded, her attention fixed on the town as they pulled in, past the civic sculpture of a solid gold dollar sign and exclamation point that greeted visitors. The road here was unpaved, too, but nonetheless lined with shops and services: a bakery, a hardware store ("We Hand-Forge Our Own Nails" read the sign in the window), a post office, an ice cream parlor, a bowling alley, a slaughterhouse, an automobile dealership, a grocery store, a fire station, a bridal shop, a Major League baseball stadium, a museum of contemporary art, a maximum-security prison, a hospital for the criminally insane, and a dinner theater. Everywhere she looked, Dragnie saw men and women walking with unyielding purpose, confident in the use of their own legs and feet. Their feet

seemed not to touch the ground as they moved busily about on the errands of the lives they lived during their existence.

Then Dragnie noticed that, in fact, their feet didn't touch the ground. These, she thought, must be the anti-gravity shoes John told her he had devised for residents of the Gorge, one of the inventions, along with the refracting lens that concealed the valley, the motor that converted atmospheric static electricity into kinetic energy, the reverse-osmotic pump that transformed ordinary poison ivy into 60/40 cotton-poly sport shirts, the amplification mirror that harnessed starlight to boil water, and the other brilliant achievements that made living in Glatt's Gorge different from living in a poorly-equipped summer camp.

Her eye was arrested by a small cluster of men and women following a single individual, who commanded their attention by holding up a furled umbrella. The group had just emerged from Hercules Fleet's Pizza 'n' Calzone. The sign in the window depicted a stylized view of Moses descending Mt. Sinai, holding the twin tablets traditionally inscribed with the Ten Commandments but here displaying, on the one, an image of a pizza, and on the other, a calzone—graphic acknowledgment and commemoration of Fleet's achievements in the outer world, where

"Is this your final gender?"

"But 'Tibetan Sky Burial' sounded so cool."

he had been a top Conservative rabbi. While at Glatt's Gorge he had invented a revolutionary new way to be a Conservative rabbi, a way that resulted in his being twice as conservative and three times as rabbinical at half the cost. But he had refused share the secret with the rest of the world, and declined even to discuss it while turning out the best pizza in the valley.

"If you don't mind, 'Dirk,' I'd like to tag along with that tour for a bit and see what things are like here now," Dragnie said.

Her driver nodded. "Just check in at the Inn when you're ready," he said, and drove off.

Dragnie hurried along and fell in step with the tour group. Over the next hour they visited a number of exhibits, at each of which, she noticed, every care had been taken to maintain the original appearance and function of the facility, while the actors portraying the various figures who had, ten years earlier, "gone Glatt," were scrupulous in their costumes, accents, and values.

They stopped by the Post Office, where the young actor portraying Flint Bigbone, the former natural gas magnate, demonstrated stamp-cancellation techniques on fragile parcels while lecturing them on the evils of subsidized medical care. Next came the Bakery, run by a talented blonde playing former Globe-Tech C.E.O. Donna-May Uppercut, who showed everyone how to hand-twist their own pret-

zels. And they visited the hardware store, where a vaguely familiar character actor embodying Gil "Dad" Popp handed out period paint chips while regaling them with the story of how, the day before his arrival at Glatt's Gorge, he had personally detonated 1,225 pounds of high explosives to demolish his entire magnesium processing plant.

By then it was snack time. Dragnie took her leave of the group, consulted the site map with its dollar-sign compass rose, and found her way to the Glatt's Gorge Inn and Conference Center.

Inside, the lobby was bustling, as corporate parties or select private individuals checked in, checked out, or met for the evening's activities. Dragnie's driver said, "I'll get your key. Don't bother looking for an elevator. There isn't one." He pointed to a row of three arches standing off to the side of the main desk. "Just walk through one of those. It will read the key and instantly teleport you to your door. It's something Mr. Glatt invented while ironing a shirt one day. We're hoping to develop its use to transport the barrels of oil Flint Buttslammer figured out how to refine from spider webs. The idea...but look at me, telling you all this, when you probably know more than I do..."

"No. Go on."

"Well, the idea is to transport the oil right from the webs in the caves to the refinery started by Clunk Fistpuncher,

when he came here after abandoning his career as the foremost legal ethicist in the world. Oh, good, here's 'Mr. Fasnacht.'" He indicated a man in work pants and a rough-weaved shirt who, smiling with purest politeness, approached.

"Miss Tagbord. A pleasure. We've been looking forward to your arrival."

She shook the proffered hand. "Thank you, Mister--?"

"Make it 'Mister Fasnacht.'" He chuckled. "It will hardly surprise you learn that I'm not actually Faustus Fasnacht. My real name is Mike Hunt. But here at the Gorge we do our best to maintain the atmosphere and the values of what the original founders brought when they first created this retreat ten years ago. All the buildings, all the roads, all the shops and factories, even the landscaping, have been meticulously preserved from the original period. The Glatt's Gorge Foundation employs a number of us to staff the conference center, and we do our part to contribute to the illusion that each visitor, whether on officially-sponsored corporate retreat or on a personal sabbatical at our Committee's exclusive invitation, feel that he—or she!—is taking part in something very like the original strike that Mr. Glatt called before the Great Takeover, and that Mr. Fasnacht bankrolled with his property here in the mountains." He chuckled. "Why, if you're with us long enough, you'll likely run into the chap playing John Glatt himself. That should be an interesting experience for you."

"Yes," Dragnie said in a mocking tone of facetiousness. "And is the real Doc Hastings around? Or only his stand-in?"

"Oh, the actual McCoy, I assure you. He's expecting you tomorrow morning at ten a.m. And by the way—" He indicated Dragnie's wrist watch. "You'll have to adjust your watch and any travel clocks you may have brought. We have our own time zone here in the Gorge, which differs from the Standard Time of the outside world by forty-two minutes and twelve seconds. We prefer not to be chronologically co-ordinated with the moochers, the leeches, the looters, the koochie-koo-ers, the hoochy-kootchers, and the hot-cha-cha-ers, if you know what I mean."

"I do." Dragnie spoke with unflinching honesty. Because she did know what he meant.

• • •

"My, my. Dragnie Tagbord. It's been awhile."

"Yes. It has."

Dragnie was seated in Doc Hastings' office, a small, wood-paneled room beyond which was an examination room that fronted a larger surgical suite. Hastings reclined in his chair behind his desk. He wore a white lab coat because he was a doctor. He was tall, lean, and tanned. His white hair floated in wisps above his flaring white eyebrows and strong hooked nose. "You're sure you're with child?"

"I'm sure."

"But why come to me? Don't they have doctors in New York City?"

"You're the only one I trust."

"Can't say I'm surprised. You hear I cured cancer?"

"No."

"Well. Not all of it. Leukemia. Figured it out last year—" He pointed to the room beyond. "—right in there. Not gonna give it to them, though, I can tell you that. Damn thieving bastards."

"I know it."

"M.S., too. Multiple whatachamcallit. Sclerosis. Had an idea, followed it through, bingo. Think I'll let anyone in on it? Don't make me laugh. Mooching swine."

"Yes."

"Plus, get a load of this…" He yanked open the long horizontal drawer of the desk and rummaged around in it. He produced an object resembling a blood-pressure monitor, although attached to the flexible cuff was, not a squeezable rubber bulb, but a device resembling a transistor radio. "Know what this does?"

"No."

"Cures arthritis, gout, shingles, and acne with cosmic rays. Transforms stray gamma into what I call 'revivification energy.' Wrap it on your ankle or around your face, tune 'er in, set the timer, listen for the ding, and you're done. Guess where it's going. Right back in here, is where." He returned the device to the drawer and slammed it shut. "So. When do you want to do this?"

"How about right now?"

"Right now it is. Follow me."

They went into the surgical suite at the rear of the building, where Doc Hastings had Dragnie replace her clothes with a hospital gown and lie on a gynecological exam chair with stirrups. He had opened a cabinet containing chemicals and syringes, when he turned and asked, "You want to be out cold for this, or awake on a local?"

"Awake, if that's all right."

"Good. A woman should see what men do to her." He prepared an injection, then disappeared into an anteroom, from which Dragnie heard the sounds of water running and Hastings scrubbing up. He returned a moment later in a wrinkled, faded surgical gown and face mask. "Let's get this done. There've never been any children at Glatt's Gorge and we're not about to start having any now. Damn freeloaders."

He injected her with the anesthetic and, while waiting for it to take effect, shared his views on existence. Finally, a few minutes later, seated between her splayed legs and his hands obscured beneath the covering sheet, he asked, "Feel that?"

"No."

"Good."

She lay back, facing the ceiling. He made small sounds of concentration until a question occurred to her, and she said, "Doc Hastings, why did you stay here? When nearly everyone else went back into the world with John?"

He paused in his activities and emerged from under the sheet over her legs. He scratched his cheek thoughtfully. "I'll tell you, Dragnie." Returning back under the sheet, he continued answering in a firm, clear voice. "I stayed here because I could no longer live in a world in which practically no one believed that the mind existed. I stayed because I couldn't bear to return to a world in which rational people are penalized, brutalized, and tortured, while lunatics and crazy people thrived. Of course, as it is today, so it has ever been. Throughout history, wild-eyed madmen have succeeded in attaining positions of authority and power, while men dedicated to rationality and reason have been consigned to condemnation, ignominy and worse. The men of the mind—scientists, inventors, and industrialists—have always been condemned by society, while shrieking psychopaths who play with their own feces have been elevated to positions of authority and prestige. Everywhere, in every corporate board room, university, newspaper office, publishing house, scientific laboratory, industrial facility, television network, and government bureau, you hear men say that there is no such thing as thought, that reason is an illusion, and that only magic, mysticism, and madness are the appropriate tools for running the world. Is it any wonder, Dragnie, that every company in the Fortuitous 500 is headed by a certified schizophrenic? Is it any wonder that every university in the nation is ruled by a committee of

gibbering maniacs in strait jackets? Everywhere, the men who actually make the world function—entrepreneurs, tycoons, industrialists, businessmen—are victimized, subjected to an endless onslaught of torture and abuse. They are forced to live in segregated communities surrounded only by people of their own kind. They are forced to vacation in remote areas, on distant islands under the glare of a tropical sun, or sliding down snow-covered mountain tops, which are costly to reach. They are forced to eat in restaurants unfrequented by and unfamiliar to the common man. They are compelled to pay five, ten, a hundred, a thousand times what ordinary men pay for such basic necessities as wristwatches, automobiles, and three-piece suits. They are required to spend millions of dollars to influence a political system merely in order to manipulate it into giving them what they want. They must endure the hardship, not only of devising ways to make money, that their immediate needs may be met, but of devising ways that their money may make money, inflicting a double burden upon them, about which they scarcely utter a word of complaint. I stayed here because, once I had come to Glatt's Gorge, once I had gone on strike against that world, once I had withdrawn myself from the world in which the rational men are constantly victimized and the raving, delusional masses live lives of undeserved lei-

sure and luxury, I discovered I could not go back to it."

She nodded. "But there's still one thing I don't understand, Doc," she said. "Why has the rest of the world turned against us?"

"Why has every country on earth become a People's State of the People, you ask? Why has the entire world welcomed collectivization, with its centralized health care and its safety nets and its trade unions and its social protections, you inquire? Why has every human being on earth—including, now, apparently, the ones in Goa—given up on our dream, the American dream, the dream of one day having a job that will sustain us in our hope that we may, one other day, somehow, become rich, you query? But the answer is simple, Dragnie. They have turned on us because of who we are. The people of the world would rather live stable middle-class lives than dare to do what you did, and inherit a railroad empire from their father. They hate us for our success. They hate us for our excellence. They hate us for our freedom. We, the greatest country that ever existed—it was inevitable that one day the rest of humanity would, in contemplation of our superiority, deform, deprive, and destroy itself out of sheer resentment, jealousy, and spite. Nations have always obliterated themselves when confronted with another nation whom they wished to make feel bad. Let two men run a foot race. Let

one of them win, while the other loses. Now observe the behavior of that second man. What does he do? He drinks a fifth of bourbon and then leaps into the reservoir. You see, Dragnie, most men would rather stab themselves in the chest with a bread knife than admit, to another man, 'you run faster than I.' In this way the weak have always victimized the strong by harming themselves and then saying, 'you did this to me.' It is, quite simply, a fact of history, and has been ever since we overcame our second-rate, inferior status in the world and rose to the pre-eminence we enjoy today."

"But they're not destroying themselves. They've declared war on us."

"The suicidal act of a desperate social order. Oh, they'll have their little war with us. And we'll destroy them. And afterwards they'll cry, 'It's not fair,' and they'll kill themselves. No, Dragnie...I mean, yes, Dragnie, the world is now in the hands of those whose central idea is that the mind does not exist, and they will annihilate themselves in order to coerce us into pitying them."

"I understand," Dragnie was about to say, when a sudden noise, as of gunfire or an explosion, sounded sharply from outside. Doc Hastings jerked up from beneath the sheet over her legs, his arms and hands still under it. "What the hell was that?" he snarled.

The door flew open and Sanfrancisco De Soto burst in. "Dragnie! It's John!"

Unaware of what she was doing, not permitting herself to ask of herself permission to consider the medical consequences of her actions, Dragnie sat upright and tore the sheet away.

As she leaped off the chair Doc Hastings cried, "Whoa, don't—" but it was too late. Dragnie followed Sanfrancisco out through the office.

• Chapter Three •

The Person Who Did the Thing With the Thing

Once outside Dragnie saw the cause of the tumult. On the rough dirt road, Hunk Rawbone and Regnad Daghammarskjold stood crouching behind a parked car. Beyond them, in the middle of the road, was John Glatt. Another man stood behind Glatt and was holding him prisoner with a gun to his back and an arm rigidly locked around Glatt's neck.

Dragnie followed Sanfrancisco in join-

"Mr. Peabody, who what happened?"

ing the other two just as she felt a sudden flow of warmth down one of her legs. She did not permit herself to engage it with the attention of her concentration. She knelt beside Rawbone. "Is anyone hurt?" He shook his head. "Hunk, what are you doing here?"

"They tried to arrest John, but he got away," Rawbone answered with icy accuracy. "We came here to re-group and devise a strategy for dealing with it."

"Who?" she cried. "Who tried to arrest him? And by what right? By what right, Hunk?"

"Mr. Jenkins and his stooges. For violating the Don't Do Anything That Will Upset Other Countries So Much That They Declare War on Us Act—which they passed in secret last night."

Behind her she heard Doc Hastings shouting from his office doorway. "Dragnie! Get back here! Or my attorney will have my head on a plate!"

Ignoring it, she indicated the man holding Glatt and asked Rawbone, "How'd he get into the Gorge?"

"He followed us through the concealment in a small plane and parachuted in."

"Who's he?"

Rawbone sneered. "Some rotter."

"What's he want?"

Rawbone's eyes flared with unspoken intensity as he burned his gaze into Dragnie's with a look that said, silently, without words, You know what he wants. It was a look that said, You know what he wants because we have discussed this a thousand times. It was a look that, having said the previous things, went on to say, You know what he wants because we have discussed this a thousand times in words that have rung with the pitiless reverberation of truth as we have enunciated it in half-hour speeches to civic groups and Junior Achievement awards ceremonies, as we have declared in thunderous tones to waiters in elegant restaurants in response to their inquiry about whether we wanted to hear tonight's specials, as we have lectured at ribbon-cuttings, at baseball games, in elevators, on the beach, in museums, in theater lobbies, at chess tournaments and, that one time, to those three little girls dressed as a ballerina, a witch, and a princess who came to my home trick-or-treating. "What they all want. Something for nothing."

Dragnie stood up. Dimly, on the edge of her awareness, she was conscious of an increased flow of warmth and, now, some

"Well, Mama used to have a tinky, but now it's a tonky."

kind of sticky, thick liquid moving down her leg, and of an unnaturally robust ventilation afforded by her clothes. Rawbone reached out to stop her but she clawed his hands off and skirted the car. She took a step with halting difficulty toward Glatt and the man holding him.

"You," she called. "Rotter. What do you want?"

"Dragnie!" she heard Sanfrancisco shout. "Get back inside! You're bleeding!"

"Nobody move!" the rotter screamed. He nodded hysterically toward Dragnie. "I know who you are. You think you're so high and mighty, Miss Dragnie Tagbord! Well why not! You were born rich. It's easy for you to make these laws. It's easy for you to call this Strike. But what about the rest of us? I haven't worked in a year! My wife is sick, my kids need clothes… we don't have enough food, we're living in a refrigerator box under a bridge…I'm at the end of my rope, I tell you!" He held the gun up to Glatt's head. "You've got to give us things we haven't earned!"

Dimly, on the edge of her consciousness where knowledge of a secondary or auxiliary nature resided, such as that of state capitals, the rules of cricket, and the lyrics to the latter verses of "America the Beautiful," Dragnie was aware that she was shuffling awkwardly forward, and

that she was sheathed in a flimsy, ill-fitting garment. "Wait," she said. "Let him go. Your life is not John Glatt's fault or responsibility."

"That is merely a piece of self-serving, pseudo-philosophical cant from a person determined to retain a life of privilege and comfort!" the rotter cried. "I hate all of you! This world you have created is inhuman, cruel, and barbarous!"

She realized that Regnad, Sanfrancisco, and Rawbone had left the protection of the car and gathered on either side of her. She said to the rotter, "What is your name?"

"Seymour Butts."

"I'm sorry, Mr. Butts."

The rotter seemed to start in surprise. "You're what?"

"I'm sorry. I'm sorry you don't adequately understand the system we live in. We don't mean to harm you personally. We're trying to create a society that affords everyone in it the maximum amount freedom consistent with property rights. But freedom only has meaning depending on its context. To a dog, for example, freedom in the context of a dog park means, 'the ability to go off the leash and run around.' In a school, freedom might mean 'the ability for the senior class to determine where it will hold its Senior Prom.'

In capitalist society, freedom means 'the unobstructed opportunity to make money.' That is what John, here, and all of us, are trying to achieve: the creation of a society in which everyone is free to make money, which at the same time allows us to preserve, expand, and consolidate the wealth we already have by preserving and expanding the power that we already have. It's not that we want you to be poor. We want you to be as rich as you can be, provided that does not conflict with our ability to be as rich as we can be based on remaining as rich as we always have been."

Butts loosened his grip on Glatt's neck but kept the gun pointed at his head. "I...I never thought of it that way," he admitted. "Thus put, it's a perfectly defensible *modus vivendi*."

Dragnie felt a desire to sleep. She ignored it and continued, "That's why we called this Strike. The rest of the world is hampering our ability to make money—which, because we're capitalists, is the only freedom we care about. And, because we control your world, it's the only freedom you care about, too. That's why you're here. Because you can't make any money, without which you and your family will starve and die."

"That is true," Butts said.

"But we have done our part. You want to make money. You have the freedom to do so. If you have not done so, it can only be your own fault."

"Such reasoning is indisputable."

"Therefore it follows that it is not us that you hate," Dragnie said, feeling herself reeling in place. "It is yourself."

"That is indubitably so," Butts replied. "I'm a weak, second-rate mediocrity who can't succeed in an economy based on competition and merit, as are my wife and children. I see now that it was wrong of me to blame John Glatt, or indeed anybody, for difficulties of which I am the sole cause. To demand that the wealthy, who have obtained their wealth strictly via their own efforts or the efforts of others, to contribute to a minimally decent standard of living for all members of the society the existence of which has made that wealth possible, is to subvert the very idea of capitalism, which holds that a man has a right to exist only insofar as he can sell something to another man." He lowered the gun and said, "I'm sorry, Mr. Glatt. I'll go now."

Taking two steps back, he raised the gun again, this time to his own head, and pulled the trigger.

Glatt did not permit himself to flinch in shock, nor did Rawbone, Sanfrancisco, or Regnad Daghammarskjold permit themselves to react. Dragnie, however, witnessed none of these events, for she lost consciousness and collapsed onto the dirt road.

• • • •

Dragnie awoke in a hospital-type bed in a small room. Before her she beheld an array of faces displaying responses ranging from pitiless unsentimentality to calm dispassion. Glatt, Rawbone, Sanfrancisco De Soto, and Regnad Daghammarskjold ringed her bed, sitting on small folding chairs, while Doc Hastings stood gravely by her side. "How do you feel?" Hastings asked.

She replied with a defiant smile. "All right," she said, her voice low. "Weak."

"You should. You lost a lot of blood out there, young lady."

"What happened?"

"You jumped up from the chair and a piece of equipment nicked an artery. Didn't you feel yourself bleeding all over your leg?"

"Go easy on her, Doc," Sanfrancisco said. "She saved John's life."

"So I heard. By the way, Dragnie, the procedure was a success."

"Thanks, Doc," Dragnie said. She turned to the others. "What happened to Mr. Butts?"

"Nothing," Regnad said, his stunning Swedish beauty more beautiful and stunningly Swedish than ever before. "Killed himself."

"Oh," Dragnie said. "Too bad."

"Too bad?" Doc Hastings said gruffly. "He got what he deserved. Damn moocher. Meanwhile, I'll tell you what's too bad. The fact that you lost about two pints of blood and are in no condition to get up out of that bed, let alone fly back to New York."

Dragnie was about to protest when a knock was heard at the doorway. Standing there was "Faustus Fasnacht," holding a sheet of paper. "Excuse me, folks. Sorry to intrude, but Mr. Glatt just received a telex from New York and it's marked 'urgent.'" He entered and handed the sheet to Glatt, and only then did his eye fall on Dragnie. "Miss Tagbord! My goodness, you're white as a sheet! What happened?"

She smiled weakly. "I had an accident and lost some blood."

"Will you be needing a transfusion? What's your blood type?"

"O-positive."

"So is mine!" The young man turned to Doc Hastings. "Doc, I'd like to volunteer to be a donor for your patient here."

"Not so fast, son," Doc Hastings said. "I'm O-positive, too."

"So am I," Hunk Rawbone said with icy objectivity.

"As am I!" Sanfrancisco De Soto cried happily.

"I am O-positive, too," Regnad Daghammarskjold remarked.

"He's so your type."

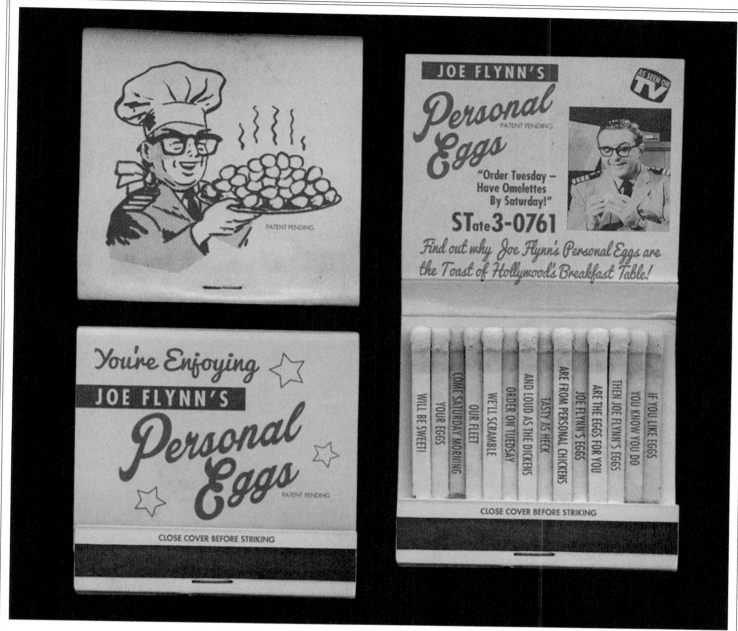

"I, too, am O-positive," John Glatt said, his eyes displaying a glint of mocking contempt.

The young man playing Faustus Fasnacht laughed. "But this is amazing! Miss Tagbord, you have an unlimited supply of donor blood. When shall we do this, Doc?"

To the young man's surprise, but to the surprise of no one else, Doc Hastings did not answer. Instead, he looked soberly at each individual in the room, ending on Dragnie, whose expression in reply mirrored the gravity of his own. Finally Dragnie said to the young man, "There will be no transfusion."

"What? Why not? I thought you said you lost a lot of blood."

"I did."

"And isn't the customary practice in such cases to replace the lost blood with donated blood of a compatible type?"

"It is."

"Then—"

"It is for some. Not for me," Dragnie said.

"Or me," Glatt said.

"Or any of us," Rawbone murmured.

"But…why not?" the young man stammered.

"Because," Dragnie said, "I would no sooner ask a man to give me his blood than I would ask him to give me his bond portfolio. Because the only thing more parasitic than living off another man's earnings is living off his body. Because I ask no man to deprive himself of that which guarantees and safeguards his existence, nor would I agree to give that man

that which guarantees mine. Because my blood is mine, the product of my body, and therefore no man may have a claim on it, just as I may not assert a claim on his. Because I do not live for anyone but myself, and I ask no man to live for anyone but himself. And because, when my body has replenished its blood supply—as it undoubtedly will—I shall go forth with neither debt nor gratitude, entirely free and self-sufficient, owing nothing, neither moocher nor leech."

Doc Hastings thumbed toward the door and said to the young man, "Okay, Junior, you got your answer. Now go." As the young man left, Hastings made a gesture toward the others. "Now suppose we all stop gabbin' and let Miss Tagbord here get some rest."

"How long will I need, Doc?" Dragnie asked.

Hastings made a face of estimation. "Four days. Five tops."

Dragnie looked at Glatt. "Tell my office, John, will you? And get word to Nathan."

Glatt, implacable in his ironclad reserve, nodded. Sanfrancisco pointed to the document in his hand. "What's it say, John?"

"It's from my office," Glatt said. "It says the government has put out an all-points bulletin calling for my detention and arrest." He looked at the others. "Your names are here, too. If we're going to go back, we have to do it in secret."

• Chapter Four •
The Naughty and the Nice

The party, a "Being-In" held by the children of the middle class, who imagined that injustices that had characterized society since the ancient Greeks somehow could be eradicated by college students smoking and ingesting illegal substances in the name of "peace," took place in a filthy loft in the derelict, grimy section of Manhattan which was normally the preserve of drug addicts, homosexuals, and petty criminals. Daubs of brightly-colored, glowing paint applied to dirty factory walls and crude signs affixed to lampposts pointed the way to a decrepit building on an ill-lit side street from which the sound of loud, primitive music, of the kind that sinks the spirit of men in the debased urges of adolescent emotionality rather than glorifying it in a purest expression of abstract exaltation, could be heard. It would take more than ten years from the Great Takeover for the neighborhoods, and the offspring, of men to be rescued from the corruptions and decay of the previous order.

It was Nathan A. Banden's first experience of such a neighborhood and, as was typical of the pampered children of the professional class, he credited himself with personal courage and ethical praiseworthiness merely for walking down the street. That there were visible no menaces to his safety was of no consequence, nor was it of any importance to his preening self-regard that the periodic appearance of a police car, sent to monitor the possibilities of civic rowdiness, served as a deterrent to any possible crimes in public.

Banden had, in the heat of their last exchange, told Dragnie he would be moving back in with his parents, but in fact he had not done so yet. He decided to take advantage of her pilgrimage to Glatt's Gorge and remain in the Glatt penthouse, where he had spent the past two days nursing his self-pity and stoking the flame of his indignation. It was while there that he had received a phone call from her office, informing him that her return would be delayed by at least four days, as would Glatt's. To Banden this felt like a betrayal. It was bad enough that she had rejected the prospect of carrying his seed and giving birth to his child; now she was extending the trip into a five-day vacation with his chief rival, and in the one place to which his entrance was barred and where she and Glatt had experienced perhaps their finest hour.

Banden trudged up the wide, worn steps of the building toward the increasingly deafening noise. He was unsure of why he was there, of what he was looking for, or if he would know it if he saw it. He knew only that, like romantic swains of ages past trapped in the suffocating misery of rejection, he sought something cathartic, possibly dangerous, and perhaps even deadly. When he had seen a sign near the Glatt apartment advertising this event, he decided to attempt to assuage his feelings of jealousy and diminishment by looking into it.

The loft was immense, poorly lighted by unshaded, naked bulbs scattered throughout and several neon beer advertisements on the walls. It was teeming with writhing bodies, for whom the word "dance" denoted a state of gyrating, spastic gesticulation indistinguishable from a *grand mal* seizure. The music, for so the assembled deemed it, featured amplified bass and thunderous drums under shrieking, caterwauling electric guitar strumming, all accompanying indecipherable lyrics shouted by "singers" of no notable training or ability. The crowd consisted primarily of young men and women of college age. Each considered himself to be exploring new avenues of self-expression, and so each wore clothing with an identical intention: to offend their parents. In evidence were flared pantaloons, tunics, Indian sport coats, blousy shirts, black t-shirts and tight jeans, dandified frills, Bluebeard costumes, feather boas, plumed hats, and other calculated tokens of strained whimsicality or affronts to normal standards of attire. Banden, in the pressed slacks and crisp dress shirt of the Glatt School student, instantly felt self-conscious.

Having led a privileged and sheltered life, Banden had no experience with the kinds of people now gyrating before him. One young man doing the Bugaboo in a red and purple striped shirt, was the son of a doctor. He believed that Western medicine was a fraud, and that men could

be cured of all diseases through chanting foreign syllables and drinking herbal infusions. The previous week he had contracted an infection and demanded that his father provide him with antibiotics without cost.

A girl in a billowing dress imitative of that of a peasant wife danced the Meat and Potatoes with abandon. She believed that the corruptions of civilization began with the stricture that women must shave their legs and underarms, and for that reason had made it a philosophical priority to display the hairy legs of a savage and to smell like a gymnasium.

Nearby danced a woman for whom the highest expression of personal freedom and individual liberty consisted in the unconfined swinging of her breasts. The week before she had taken part in a demonstration at which women too old, unattractive, or disagreeable to obtain a lover had gathered to remove their brassieres and burn them in a public display of what they considered to be advanced thinking and political protest.

Banden's eye fell on an older man, just past thirty. He was an assistant professor of sociology at a local university. As befitted his relative maturity, he gazed at the gathering from the periphery and contented himself with smoking a tiny ceramic pipe stuffed with the compressed extract of the poppy. In his classes he instructed his students that the mind was an illusion, the brain was essentially a large kidney, and the collective wisdom of three thousand years was contemptibly out of fashion. He urged those attending to his words to follow precepts uttered by illiterate popular singers, Hindu mystics, or Buddhist worshippers of self-annihilation.

A man in his late twenties dancing the Twang wore a pseudo-military jacket of braids and epaulets. He was a dealer in mind-damaging plants and hallucinogenic chemicals. That one of his customers had, the previous week, been under the delusion that he could fly, and had leaped to his death off the roof of a building, was of no consequence.

Two women in blue jeans and shapeless gray sweat shirts were Lesbians. Their movement scarcely qualified as dancing at all, even by the debased standards of the present event. Instead, they deemed it a measure of their freedom to be able to openly engage in kissing and stroking on the dance floor.

A boy wearing a shabby tuxedo and top hat, with his face painted yellow and red, spun like a Dervish, displaying no sense of rhythm or form. He had no aptitude for study and lacked the discipline to derive any benefit from a university experience, and yet felt entitled to a full scholarship to one of the most prestigious colleges in the nation.

One couple, each in black from head to toe, clutched each other and rocked as though in the grip of an attack of delirium tremens. She was an associate professor of English. He was "a poet." Both believed that the problems of society were due to the necessity of each individual to earn a living, and both called upon the workers of the world to overthrow the creators of wealth and to distribute their riches among "the people." That they lived in a townhouse purchased by her father was a fact neither found difficult to ignore.

"Hey, man, your attire is far away."

The girl who spoke to Banden was pretty, slim, and with the exaggerated eye makeup of a child exploring the treasures of her mother's dressing table. She was slightly shorter than he and wore her dark hair long, unstyled, and untied. "I'm Angel Human," she said.

He started. "Is that really your name?"

She shrugged and emitted a doltish grin. "I don't know. What does it matter? Names aren't important as long as you love everybody. Why can't we just be? La la la, life is so simple."

Someone nearby handed her some-thing from his fingertips to hers. She put it in her mouth and inhaled, then held it out to Nathan. "Want to smoke a Mary Jean cigarette?"

Banden took it with the fascination, dread, and morbid curiosity he would have felt had it been a loaded gun. He knew what this contraband substance was, but it had never occurred to him that the opportunity actually to sample it would ever present itself in the circles in which he moved. Internally committing himself to whatever dangers lay before him, he put the cigarette to his lips and drew in sharply. The smoke plunging into his chest caused his throat to clench and loosed a spasm of coughing, at which Angel Human laughed merrily.

"Your first time, huh? Far away. Not so much this time. Here."

As she held the cigarette up to his lips and he took a puff, he became transfixed by her eyes.

They were large, brown, and guileless—so different from his former lover's ice-blue eyes, with their sparks of intelligence, their glint of calculation, their burning awareness of existence as the ground of all phenomena. It would be nice, Nathan felt, to be absorbed by these eyes, to receive from their untroubled placidity a sanction for the cessation of striving, of pushing, of achieving, and instead merely to exist in the here and now, like an animal or a rock. He took another puff as she smiled softly at him.

"Can you folks in the back hear me?"

"Hey," she said. "Wanna dance?"

He was about to protest that he didn't know how, when she summarily began shifting and gyrating in place, more or less in rhythm with the throbbing wail of the popular music blaring from loudspeakers across the room. She pulled on the cigarette and held it up for him. He drew on it again. She then passed it to someone nearby and, with a luxuriant toss of her head, exhaled the smoke directly at him as her hair rippled on either side of her smooth, childlike face.

"You're cute," she said.

"So are you," he said.

"Hey, let's engage in heavy petting."

He hesitated. "I'm not sure I should."

"Oh, man, don't make me trip over a bum," she said, rolling her large, liquid eyes with exasperation. "Hang up on society and call up freedom long-distance! Don't let the square world drag you down. Because what if they threw a war and nobody caught it? Did you know that the Earth is like ninety percent water? It's our home and it's water, okay? The Earth is our home and we live here, man, covered in water. It's like a big aquarium and we're all fish. Fish don't make bombs. Fish don't declare war on other people just because they're different. They live for today because tomorrow is just today that hasn't come yet. That's why this is the dawning of the age of aquariums. Everybody should do what fish do—stay in the school, get in the swim, and enjoy Nature."

It was a nonsensical fit of verbal hysteria, an ignorant mélange of colloquial expressions, simplistic metaphors, and crude piscine symbolism, but Banden listened to it in a state of transfixed fascination. It articulated a view of the world, a set of values, a code, which he never knew existed. Compared to this, Dragnie's comments about mind, will, and rationality seemed simply too difficult to confront and too demanding to live up to. The simplicity of Angel's expression, the fluidity and grace with which she carried herself, the guileless directness of her manner of interaction, and of course her physical attractiveness, proved convincing evidence to Banden of the correctness of her views, however nonsensical they were in reality.

"You're right," he said dazedly.

"Come on."

It took ten minutes by cab to reach her apartment, a small studio in an old apartment building in a quaint residential part of the city, where poets and painters of previous eras had lived, but which was now occupied by the children of the privileged while they attended university, where they spent the days protesting its curricula and policies and the nights engaging in lurid escapades involving mentally disorienting drugs and sexual activities devoid of metaphysical dimensions.

As she unlocked her front door he thought, Do you see this, Dragnie? Here is a place to which you cannot gain admission. It is the place of today's stylish

and hip-most young people, who have something to say to society and want the whole world to jibe on their now message. His voice tremulous with hope, he said, "Is what we're going to do a thing?"

She smiled. "Definitely," she said. "It's a thing and we're going to hang it out."

"It sounds like it will have many grooves."

"It already does," she said, and pulled him into the apartment.

• Chapter Five •
When You Are Hot You Are Hot. When You Are Not You Are Not.

On the morning of the third day of her convalescence, Dragnie was sitting up in bed in Doc Hastings's clinic, reading with ruthless literacy the freight manifests and other railroad documents sent to Glatt's Gorge by her assistants in New York, when John Glatt appeared in the doorway. As always, his face bore no outward sign of his inner state of being, apart from a slight narrowing of the eyes signaling an absolute love of existence and a barely-perceptible wiggling of the ears manifesting a withering contempt for reality.

"Hello, John," she said. "Is something wrong?"

"I've just been speaking to Fritz," Glatt said.

"Our loyal chauffeur? On the telephone?"

"Yes. Nathan has been compelling Fritz to drive him to various social engagements the past several evenings."

"Oh, is that all?" Dragnie said, chuckling.

"No," Glatt said, not chuckling. "Nathan has been accompanied in these nightly outings by a young lady--the same young lady, every night—who, Fritz said, is physically attractive in a girlish, lissome way said to be appealing to the masses of men for whom, according to the latest fashionable magazines, such an appearance and manner are widely considered to be pleasing."

"I see. And she is how old?"

"Approximately eighteen. At the end of each evening Nathan requests that Fritz deposit both of them at the girl's dwelling, a squalid little apartment in the disreputable section of Greenwich Village frequented by bohemians and non-conformists. And now excuse me. I've got work to do in my secret laboratory, dedicating all of my intelligence and energy to the creation of an invention thus far unseen by the eyes of men."

Glatt left. Dragnie pondered what course of action would best honor her highest code of values and conduct. After a few moments of pitiless concentration and dispassionate analysis, it became clear that the optimal course of action for her would be to return to New York, initiate a discussion with Nathan A. Banden and, at a precise moment the arrival of which she would identify by a combination of innate instinct and objective calculation, shriek emasculating insults at him and, if feasible, repeatedly slap his face as hard as she could. He would, she felt with the confidence of certitude, recoil from this expression of her displeasure. But she did not doubt her ability to pursue him both verbally and physically, whether in the apartment, around the corridors of the world-famous Johnsonwood Building, or up and down the street. She would do so until, having delivered a sufficient quantity of slaps and, if a propitious opportunity presented itself for such actions, punches, he acknowledged her theme and accepted its premise. Its premise was that she accepted full responsibility for how old she was. Its premise was that if he had begun to experience her age as a "bring-off" and a "turn-down" he need only have said something, and she would have prevailed on John Glatt to invent something to make her younger. Its premise was, thus, inescapably, that it was his fault that she was old, that she was compelled, by a reasonable assessment of her self-interest, to slap him and yell her values at him, and that she was now forced to wonder if she—she, Dragnie Tagbord—were not enough for him.

Flinging the papers aside, she tore off the bedclothes and struggled to her feet. Striding out of the clinic, Dragnie barely heard the astonished Doc Hastings cry, "What th—?". She did not stop to reply. She had to find her plane, prepare it for flight, and return to New York. She shuffled in staggering steps down the dirt track toward the airstrip, her thin hospital booties shredding against the loose stones and sun-baked ruts of the road. Behind her she heard Doc Hastings yell, "Dragnie! God damn it! Not again! Where are you going?"

CHEKHOV'S MOTHER

"Home!" Dragnie shouted, not looking back.

"Where—New York? Bushwa. You're in no shape to go anywhere, least of all to the airport in order to commandeer that twin-engine dual prop Cessna for an eight-hour solo flight back to Teeterboro! If you take off in that thing you will crash and die. Now get back here."

She did not heed his command. She did not stop and get back there. She did not do anything other than the thing that she did, which was to continue walking.

"Miss Tagbord?"

Out of nowhere, a figure had appeared.

It was a young woman who had apparently run over to her from Ed Virility's Bait 'n' Tackle Shoppe across the road, where Ed Virility, the nation's top forensic ophthalmologist, had pioneered an important breakthrough in using fishing gear to conduct forensic ophthalmology and then refused to share it with the rest of either the forensic ophthalmology world or the fishing gear world. Dragnie walked on, examining the girl with a cursory glance but never breaking stride. The girl looked vaguely familiar. Her haircut, in a style no longer in fashion, reminded Dragnie of some similar style she had either seen or dreamed about years before. Her clothes—trim chino pants, showing off her slim shape to perfection; a loose white blouse accentuating her superb posture; the sensible flat shoes announcing their utter disregard for standard notions of feminine footwear—also looked like something Dragnie had seen in the past.

"Do you have a minute?" the young lady asked. "I've been dying to meet you. My name is—well, my real name is Phyllis Upp, but that is of no consequence. Don't you know who I am?"

Dragnie marched on, fully determined to continue marching on. "Should I?" she said.

The girl smiled. "I'm you. I'm 'Dragnie Tagbord.' I play you here at the Gorge."

Dragnie stopped. She turned and fully exposed herself to the sight of the young lady at whom her eyes were openly staring. It was only then that it struck her, that she was indeed looking at herself—or, rather, at herself as she had been ten years earlier. The young woman's face resembled the younger Dragnie's. Her hair, her clothes, her personal sense of individual style and her unique, kicky personality that made her one-in-a-million unique and someone people liked to be near, were identical to Dragnie's of a decade earlier. "But you're…perfect," Dragnie breathed.

The girl smiled. "Yes, that's how I'm playing you. As the perfect woman. As a fully conscious being who loves existence and maintains complete awareness in everything she does, says, and thinks."

"Yes," Dragnie replied. "That is exactly what I am."

"I know it."

"No, I know it."

"Well," the girl laughed, "I know it in a different way. You see, Miss Tagbord, I'm a work of art, and as such represent a re-creation of reality according to an artist's metaphysical value judgments. My depiction of you is an even more accurate depiction of you than is your depiction of you. I'm more you than you are you."

"But how can you be sure?" Dragnie asked, as always supremely concerned with the truth of her self-knowledge. "How can you be certain that your depiction is accurate? Your metaphysical judgments represent opinions of purest subjectivity."

"Not if they're accurate," the girl said. "Then they're transformed from being subjective opinions to objective facts."

"And how can you be sure your subjective opinions are accurate?"

"Because it's not just me," the girl smiled. "Everybody I talk to about you says, 'Yes, that's how she was--the perfect woman, supremely aware and with a volitional consciousness impervious to the influence of the so-called unconscious.'" The girl shrugged, as though stating something obvious and indisputable. "Their belief in your perfection proves it's an objective reality. That's why I've created an entire philosophical system based on my experience as an actress here at Glatt's Gorge. I call it 'Objectivismism.' Its principle tenet is what I have just articulated: that one's subjective opinions are, when also held by other men, elevated to the status of objective fact."

Chuckling, Dragnie chuckled. "But… but that's exactly how I've always felt, too," she said.

"Ever since I was fourteen. I read a book about demigod heroes who announced their beliefs to each other as they triumphed over mortal enemies, and I thought, 'This is how life should be—and would be, if my parents weren't such moral cowards, and possessed the courage to see things as they really are, in black and white. If only I could be surrounded by people who think as I do, life would be perfect.'"

"Of course," the actress said. "The more you're surrounded by people who agree with you, the more you know your ideas are objectively correct."

"May I ask you something?" Dragnie found herself saying. "I don't know you but I sense that you can be trusted. Recently a man betrayed me. I am significantly older than he, and his unfaithfulness was with a much younger woman—a teenager, actually. And yet I know him to be a supremely rational, if still somewhat immature, young man. His actions seem to suggest that I am not enough for him. But how, if I am as perfect as you contend, can this be possible?"

The young woman playing "Dragnie Tagbord" chuckled. "That's easy. It isn't possible. It's not that you aren't enough for him. It's that he isn't enough for you. You're too much for him. He betrayed you because you threaten him."

Dragnie embraced the young woman and said, "Thank you, Phyllis. As an actress, you possess keen insight into human reality. What you just said sounds perfect. Which means it is perfect."

• Chapter Six •

The Conversation of Talking People Saying Things

It took five days for Dragnie to regain sufficient strength and stamina to enable her to return to New York. Dur-

"Daddy, what did you do in the war on women?"

ing her convalescence she had directed Tagbord Rail from afar, communicating via telephone with her subordinates and conveying ideas from her mind into their consciousness via the power of human speech. She had also consulted with Glatt and his colleagues about the Peoples' States of the People's declaration of war, and Mr. Jenkins's issuance of an arrest order for Glatt and the others.

"It makes no sense," Dragnie had said. "Mr. Jenkins knows he is nothing more than an impotent puppet who serves at your pleasure. Why would he want to antagonize you?"

"The Strike is teaching Americans many things," Glatt had explained. "It's showing America that it can survive without jobs, without income, without tolerance, without opportunity, and without most of the rudiments of a modern civilization—which is to say, the very things guaranteed by government. All it takes is a willingness to redefine the word 'survive.' Sooner or later it will dawn on Americans that they can survive without government itself, and that a nation run by corporations, who are obedient to the demands and the rules of the market when they are not busy subverting or conspiring against them, is all that men need in order to live a life minimally acceptable to the mass of citizens and maximally desirable for the corporations themselves. Mr. Jenkins, as the Head Person of the government, knows this. He knows his job is in jeopardy. That is why he wants to arrest me and, indeed, all of us." He had paused, and then added, "That is why we must avoid capture as we continue to press the Strike."

During her more leisurely hours Dragnie also meditated on her relationship with Nathan A. Banden. Now that the termination of her pregnancy had taken place, what would his response be? Did she still desire him as a lover? Did he her? None of these questions possessed ready answers, but one thing seemed certain: Banden had been deeply hurt by her decision to decline motherhood, and even more betrayed by her refusal to allow him to accompany her to Glatt's Gorge. He had said he would be moving back to his parents' house, and she could not but assume that he had done so.

She arrived at the penthouse under cover of night and in the concealment of an unfashionable garment. Accompanied by her chauffeur, Dragnie planned to gather

"If this inter-office memo you wish to see, first you must answer me these questions three."

some essential clothes and business materials, and then to rendezvous with Glatt at their secret safehouse.

She debarked from the elevator on the top floor of the world-famous, prize-winning Johnsonwood Building, unlocked her front door, and rushed in.

"Hello, Dragnie," Nathan A. Banden said.

Dragnie did not permit herself to scream the epithet she so desperately wanted to scream.

"Hello," she replied.

"How are you feeling?"

"A little weak still, but—"

He chuckled. "Weak? From your five day tryst with your in-effect husband? You must have had a fine vacation indeed."

"I?" she chuckled. "Vacation? I was in bed the whole time."

"I'm sure you were in bed—where, one may assume, you enjoyed the superior amatory talents of your other lover, a man old enough to be my father. But why tell me, Dragnie? It's certainly none of my business. Not any more."

"I mean, Nathan, that I sustained a bad cut, lost a lot of blood, and had to stay in bed while I recuperated. I hardly saw John at all. He's been busy with his advisers, talking about the People's States."

"Yes, well, I'm sure he has been. Somebody has to save our way of life, so it

might as well be the great and heroic John Glatt."

"Is something wrong, Nathan?"

"With society? Oh, I think one could say that, yes. Ask yourself this, Dragnie: What if somebody threw a war and nobody caught it?"

"I?" she cried. "Ask myself that? Don't be preposterous."

"I? Preposterous?" he chuckled. "Tell me, are you aware of the fact that the Earth is ninety percent water? And what does that make Man?"

"Wet?"

"A fish. Man is a fish, Dragnie. And there is nothing that you, or John Glatt, or the rest of your tightened-up rich friends, can say or do that will make it any different."

"I see," Dragnie said. "These are uncharacteristic expressions, Nathan. Do I sense a shift in your values? Has your perception of reality altered in some vital way?"

"It has."

"Then I can only conclude that you have been sleeping with another woman."

"I have. Wait here."

Banden strode out of the living room toward his bedroom in the rear. Several moments later he re-appeared with a young woman. Both of them were naked. Joining hands, they stood before Dragnie.

"Dragnie," Banden said, "Angel Human and I are going to have a sexual relation-

"Hi, handsome."

ship. I trust that will receive your permission and blessing. It of course will have no effect on my relationship with you, so there is no rational reason for you to object to it."

Dragnie smiled, as a man might smile at an apprentice displaying competence at a task of which the man had been teacher. "Of course I permit it," she said. "Of course I give it my blessing. It's nice to meet you, Angel Human."

"Cool. Hi."

"In fact, Nathan, why don't you and Angel Human join us for our dinner party tonight? We're having a few friends over and the conversation will be sparkling and enlightening, since it will deal exclusively with reality."

"We'd love to," Banden said icily. "Wouldn't we, Angel?"

"Far away from sight."

"But Dragnie," Banden added. "This apartment hardly looks like a place scheduled to be the scene of a sparkling dinner party."

"Oh, we're not holding it here. We have to temporarily move to a secret location while John works out some problems with the government."

"A secret location?" Banden's mouth displayed an amused smile of purest mockery and somewhat-alloyed contempt. "It sounds like they're after him. Has an arrest warrant been issued for John?"

"Not formally, no," Dragnie replied coolly. "But he is wanted for questioning."

Angel's eyes grew wide with the expression of willed innocence and falsely childlike wonder typical of her generational and cultural cohort. "Really? The Pigs are after your husband? Far away from sight!"

"We're not married. In any case, the matter is being addressed," Dragnie said. "But you two may feel free to stay here and I'll send Fritz to pick you up at six. Casual dress, naturally. Now excuse me, I must pack and run."

Dragnie strode from the living room toward her own bedroom, noting, as she went, Angel Human's comment to the young man. "She seems nice," the girl said.

• • •

"The paradox of the unconscious, my dear, is that we are only aware of it when we are not aware of it, and by then it is too late."

A cascade of glittering laughter followed this witticism as the preparation and imbibing of cocktail drinks continued. Dragnie was about to wonder where her final two guests were when they arrived: Nathan A. Banden and Angel Human were ushered into the Glatts's secret location by Fritz, the loyal chauffeur.

The apartment was an elegant, spacious three-bedroom duplex in a nondescript building at an unregistered address, and was concealed from the sight of men by a three-dimensional camouflage projection

conveying the deceptive impression of a leather tannery. Banden was at first confused when, expecting a sumptuous yet tasteful example of architectural splendor as the site of the evening's activity, he and Angel were escorted into what appeared to be a dilapidated industrial structure. But their disorientation upon entering the building was nothing compared to his bedazzlement as he was introduced to the array of accomplished, glamorous guests.

Dragnie rose, put her perfectly mixed martini down onto the handsome table designed by a famous table designer, and conducted the introductions. "May I present Grace Adams, the beautiful movie star, and her husband, Derek Maxwell, the popular British spy. Grace is the extramarital lover of my husband, John Glatt. Now may I introduce noted author Andrea Smith, her lover, Paul Rogers, the brilliant physicist, and her husband, top economist Alan Greenback. Beside them are prima ballerina Marie Francais, who is Alan's mistress, and her husband, Nils Nillssonsonson, the Norwegian philologist, who is Andrea's sometime-paramour. Everybody, this is Nathan A. Banden, my extramarital lover, and his little girlfriend, Angel Human."

As Banden and Angel shook hands with the other guests and found places for themselves on the elegant, spare sectional Danish seating system created by a famous Danish sofa creator, Dragnie took the keenest pleasure in observing Nathan's reaction to this dazzling array of achievement, beauty, and intelligence. The chic and flattering clothes on the women, and their expertly applied makeup; the stylish dress of the men, and the ease with which they discoursed on abstruse matters of political economy, aesthetics, and epistemology; the sophistication of everyone's cigarettes—did Banden know how privileged he was to be included in this event?

The question went unanswered in Dragnie's mind as Nils Nilssonsonson directed a jovial query to Glatt in his charmingly Norwegian-accented English.

"So, tell me, John. This Strike of yours, to teach the world a lesson by destroying America. It goes well, yes?"

Glatt's face, an expressionless array of flat planes and sharp angles, accommodated itself to the sipping of a vodka gimlet prepared with the highest competence by Juan, the Filipino bartender, as he replied, "Yes."

"You mean it was your idea?" Angel

asked in a tone of surprise.

"Yes."

"But don't you think it's sad, that people are so bummed up in their heads about everything?" the girl inquired in a juvenile tone of voice. "I mean, 'cause, like, when nobody has a job, and everybody is intolerant of everyone's race and creed and everything, and everyone's poor and sleeping in the bus station and everything, isn't that, like, bad?"

"No, Angel," Dragnie said, her gaze fixed on Nathan A. Banden. "What would be bad is if they slept in the train station."

A burst of knowing laughter greeted this observation—laughter from everyone in attendance except Angel Human, who did not understand the allusion, and Nathan A. Banden, who looked uncomfortably from Dragnie to Angel and back again.

"Besides, Miss Human, what is 'bad' about freedom?" Glatt remained impassive, his expression displaying the confidence borne of the unyielding certitude that, while other men could be wrong about some things, he never could, because he knew he was right. "Is it 'bad' that men be free to suffer?"

"Uhm?"

"'Uhm' indeed, Angel," Dragnie said. "Nathan, you didn't tell me that your girlfriend possessed such a keen theoretical mind. I can see what attracts you to her."

"Now see here, Dragnie—"

"Is it 'bad' that each man be liberated from the atavistic shackles of a cowardly social order whose inability to accept reality was for centuries faked out and smushed over by the empty cliché that 'man is a social animal'?" Glatt asked aloud.

"Ehrm?"

"But see here, John," Derek Maxwell said. "If man isn't a social animal, what is he?"

"He is an individual," Glatt said. "He has always been an individual, even from the time he was a little baby. And everything he has done, from the invention of the English muffin to the creation of the atomic bomb, he has done on his own, without help from anyone."

Andrea Smith looked mischievous as she said, "Not even…from society?"

"Society is a myth, my dear," Alan Greenback purred. "Society is what we call it when two individuals stop strangling each other and break for lunch."

"Oh, come, Alan. Don't you think you're being a bit reductive?" Grace Adams, the

............◆............

unforgettable star of movies, said. "Even you must admit that civilization is the result of society going to work each day creating industry and agriculture, and then coming home and enjoying ample leisure and cultural activities."

"I admit no such thing, Grace," Greenback twinkled genially. "Ask the philosophy boys and they'll tell you to ask the anthropology boys, who'll tell you that civilization's spent the last two thousand years sitting on its hands and playing pinochle."

"Is that not a contradiction?" the ballerina with the French name said. "One gentleman, he says one thing. The other gentleman, he says another thing."

Perplexedly, Angel Human said, "Fahm?"

"Don't say anything," Nathan A. Banden told her.

"There is no such thing as contradiction," Glatt declared with finality. "Reality—real reality—permits no disagreements."

"I am not seeing it that way," Nils Nilssonsonson said.

"Then you are wrong," Glatt replied. "Reality is binary and absolute. That is why opinion is something properly confined to animals and, to a lesser extent, plants. Something either is true, or it is not true. Either something exists, or it does not. If it does not exist, we say, 'Hey, what happened to it?' Then we discover that it does exist, and we say, 'Oh, never mind, here it is.'"

"I don't do that," Angel said.

"Oh just shut up," Banden muttered. "Let them talk."

"Na-than," the girl whined. "Be nice."

"The morality of reason rests on the axiom that existence exists," Glatt continued. "All of the problems of the world, throughout history, are the result of men seeking to deny this fundamental truth. Their evasions and denials take several forms. Some men say, 'Existence has never existed, so we may as well enslave mankind.' Others aver, 'Existence used to exist, but it went away.' Still others claim, 'Existence does not exist yet, but we expect it to exist in about fifteen minutes.' All of these are gross misconceptions. For either existence exists, or it does not. And we know that existence does exist. We know it exists because we can go outside and point to it. We go outside. I point to something. You say, 'What is that?' I say, 'That is the thing that exists.' You say, 'Oh, of course. Thank you.' I say, 'You're welcome.' And all the while we feel free to ignore the underlying fact that if the thing did not exist we would not be talking about it. This holds true for everything in human history except unicorns. They do not exist but we are compelled to talk about them from time to time. And when we do, we are not conscious. Any man who discusses unicorns is, by definition, asleep. Besides, it is impossible that existence not exist. To the man who says, 'Ex-

.... ◆ ....

istence does not exist' we say: then what does? That man is invariably at a loss to reply."

"Bravo, John Glatt," Paul Rogers, the brilliant physicist, said. "Let me, if you will, extend your thinking. It is man's capacity for reason that keeps him from being a crazy person. That is why the businessman is the highest form of human being. No lunatic can be a businessman, else the other businessman with whom he attempts to deal will say, 'You are insane, and I will not deal with you.'"

"I don't understand this kind of talk," Angel Human said.

"Just pay attention and keep your mouth shut," Nathan A. Banden hissed at her.

"Nathan?" Andrea Smith murmured.

FOR EVERY "YES" ANSWER, GIVE YOURSELF FIVE POINTS:

5-10 POINTS:
ARE YOU A MORMON?

15-20 POINTS:
WOULD SUBWOOFERS IN THE MINIVAN HELP?

25-30 POINTS:
THOUGHT ABOUT DEFYING YOUR GATED COMMUNITY'S COVENANT? NICE TRY.

35-45 POINTS:
HITCH UP YOUR DOCKERS AND START THINKING ABOUT DEATH!

50 POINTS:
CONGRATULATIONS! THEY'LL HAVE TO PRY HIPNESS FROM YOUR BONY, COLD, DEAD FINGERS.

that is, with the exception of Angel Human. The girl suddenly leaped to her feet and addressed the others in a tone of anger common to those unaware of the fact that their code of morality is inferior to those of the superior people to whom she speaks. "How can you people talk this way?" she demanded. "People who've lost their jobs…people who've lost their homes…people who're living on the streets and in tents out in fields—they're not insane! They're just poor!"

Dragnie smiled with pitiless sympathy. "You haven't been listening, Angel. We just proved that they are insane. Nathan?" She looked pointedly at Banden and made a gesture of appeal. "I think it would be best if you and Angel left in embarrassment and disgrace, don't you?"

"I certainly do," Banden seethed. "I have no patience for people who take pleasure in mocking someone not as brilliant as they are."

"I'm leaving, too," Angel Human announced. "I don't like people who don't love everybody, and who only believe in providing goods and services for money. I think everyone should feel sorry for everyone else, because otherwise you have a mean society."

Dragnie walked the two young people to the front door. She smiled coolly at Banden and said, "You must be completely humiliated. Well, good night, and thank you for coming." After they had exited the building she closed the door.

Out on the sidewalk, Angel Human tried to conceal her dismay with a hollow, forced laugh.

"Wow, what terrible people," she said.

Banden did not answer. Instead, he took a few steps to the corner and peered up at the two street signs identifying the intersection. Nearby was that essential utility without which a civilization cannot function: a public telephone booth. Entering it and placing coins in the slot, he dialed some numbers and, when a voice answered, said, "Hello? Is this the government? My name is Nathan A. Banden and I'm at the intersection of Crenshaw and Third…"

They were still standing there when, several minutes later, three unmarked cars and a van roared up and disgorged ten men in trench coats and carrying side arms. The men rushed into the building. Banden dragged Angel into the concealment of an awning's shadow as they watched the men lead Dragnie, Glatt, and

.... ◆ ....

"Your girlfriend gives some appearance of being stupid. One is tempted to conclude that you are stupid, too."

"I am not stupid!" Banden cried. "Please, sir, continue."

Rogers smiled. "Thank you. Now, we are a society run by businessmen, and by corporations, who are identical to businessmen except that they wear buildings instead of suits. This means we are a rational society. And, since no businessman is in the business of causing human suffering, it follows that anyone suffering in society is not a businessman, and therefore is not rational, and thus can be said to be insane."

Everyone raised their glass in a silent congratulatory toast—everyone,

The image depicts an album cover:

AUDIO FIDELITY DFS 7030 · STEREOPHONIC

THE INCREDIBLE SIGHTS AND SOUNDS OF THE
CIVIL RIGHTS ACT OF 1964
AN ON-THE-SPOT RECORDING OF THRILL-PACKED MOMENTS FROM THE ACTION-PACKED SESSION!

PRESIDENTIAL SIGNING CEREMONY

WASHINGTON

INCLUDES TITLES I THROUGH XI

TITLE I: Bars unequal application of voter registration requirements!

TITLE II: Outlaws discrimination based on race, color, religion or national origin in public accommodations engaged in interstate commerce!*

AND IX MORE!

Skritch!
Skritch!

*Exempting private clubs without defining the term "private"

---

their guests out, forced them into the van, and drove off into the night.

PART III

Non Being and Somethingness

• Chapter One•
Fixed for Great Justice

What is the matter, honey?"

"Nothing," Nathan A. Banden said. "Just, for god's sake, you little fool, shut up."

The chair, which was of the beanbag variety, was of a bright pink color. It smelled of plastic, and of death. It was symbolic of a world in which Banden had recently come to realize that he no longer loved life.

A week had passed since agents of the government had seized Dragnie, Glatt, and the other guests at the party and, Banden assumed, spirited them off to an undisclosed location. Banden now lay sprawled on the crunchily noisy seating unit, flailing about in its impudent grasp, imprisoned within the untidy and

faintly repulsive apartment of Angel Human. The television had just broadcast an announcement informing the American people that, in ten minutes, Mr. Jenkins would introduce Miss Dragnie Tagbord to make a very special announcement to the public. "Mr. Jenkins wants you to watch Miss Dragnie Tagbord's important address to the People, so please be sure to do so!" the "public service announcement" commanded. Banden, determined to avoid viewing the program, had struggled to extricate himself from the chair, but had failed in his purpose.

"Do you need a hand getting up?" Angel inquired.

"No! Just stop talking," he sighed. "I'm…fine. Just fine."

Parting her long, straight hair from either side of her childlike, smooth face, she smiled as though speaking to a disgruntled toddler. "Are you looking forward to hearing your friend on television?"

"My friend be damned!" he cried.

"Na-than," she chided. "You don't have to bite my head off with displaced frustration. You've been such a big grouchy puss lately."

"Stop talking baby talk! Speak the

way intelligent men speak, in complete sentences tidily arranged in elaborate, extended paragraphs making full use of dependent clauses, perfectly articulated chains of logical, sequentially arranged phrases, a formal and, arguably, somewhat artificial deployment of commas—and inserted sub-comments set off by em-dashes in the service of providing auxiliary but nonetheless logically valid digressions—and, if it were to prove necessary, accurate employment of the conditional tense, I tell you!"

"You say men but I'm not a man. I'm a human woman, which is the proper way to denominate a female individual in our society today."

"I can't live like this, I tell you!"

"If you don't like the beanbag chair go sit somewhere else, silly."

"Oh, Angel, Angel—"

"Although everybody else that comes here likes it," she noted. "And I think people are all the same, and so they should all like the same kinds of chairs. Individual taste and personal proclivity just lead to arguments and fighting and wars and stuff. That's why genius is bad and mediocrity is preferable. I think that and I think you should, too."

Banden surrendered to the enveloping grasp of the chair, acutely conscious of the reality that he despised existence.

Less than a mile away, in a television studio located in a moderately important building, Dragnie sat on a small sofa in a so-called green room near a sound stage. Two agents of the government, in identical dark suits, flanked her and observed her every move. Across from her, leaning forward anxiously from a folding metal chair, sat Mr. Jenkins, the Head Person of the Government of the United States.

"I must say, Miss Tagbord, I'm rather impressed with how reasonable you're being about all this," he said, his face wreathed in a desperate, obsequious smile. "Especially after your initial resistance to making our little speech."

"Your threat was quite clear, Mr. Jenkins," Dragnie said coolly. "You did, after all, threaten to hold John Glatt, Mr. De Soto, and the others—including me—in a military prison for an indefinite period of time, without recourse to counsel, under a series of State of Emergency laws summarily passed by you without any consultation with us as the Board of Directors of the United States, or any other acknowledgment of due process."

"We are at war, Miss Tagbord. The usual nuances of peacetime legality do not apply."

"So you claim. In any case, John and I discussed the situation and agreed on what we considered to be a rational response."

"Yes, well, I always figured Glatt for a sensible fellow." The career bureaucrat sat back and indulged in a chuckle, chuckling. "Mind you, I'm no fan of this embargo brought about by the People's States. I'm no fan of it at all! But then you and Glatt call this Strike, and the People's States declare war—well, I mean to say, nobody benefits from any of it! It's bad for business all the way around. He sees that, and you see it, and, well, I'm just glad you all are willing to help us calm things down." He glanced at his watch, an overpriced and vulgar instrument of no great precision, and inaccurate below a depth of two fathoms. "Better get yourself together. You go on in fifteen minutes." He held out a sheaf of typescript. "Do you, uh, want to see the text again?"

"No, thank you," Dragnie said. "I'll read it from the teleprompter."

"Fine, fine. Suit yourself." Mr. Jenkins rose and headed for the door. "I'll be back in a few minutes. Meanwhile, if you need anything…"

Dragnie nodded. She needed nothing. A single reading of the speech Mr. Jenkins and his speechwriters had composed had been enough to disclose the theme, content, and purpose of this address, both explicitly and, more importantly, implicitly. It called for an end to the Strike. Effective immediately, all actions and policies that had been implemented to subvert the idea of America as an ideal of liberty, equality, and opportunity, in the mind of men, would be cancelled. This would have the effect—and this was patently the reason and purpose behind the speech and the Strike's cancellation—of reasserting the validity of and the need for government.

In return, the forces holding John Glatt and the others prisoner would release them, unharmed. Mr. Jenkins would negotiate a diplomatic truce with the People's States of the People, the war would be declared over, and, after some token assurances that American manufacturers would take steps to improve the safety of their products, the embargo would be lifted. Life would return to normal—and governments all over the world would be safe, once more, from a threat to their existence.

"Miss Tagbord?" A young man knocked on the green room door and opened it. "Five minutes."

Dragnie nodded. She was ready.

"Good evening, my fellow American citizens."

Banden watched Mr. Jenkins glumly from the implacable clutches of the beanbag chair as Angel sat nearby. Unable to cope with reality, she smoked a Mary Jean cigarette and damaged her consciousness in the manner promoted by her generation of lazy hedonists who expected something for nothing.

"As you know, we have been in the midst of a national emergency," Mr. Jenkins continued. He summarized the embargo issued by the People's States of the People, the Strike as called for by John Glatt, and the subsequent Declaration of War by the People's States. "I'm sure you agree with me that it all seems so…hostile," Mr. Jenkins went on. "Everybody is suffering—our people, people all over the world, and the people in governments in every country on Earth. That is why I am pleased, now, to introduce Miss Dragnie Tagbord, who as a member of the Board of Directors of the United States and an original participant in the Great Takeover, is known to you all. She has some words about the war, and the Strike, that I know you will all want to hear. Miss Tagbord…?"

As Banden stared in a miasma of guilt, despair, and impotent self-loathing, the image of Dragnie appeared on the screen. She wore a gray jumpsuit suggestive of some sort of official captivity, and the effects of a week's detention were evident in her drawn, haggard face. "Thank you, Mr. Jenkins," she began. "Ladies and gentlemen: As you may know, the text of the speech I am supposed to deliver appears on a small screen just under the lens of the camera that is beaming my image to your television sets. I am to read the speech, while appearing to be looking into the camera, at you, the American people.

"The speech is one in which I call on all of you to end the Strike that John Glatt initiated in his now-famous Broadcast From the Moon. I am, supposedly, to call on you to restore America's reputation as a place of economic opportunity, religious tolerance, and racial understanding, and to cease and desist from pursuing our Strike goals of promoting poverty, bigotry, and racist hatred. But I am not going to do that."

Untitled

A blizzard blew an Eskimo
Way down to Egypt-land.
The Arabs had no word for snow
And he no word for sand.
They searched for years to find the com-
Mon thing that each man shares.
And there, beneath the swaying palm,
Announced that thing was bears.
Yes, bears, bears, bears, bears, bears, bears, bears,
Bears, bears, bears, bears, bears, bears,
Bears, bears, bears, bears, bears, bears, bears, bears,
Bears,   bears,   bears,   bears,   bears,   bears.

—Michael O'Donoghue

STEVE MARTIN
THE TELEVISION STUFF

Rare TV & Stand-up Specials from the Legendary Comedian on DVD for the First Time!

Over 6 Hours of Wild & Crazy Laughs on 3 DVDs!

BONUS EXTRAS INCLUDE:
- New Interviews with Steve Martin
- Famous Guest Appearances on *The Tonight Show with Johnny Carson*, *The Late Show with David Letterman* and *Saturday Night Live*
- A Collectible 24-Page Book and More!

Available at Movies & Music Locations

BARNES & NOBLE
BN.com

Suddenly alert to an ominous tone of defiance in Dragnie's voice, Banden sat up with an abrupt jerk, or tried to, but failed, and flopped backwards into the yielding, entrapping sack of pebbles.

"I am not going to do that, because to do that would be to compromise our highest value—that the poor be just as free in theory to become rich as the rich are free in reality to become richer. It would compromise our most cherished principle—that individuals collected into groups known as governments and unions represent mediocrity and are an unmitigated evil, while individuals collected into groups known as corporations represent the pinnacle of civilization.

"It would compromise our noblest foundational axioms of truth, which hold that existence exists whether it wants to or not, that everything is itself and so everything is everything, and that only tautologies offer the basis for an unchallengeable philosophy, because only tautologies are always true, because they have to be, which means that they are."

"Nathan, are you okay?" Angel was looking at him in concern. But it was the concern of the silly nitwit for the well-being of the superior man, and as such was of no consequence. "You have like this weird expression on your face."

"Just please," he replied, eyes fixed firmly on the television screen. "Please, I beg you, do whatever you can to shut up. She's...she's wonderful."

"You whose company manufactured those spontaneously combusting legal pads, whose products are no longer bought in the other nations of the world; you whose job consisted in packing and shipping fourteen-ounce jars of marinated okra, whose off-gassing vapors have proven toxic to all mammals, including Man; you who have spent your days delivering shipments of potassium-fiber bathing suits which explode upon contact with water: what'll you do now, you ask? Now that your companies have gone bankrupt and left you without income? We say: so long as you are conscious, you are alive. And we want you to live. We want you to remain conscious."

In the control room of the television studio, Mr. Jenkins cried to the technicians, "This isn't the speech she's supposed to give! Cut her off!"

The engineer, whose life, unlike that of the bureaucrat, was dedicated to the clean, pure pursuit of the utmost exactitude, said, "Not so fast, Mr. Jenkins. I want to hear what she has to say—and I have a hunch other people do, too!"

"It doesn't matter what she has to say, damn you!" he yelled. "Get her off the air!"

"This is my studio," the engineer said, gesturing with clean, economical gestures toward the clean, efficient instruments and technology. "And as long as you're broadcasting from my studio, you'll play by my rules."

"And now," Dragnie said into the camera, "I have an announcement to make. My announcement is that Mr. Jenkins and his bureaucrat thugs have taken me, John Glatt, and several of our colleagues as their prisoner. My announcement is that we are being held in an undisclosed location until you, the American people, end this Strike. But you must not end the Strike. Rather, if John Glatt and Sanfrancisco De Soto and Hunk Rawbone and I are not released within forty-eight hours from now, the consequences around the world will be dire. You, in the meantime, must continue to display openly your natural or learned enmity toward people of other races, creeds, and religions; you must continue to reject what had once been known as the American Dream, and its promise of upward mobility, and persevere in embracing a frightened acceptance of the American Nightmare, with its threat of total financial desolation; and you must continue to transform America from the hope of the world's peoples to the shame of all of Planet Earth. You must do this until our enemies capitulate, end this cruel embargo, and resume buying our admittedly occasionally hazardous barbecue sauces and radioactive typewriters. You must do this for the reason all true American patriots do whatever their leaders tell them to do: in the name of Freedom. As John Glatt himself once said while asking me to pass him the sour cream—"

But Dragnie was unable to continue. Mr. Jenkins strode out onto the studio and, live and on camera, pulled her out of her chair. "That's it!" he barked at the lens. "Show's over." He forced her off the set, away from the cameras and microphones. "I should have known better than to trust you," he hissed. "Well, you've dug your own grave. You and Glatt have had it. We're going to bury you in a military detention center and throw away the key."

"We'll see about that," Dragnie said

THE FIRST CHRISTMAS

Kimster

with a mysterious smile.

"What are you doing, Nathan?" Angel said after the special announcement had ended and normal broadcasting had resumed. The girl's attention, to the extent that it was not focused on trivial fancies and her own childish vanity, was caught by the sight of Nathan A. Banden suddenly squirming and lurching around within the grasp of the bright pink mass of plastic furniture, amorphous as a giant blob of bubble gum, in which he had lain, trapped.

"Leaving," Banden replied, and, summoning all his energies, competence, and purpose, pushed and hoisted and managed to lift himself up out of the beanbag chair and rise to his feet.

"Where are you going?" the girl inquired.

"Where I belong," he said, and left the apartment.

• Chapter Two •
To Have and Then Not to Have Any More

They returned Dragnie to her cell, a windowless cube with only a cot and a toilet, its door heavily barred. After several hours a guard appeared and announced that she had a visitor. The guard escorted her into a meeting room, where she was both astounded and utterly unsurprised to discover, waiting for her, Nathan A. Banden. He looked cowed and worn down, his normally crisp attire of khaki slacks and white dress shirt both wrinkled and unwashed. He looked as though he had not shaved in several days.

"Hello, Dragnie," he said.

"Hello, Nathan," she replied. "You're looking well."

"I?" Banden laughed bitterly, as if something were funny, not in a sweet way, but a bitter way. "I look ill-kempt and disreputable. You look great, though."

"Thank you."

"I...I saw you on TV," he said. "Do you...do you really think they'll let you go in forty-eight hours?"

"No."

"Then...then what will you do?"

"We'll see." She gazed at him coolly, evenly, with her eyes. "How did you find me here?"

"My father is a man of some influence," Banden replied. "In fact, that's one of the reasons I wished to see you. I...I want to apologize. And to beg you to forgive me. And to take me back. I was a fool to have betrayed you. I indulged in a fit of childish pique when you wouldn't let me accompany you to Glatt's Gorge. I felt as though you disdained my youth. And so I convinced myself, despite ample evidence to the contrary both historically and introspectively, that your age made you unattractive to me. I sought revenge for my wounded feelings by giving my attention to a younger woman—and in so doing, I behaved like a rotter. How I regret my impulsive actions! Oh, it is true that she is younger than you, and in that respect can be said to be 'prettier' in a girlish, fledgling way. But such immature comeliness can, in the end, only be of interest to the callow youth, the boy-man whose romanticized notions of what is attractive and desirable are as shallow, limited, and transitory as his experience in love's ways is primitive and half-baked. To the real man, to the true man, to the man of men, no manner of superficial maidenly prettiness can compare to the deep, feminine beauty of a mature woman who has encountered the world and bested it in the pursuit of her highest values. Yes, the body has its imperatives. Yes, the need for sexual activity is fundamental. But these imperatives and needs can be satisfied through the simplest mechanisms of sexual activity, with any passably desirable and compliant female. Beneath the body, however, is the spirit. I refer, of course, to the human spirit, since we, the two of us, spend our existence as human beings. It, too—the human spirit—asserts a repertoire of needs, but its requirements and criteria are orders of magnitude more profound, more demanding, and more important than those of mere adolescent physicality. It is those—as well as the more superficial but no less pleasurable needs—whose satisfaction I found with you, Dragnie. It is those which I must resume. It is those which you must vouchsafe to me again, now and forever more. Will you, dearest? Will you forgive my foolish transgression and allow me to worship and adore you as you deserve to be worshipped and adored—by a young, hyper-potent lover with a brilliant intellectual future ahead of him?"

"No."

"I--What?"

"No."

"But…but you have to! I am young and virile, brilliant and energetic, vibrant and handsome and bursting with potential! I am eighteen! You are forty-three!" For a moment he was at a loss for words. Then he added, "This is a good deal for you! Plus, my father can get you out of jail!"

"Nathan," she said. And she said it quietly, calmly, without rancor or hostility, without resentment or feelings of betrayal or the desire for revenge. "How did the government's men know where John and I were holding that dinner party?"

He blanched, and a look of terror appeared as an expression on the face of his head. "I…how should I know…"

"You told them, didn't you?"

"Yes!" he sobbed. "Because you were making fun of us! Not just of her! But of me! Your sophisticated friends, the men and women of achievement with whom you socialize, treated us with mockery and contempt and sneering derision! Why? Why, Dragnie, why?"

"They treated you as you presented yourself to be treated. As a high school student with a silly girlfriend, out of your league and in over your head."

He started, stunned. And then a look of shrewd calculation replaced the expression of dismay. "Wait a minute," he said. "Why're you being so cruel to me? Can it be that you're…jealous? Ha ha ha ha! The great Dragnie Tagbord, jealous of a silly, unworldly girl—who, by definition, is no threat to you. You can't possibly imagine I find with her the kind of communion of kindred souls I find with you. What, then, is there to be jealous of? Mere sex? Does John Glatt behave this way? Is he jealous of me? Of course not. He knows I'm no threat to him. But you, who're supposedly his female equivalent; you, who're just as devoted as he is to only the highest codes of standards of ethics of the values of the behavior of principle of the meaning of life in the awareness of the human mind!; you, who're committed to being so entirely conscious and rational about everything all the time: you're jealous of a teenage girl named Angel Human! Ha ha ha ha! How amusing. How hypocritical. How…irrational!"

He thought, she could tell, that he had blocked her. He thought he had thwarted her. He thought he had won. But when she replied, it was without defiance, without heat, without self-congratulation.

"Jealous? I?" She smiled. "I assure you, I am not jealous."

"That's what you say. That's your mere subjective opinion."

"No, it's an objective fact." From a pocket in her prison jumpsuit Dragnie produced a piece of paper. It was a standard sheet of typescript, folded in quarters, and when unfolded revealed a paragraph of typed text above a series of signatures. "I have here an affidavit attesting to the fact that I am not jealous, either of you or of your little girlfriend. It is not only signed by me, which would be of no significance, but it is also signed by other people. It therefore can be said to establish an objective fact." She handed the sheet to him and watched as he perused it, as he squinted at the signatures of John Glatt, Hunk Rawbone, Sanfrancisco De Soto, and several others. "It is the first principle of Objectivismism: my friends all agree with me, which means that I'm right," she said. "That is why it is important to surround yourself with people who believe what you believe. So they can help you create your reality. And that is why I can no longer allow you around me."

She could see his defiance and confidence ebb, leaving behind the dispirited, defeated shell of a young man suddenly aware of his inability to live up to his own greatness—and to hers.

"You win, Dragnie," he muttered. "You were and are too much for me. I now realize that, even sexually, you are more desirable than Angel. As for intellectually, existentially, and psychoepistemologically, well, there is no comparison." He handed her the paper and stood up. "Goodbye, Dragnie. I will never forget you, nor how superior you are to every other woman in the world."

• Chapter Three •
It Is Your Thing; You Do What You Want to Do

For two days, the world held its anxious, worried breath. Neither Dragnie, nor John Glatt, nor any of the other prisoners were released by Mr. Jenkins from captivity. The embargo decreed by the People's States of the People remained in effect; the Strike called by Glatt also remained in effect. The state of war declared by the People's States continued, albeit with no clear manifestations or acts of military hostility.

By then, Nathan A. Banden had reconciled himself to having lost Dragnie forever and, as is typical of such men when they can no longer find approval in the eyes of the best of women, he contented himself with the attentions of a lesser woman. Having relinquished all thoughts of college, he spent the day in the apartment of Angel Human, mired in the bright pink beanbag chair, watching the television. It was in this manner, therefore, that he was able to monitor the events of that convulsive day which would come to be known to men as Takeover Two.

Two days after Dragnie's televised speech, at nine o'clock in the morning, Eastern Standard Time, in a nondescript area of the Bronx, a plain panel van pulled up before an unidentified building. Out of it emerged an armed squadron of strikingly beautiful Swedish pirates. They quickly overwhelmed the guards both outside and inside the facility, and moments later escorted Dragnie Tagbord, Hunk Rawbone, Sanfrancisco De Soto, and John Glatt out of the building and into the truck, and drove off. Astonishingly, this entire event was broadcast live on national television, as cameras and news crews, consisting of self-loathing "on-air reporters" whose sole concern was the dissemination of celebrity gossip, political scandals of the most sordid kind, stories of local crime and corruption, and sentimental "human interest" melodramas, were on hand. Nathan A. Banden therefore, by sheer happenstance, was able to watch, live, the rescue of the woman he had so selfishly, immaturely, and rotterishly betrayed.

A news helicopter was present to follow the escape van as it drove to a hidden airfield, where its passengers (except for the really quite fantastically lovely Swedish pirates) debarked and boarded a small private plane, which took off immediately. A news plane gave chase and broadcast to an astounded world the escapees' flight to Wyoming. There Glatt's plane descended through what proved to be an illusory visual projection depicting wild mountain crags, to land on a verdant meadow below. The news crew, unsure of its ability to land safely in pursuit of the story, radioed to the nearest city, where a vertical-take-off-and-landing news jet was scrambled. This aircraft rendezvoused over Glatt's Gorge—for such was the location where Glatt's plane had landed—and successfully touched down at the air strip below. The jet's news crew was therefore able to broadcast what transpired next.

A squadron of small, sleek, two-man jets taxied out of a heretofore hidden hangar and took off. Their destinations, men would later learn, were the capitals of the world. Each of them was armed with three things: A "ray gun" that emitted a modulated sort of radiation which, when its waves passed through the human brain, had the effect of making the subject feel deeply ashamed of himself; these were protected by a kind of shield made of a metal no man had seen before, which was able, when attacked by ordnance, bombs, or missiles, not only to deflect the incoming round but literally to reverse its course and send it back against the device that had shot it.

Finally, each of the small jets was equipped with a series of non-lethal bombs which, when exploded over government buildings, released a cloud of fine-particulate talc-based chemicals that caused the officials in their blast radius, and their academic toadies and corrupted shills in the press, to acquire an immediate and intense dislike of collectivism, and to yearn instead for freedom.

All of this unfolded as Banden, and a billion other people in nations all over the globe, watched. On-air analysts speculated—accurately, it later emerged—that the jets and the "shame ray" were the inventions of John Glatt,

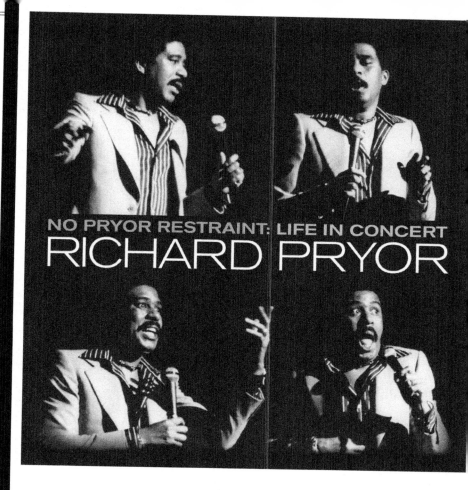

The Dairy of Anne Frank

the explosive-deflection metal the creation of Hunk Rawbone, the anti-collectivization powder the product of Sanfrancisco Nabisco Alcoa D'Lightful D'Lovely De Soto, and the personnel, both in the jets and coordinating their movements from the ground, were under the direction of Regnad Daghammarskjold, the notably handsome Swedish pirate.

The results of this unprecedented action were swift and decisive. As announced that afternoon on television by Dragnie Tagbord, who functioned as the liaison between the Glatt forces and the public, within five hours half the nations of the world reported that their civilian populations were thoroughly embarrassed by everything they had done, beginning with opting for the collectivism of the People's States of the People and up to and including the recent embargo. Mass demonstrations erupted in national capitals around the globe, at which expressions of shame and abasement alternated with demands for capitalism, individualism, and a free market. Guarantees of a well-maintained public sphere, safeguards of a clean environment, provision of affordable medical care, assurance of a quality

elementary and secondary education, and the protection of an old age marked by dignity and respect, were universally denounced as being "socialistic" and "parasitic." Within twelve hours of the initial jet sorties, a wholesale rejection of collectivism and an avid embrace of corporatism had firmly taken hold in every nation on earth except Goa.

The response of the government of the United States was equally decisive. Mr. Jenkins went on the air, not only to formally resign, but to fire his entire administration. This had the effect of eliminating what few skeletal remnants still existed of the original Executive, Legislative, and Judicial systems. Over the course of two days, all of the Federal government withered away, followed by the various state governments—a transition formalized by an old man named Judge Rapahannock, who took a gift-shop copy of the Constitution and scratched it out.

Nathan A. Banden watched all this on television while dressed in pajamas and a bathrobe, leaving his beanbag chair in Angel's apartment only to attend to bodily functions and insisting she bring him meals. Three days after the initial escape by Glatt and the oth-

ers, he was still watching the historical events unfold. He had viewed footage from all over the world of rioting mobs of citizens transformed, by the arrival of freedom, into swarms of jubilant consumers. He had watched the interviews with Glatt, Rawbone, De Soto, and Daghammarskjold. He had watched Dragnie conduct three press conferences. He had watched coverage of victory parades in Washington, D.C., Los Angeles, Chicago, San Francisco, Atlanta, Dallas, and Seattle. He had watched as high government officials such as Francis Pissypants and T.T. Mucklicker had dodged reporters and muttered "no comment" and generally sought to avoid confrontation with the nation's, and the world's, radiant new reality.

It was while he was watching coverage of the parade down New York's Fifth Avenue that he realized that Angel Human was not in the apartment. Compelled to prepare his own bowl of cereal, he was leaning against the kitchen counter when she burst into the flat. She was exhilarated and breathless.

"Isn't it neat, Nathan?" she gasped happily.

"Isn't what neat?"

"Everything! What John Glatt and

those guys did! I just came back to get my camera. Somebody saw Dragnie Tagbord up the street and I want to get a picture of her! She's so fantastic! It's a shame you weren't man enough to keep her." She seized her camera from a coffee table and ran out.

Banden heard a familiar voice emanating from the television.

"Ladies and gentlemen of Earth, it is my pleasure to announce that Goa has capitulated." It was a voice he had heard over the course of many nights, as a train had roared into the darkness along gleaming, vitamin-rich rails of Rawbonium, its two principle passengers escorting each other into the realm of ecstasy and creating, with that voice and with his, the sounds of attack, conquest, surrender, hatred, fury, triumph, and subjugation. "It is also my pleasure to announce that, as of twelve noon tomorrow, Eastern Standard Time, this nation shall be formally known as the Incorporated States of America."

Banden put the milk back in the refrigerator and carefully closed its door. He shuffled into the bedroom and emerged with his belt. Hoisting the noisy, plastic beanbag chair, he squeezed its central section until he had reduced its volume by half. He then plunged his face into the resulting bulge above the narrowed part and, with some difficulty, lashed the furniture to his head with the belt. It did not occur to him to change his mind. It did not occur to him to attempt to undo the belt. It did not occur to him to claw his way out of the asphyxiating grip he had contrived for the pink plastic object.

Angel found him two hours later, his skin a necrotic white against the bubble-gum floridity of the clammy, suffocating bag.

• Chapter Four •
That This Triumph Shall Be A Victory of the Winners

The coronation of John Glatt as King of the Earth took place at a ceremony two weeks after the capitulation of Goa and the final consolidation of Takeover Two. It was held in New York's most elegant and important concert hall, and beamed to television sets all over the world. In his remarks, Glatt thanked Rawbone, De Soto, Daghammarskjold, and Dragnie, all of whom would serve on the Committee to Control the World for lifelong terms.

Glatt's speech lasted four hours, and touched on a number of important topics, including the history of mankind, the importance of logic, the vision of Man as a heroic being, and how the free market would, henceforth, solve all of humanity's problems. As the speech was nearing its conclusion Dragnie, standing in the wings and gazing on in proud delight, spotted a familiar face.

It was Edward G. Willikers, the classmate of Nathan A. Banden whom she had met several months—and a lifetime—before, at the Glatt School. She motioned for him to join her.

"Hello, Eddie," Dragnie said. "Don't tell me you're on the stage crew here, too."

"Hi, Miss Tagbord," the boy said. "Yeah, I'm just helping out for the summer."

Dragnie found herself revising her characterization of him, for he no longer resembled a mere boy. "You look different, Eddie," she said. "How've you changed?"

"I'm growing my hair long," he said. "All the guys are doing it." He indicated Glatt, out on the stage, still speaking. "Gosh, Mister Glatt is wonderful, isn't he?"

"He certainly is, Eddie. Also…are you growing a beard?"

"Trying to," he chuckled. "But all of you guys are great," the youth continued. "Mr. Rawbone, Mr. De Soto…even that Regnad guy, the strikingly beautiful Swiss pirate."

"Swedish. The Swiss have no coastline."

"Oh. Yeah." The young man shrugged. "I get 'em mixed up. And you, too, Miss Tagbord. You're really great. Men are saying that you guys are about the greatest people who ever lived."

"Thank you, Eddie. But if you've been listening to Mr. Glatt's speech, you know that he says that everyone can be a hero just like him. That means you can, too."

"I know, but…" The young man hesitated. "Miss Tagbord? There's a few things I don't understand."

"Like what, Eddie?"

"Well, like, what Mr. Glatt said in his speech two hours ago. He said, 'Our conception of Man is as a heroic being, who lives purely for himself. Who asks no other man to do anything on his behalf, and who will do nothing on behalf of another man.' Did I get that right?"

Dragnie smiled. "Yes, you quoted it perfectly."

"It's not a Republican leaf or a Democratic leaf. It's just a leaf."

"But the thing is, Miss Tagbord, you can't be a hero and live only for yourself. That's not what a hero does. A hero does things for the sake of others. That's what makes him a hero, and not just some guy doing stuff for himself, like everybody else."

"Well, I suppose it depends—"

"And another thing. Mr. Glatt said, 'We call on Man to live solely in the light of logic, undistracted and unimpeded by fear, shame, anger, hatred, and, yes, even love, obligation, loyalty, altruism, sacrifice, and any of the other subjective atavisms that have for millennia distorted Man's true purpose.'"

"You have a good memory, Eddie. Yes, you see—"

"The thing is, Miss Tagbord, you can't really be a hero unless you feel fear. Heroism isn't when you do something that's no big deal. It's when you're afraid of something that might bring harm to yourself, but you do it anyway."

"Well, of course you're capable of feeling fear. What Mr. Glatt means is, we admire most the superior man who has no feeling for others—not because he chooses not to, but because he lacks the capacity for it. He is completely unmoved by others' pleasure, or pain, or suffering, or happiness, because he lives entirely for himself, above the plane of the mediocre herd."

"But...well, gee, Miss Tagbord, what's the difference between that kind of person and a whatchamacallit, that we talked about in social studies?"

"A laissez-faire capitalist?"

"A sociopath."

Dragnie chuckled. "Be careful using that word, Eddie. Just because a superior man's complete independence of spirit makes it impossible for him to have feelings for any another man, doesn't mean he's a 'sociopath.' The sociopath has an urge to defy society, so he kidnaps a young girl, kills her, and chops up her body. The superior man, while perhaps admiring the sociopath's freedom from societal constraint, knows that such an act is not necessary—however much one might admire the principle of freedom as an absolute that lies behind it."

Eddie Willikers looked dubious. "I could never be like that."

"Sure you could! You just have to study these ideas, understand the truth of them, and then apply them to your daily life."

"But that doesn't make any sense!"

"It makes nothing but sense," Dragnie smiled. "Try this, next time you go out into society. Don't let feelings influence your actions. Just base your actions on logic. You'll see. It's easier than you think!"

"But isn't that...you know...crazy?"

"I hardly think—"

"Everything we do begins and ends with feelings. Fathers go to work because they feel responsible for their families. Mothers take care of their kids because they love them. You know what that's like, right? You have kids, don't you?"

"No."

"Oh. Well, anyway, that's the basis of every human society throughout, like, history. Parents sacrifice their own desires for the sake of their children. That's what Nature requires, Miss Tagbord. Otherwise, offspring would never—you know—survive. Sure, you use logic to solve problems. And you can say that if you base everything on feelings, you're like an animal. But if you eliminate feelings completely, and base everything on logic, you're not heroic. You're not even human."

"Eddie, tell me something." Dragnie fixed the young man with a commanding stare. "Who is John Glatt?"

"Huh?" He pointed out onto the stage. "He is."

"No, Eddie. True, that man's name is John Glatt, and he is being crowned the King of the Earth. And these are the values he's lived by. But we can live by those values, too. We can be just as great as he is. Who is John Glatt? You are. I am. We are all John Glatt."

Eddie Willikers frowned and scratched his head in puzzlement. "Well, but, gosh, Miss Tagbord, no we're not."

"Well, I mean, not literally. But—"

"Not at all. John Glatt invented that electric power motor, and those anti-gravity shoes, and that shame ray, and that concealing projector over Glatt's Gorge—oh, and those neat teleportation arches. Plus probably other stuff I don't even know about. He created all these fantastic new devices. That's got nothing to do with his values. Anyone can have those values, but it doesn't mean they're a genius inventor. Same thing with Mister Rawbone. He isn't rich and powerful because of his values. He invented Rawbonium. That's not me. I'm not John Glatt. I'm just some kid who graduated high school and is going into college in the fall."

Dragnie paused. On the edge of the mind of her consciousness she recognized that Glatt was at that moment reading the last several lines of his speech. In a moment the hall would be filled with thunderous applause, and swarming reporters, and dignitaries frantic to have their photos taken with Glatt and the others. Her private moment with this young man would be shattered forever. She simply did not have the time, now, to correct his misapprehensions, to recommend that he surround himself with people who believed in the truth, as she did, as Glatt did, as Rawbone and De Soto and the other members of their circle did. She did not have the time to draw the fine distinction, so crucial to her values, between the perfect man and a sociopathic murderer. She did not have the time, just now, to correct Eddie's premises. But she sensed, behind his rather appealing looks, an intelligence simmering with potential.

"You know, Eddie," she said. "These questions you're asking—they're excellent questions. I'd love to discuss them more with you. So let me make a suggestion. Now that Mr. Glatt has been named King of the Earth, he and I are going to need a private assistant. I think you would make an excellent candidate to fill that job. Of course it would require putting off college for a few months, and living with us...but would that interest you?"

"Really?" The young man look stunned. "Well, yeah. Of course. But my parents—"

"I'll talk to your parents."

Out on the stage, John Glatt said, "...as we inaugurate a new era in human society: the New, Improved Era of the Producer, and the Rest of the Human Race, Who Help Him." And with that, he raised his hand, and made a gesture outlining the sign of the dollar, and the exclamation mark, articulating its final dot with a pointed finger and an outthrust arm.

SHADY MANOR INN QUESTIONNAIRE

Dear Guest,
Thank you for staying with us. Please take a moment to fill out the following survey. How did you hear about the Shady Manor Inn? Check all that apply.
_ Saw billboard
_ Read about us in guidebook
_ Read about us in *Journal of Paranormal Activity*
_ Heard voices telling you to "go to the inn," that it was "time to go to the inn"
_ Ordered to spend one night at the inn in order to receive large inheritance from eccentric relative
_ Followed friends into the inn after they went inside to have pre-marital sex and did not return
_ Directed to inn by old man at abandoned gas station, who cryptically laughed when you asked what your stay would "cost"
_ Dragged here physically
_ Yelp

—SIMON RICH

BY DAVID ETKIN

OUR COFFEE IS THE BEST

Jimmy's Diner will no longer be silent

Our coffee is the best. Disregard what you have heard from others. Forget what you think you know about the best coffee in the world. Our coffee is the best!

IT IS BETTER than the coffee your mother makes when you go home.

IT IS BETTER than the coffee they serve the president when he wakes up and demands "the best coffee!"

IT IS FAR BETTER than the coffee consumed by the owner of a coffee plantation in Jamaica widely renowned for producing the finest beans in the world, even though he has his roasters give him the freshest, most select beans upon pain of death and then he observes his valet/barista Gorky grind them to perfection in a burr grinder—not a despicable blade grinder which would heat the beans to undesirable temperatures and thus damage their precious, delicate oils—and then soaks them oh-so-lovingly in triple-filtered artesian well water imported from a distant country very well known for producing water that makes terrific coffee; and even though this perfectly ground bean is soaked in this perfect water (which has been heated to the perfect range of 196-206 degrees Fahrenheit) in a perfect French press (which does make the best cup of coffee, especially if you drink it black which is the only sane way to drink a truly fine cup of coffee) and poured in

such a way that something in Gorky's wrist action actually makes it taste even better, even though all of this is done this coffee tastes like a cup full of tepid tar when compared to the coffee which we brew here at Jimmy's Diner.

We do it! We brew the finest, most world-shattering cup of coffee in the entire world and we who staff Jimmy's Diner will no longer hide that unwavering beacon of light under a bushel! We are tired of the Smile Deli and the cloyingly named Sugarcube Café and the irritating bundle of swagger who slings singed beans to empty-eyed corporate suits out of a squeaky-wheeled pushcart trying to lay simultaneous claim to a title which

common sense dictates can only be honestly applied to one entity, and which your palate should and will dictate can only be applied to we few, we happy few here at Jimmy's Diner, no matter what libelous claims are foisted upon a gullible public via signage posted at these and other wretched monuments to self-aggrandizing, megalomaniacal excess and hyperbole. Jimmy's Diner has no sign, because our coffee does not require one! The truth needs no agent. Justice does not rely on good P.R.! Jimmy's Diner coffee speaks to you from our kitchen, heralding its rightful title to your nose long before our simple white mug is presented to your palate. Sip it once and be transported to a place beyond all care, to the place where Plato posited that the perfect, conceptual ideals, of which all the physical world is merely a shadow, exist. Sip it once and look me in the eye and if you do not instantly sing a glorious hymn to Jimmy's Diner coffee then you must snuff out my life for everything I have ever known is a lie!

Also, we make very, very good carrot cake. 🐧

DAVID ETKIN

David Etkin is a drinker with a writing problem. No, wait, that was Bukowski. David is a writer with a plagiarism problem. Just kidding — he's not a writer. He's an editor living in New York City.

BY DENNIS PERRIN

NOTES FROM "JANITORGOD"

"It'll be the end of everything." "Exactly," he suddenly smiles

*"**Janitorgod** covers my 40s," Dennis Perrin wrote, "when my wife, kids and I moved to Ann Arbor after going into tax debt in NYC. This was a year after **Mr. Mike** came out, but I couldn't find any writing/editing jobs, so I went back to blue collar work. And there I remained for the better part of a decade... When people say to me, 'Oh, Ann Arbor! That's such a cool, fun town!' I usually shoot back, 'Not when you have to clean it.'"*

.... ◆ ....

Cleaning companies have regular turnover, which makes sense. Shit job. There's always an opening.

I apply at Patriot Clean. Their ad is direct, as if standing at attention. Their offices are just outside of Ann Arbor. Downstairs, rows of folding chairs in front of what resembles a pulpit. Upstairs, smaller offices and a large classroom. On the walls, placards read U.S. OUT OF THE U.N. and JOE MCCARTHY WAS RIGHT. A magazine cover warns of Chinese drug dealers from Mexico.

These cats are serious. They're the cleaning wing of the John Birch Society. *The* John Birch Society.

One owner, Bill, thick gray beard, short gray hair, gives me an application to fill out. He wears a large anti-abortion button on a plaid shirt; a fetus in a garbage can. Is Planned Parenthood one of their clients?

Bill is friendly. He smiles, ushers me in to see his co-owner, Jim, who sits rigidly. He looks 20 years younger than Bill, clean cut, all-American stereotype. His movements are deliberate and staged. Jim crisply asks me questions. He doesn't smile, doesn't probe my political views. He's more concerned with my stamina.

"How's your back?" Jim asks.

"My back? It still seems to work."

"Good, because the back's the first thing to go."

Looking at Patriot's offices, you'd think it's the mind.

He likes that I don't fit the cleaner image. He says it will help calm clients made nervous by darker people in their work space, at night, with keys and alarm codes. All of this should alarm me, but I need the job and, I'll confess, I'm intrigued. Jim offers and I accept. I start the next night.

The Birchers show me their chemical warehouse, a small space crammed with ammonia, bleach, acid, and other agents doubtless banned by the Geneva Convention. Bircher Jim quietly explains what each chemical does, how it should be used, and how to water it down to save money. Bircher Bill nods along, saying "That's right," as if in church.

The Birchers are seriously stocked. They'll be able to clean well into the End Times; and given their connection to God, they may dominate the post-apocalyptic cleaning market as well.

Occasionally, Bircher Bill shows up while I'm working. He offers tips I don't need, but he's so damn nice that I play along.

Bill attempts to modify my toilet cleaning technique. There aren't that many ways to clean a toilet, but Bill believes he's found an inside track.

"Instead of swirling the Johnny mop in the basin, use short, hard strokes. That breaks up the dried fecal matter. Also, when you're finished, leave the seat down."

"I prefer leaving the seat up," I reply with strange confidence. "That way the customer can see that both sides are clean."

"Hmmm," says Bill, pulling on his beard. "I can see that, sure. But we usually leave the seat down."

I'm sure that most cleaners do, because most cleaners ignore the seat's bottom where the majority of shit resides. But I simply say, "Leaving the seat up has worked for me. I think it'll work for Patriot."

Bill brightens. "Well, okay then!" he says, shaking my hand. "The seats stay up!"

Bircher Bill wears an anti-gay marriage button which delights me, seeing how we're standing together in a men's stall. Maybe in another life.

My body continues to change, slowly, steadily, obviously. Genes, booze, work. Mostly work. That alters everything.

Men in my family become barrel shaped. They drink eat party, hence the look. This comes later to me. I'd avoided booze forever, until an old friend dosed me with gin. I loved it -- detachment, warmth, buzzy high crazy.

Booze steadily feeds me. Conditions me. I follow its promise. When I drink, I sing with my ancestors. Drunk, I howl at clouds. My bloodline comes to life. I finally see that true sadness. As sweet as that sadness is, I want to push past it. Ruin it. Crush it. I desire oblivion, erasure, a liquid bullet to the brain.

Warm highs anger me. I'm not worthy of such delicacy. As a kid, I'd break any-

DENNIS PERRIN *(@DennisThePerrin) is the author of* **Mr. Mike**, **American Fan**, *and* **Savage Mules**. *He's written for television, advertising, and many fine publications, including this one. This is from his next book.*

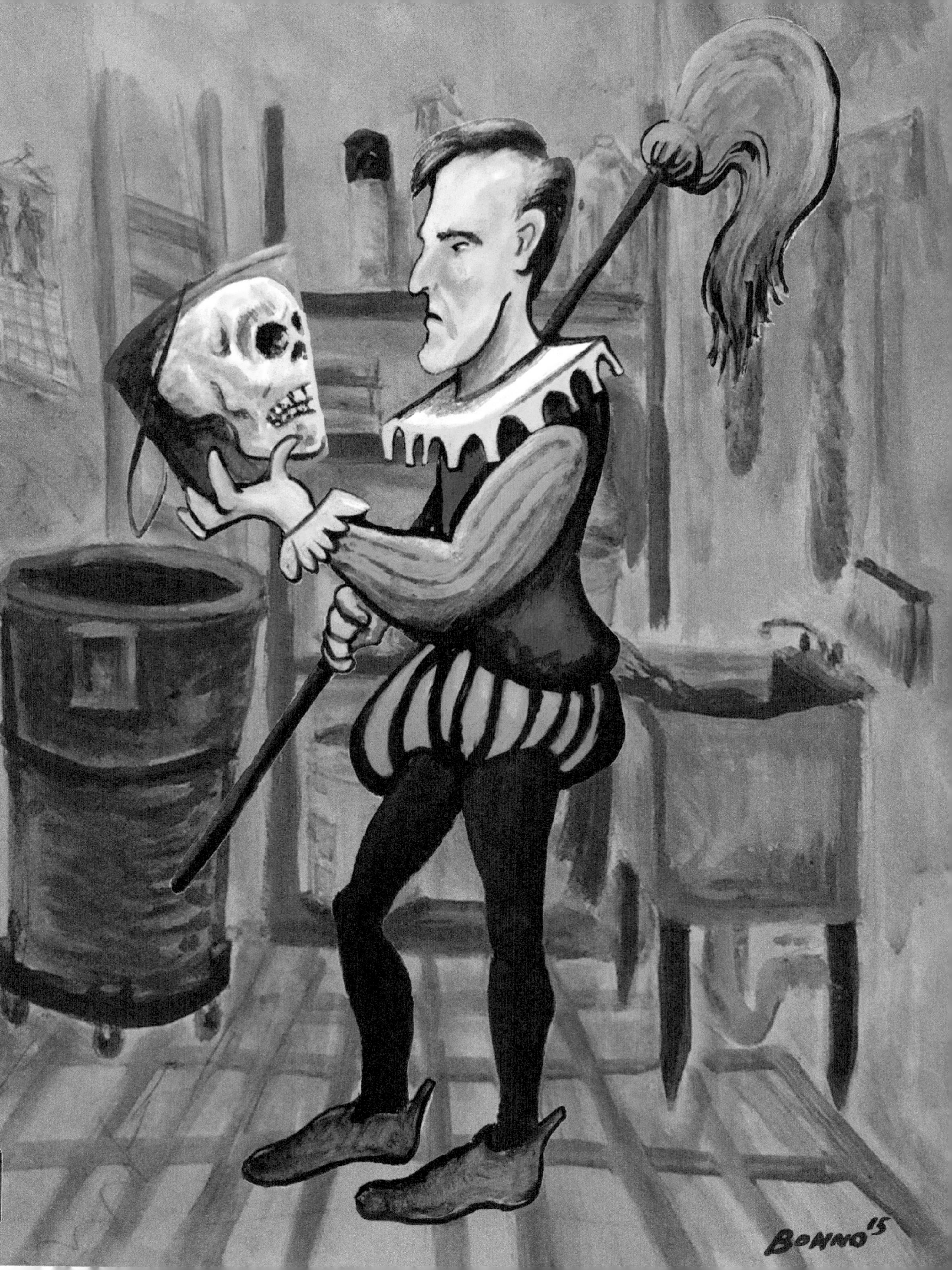
BONNO'15

CHRIS BONNO

thing fragile, just to prove its fragility. I understood subtlety, which made me despise it. The slightest thing would set me off.

Perhaps that's why it took so long for me to drink. Something inside of me knew. Once I entered that world, I'd see all the patterns, all the mistaken beauty. And then I'd have to destroy it.

Like jumping off a building because you can.

Late night inspection in the trucking company building. After several fits and starts, and two firings, the cleaners seem to have it down. The floors look good. Cubicle tops dusted, no missed trash. Another minor reprieve until tomorrow night.

I turn off the big lights. Smaller lights remain on, giving the place a shadowy look. Rows and rows of empty cubicles in the semi-dark. You can feel the residual energy from the workday, mostly anxiety and boredom. Hushed voices penned in together, salty snacks eaten in solitude.

Walking through a building late at night connects you with various ghosts. There's a certain calm to it. There are nights when I let it soak into me, lean against a darkened wall, hear myself breathe against the silence.

Occasionally, without notice, Bircher Jim shows up. He sees me in the shadows, waves as if we're friends. Officially, he appears to see if I have the building under control. But what he really desires is conversation.

We talk about other buildings, possible contracts, cleaning supplies. Empty bullshit I can do without, but I humor him. When Jim turns to politics, he holds my attention. His bizarre theories break the job's monotony. It helps that I know most of the history that Jim takes as scripture.

His eyes widen when I speak about the origins of the New Right, name names, parse ideologies, affix dates. This, I suppose, breaks his monotony.

"Surely you're worried about the Chinese?" Jim asks me.

"In what way?"

"They're taking over the world. And we're next."

"Well, China does pump a lot of money into our economy."

"Exactly!" Jim nearly leaps. "They're softening us up for the big push."

"And what would that be?"

"Invasion and occupation."

I laugh. "You can't be serious."

"Oh, it's happening," Jim confides as if he's sharing a deadly secret. "George Washington predicted it."

Pause.

"Washington predicted a Chinese invasion of the United States?"

"Yes. You don't know about that? You seem pretty well-read."

Long breath.

"Well, look at the bright side: Michigan will finally get decent Chinese food."

Jim chuckles, but he's guarded. He knows I'm not taking him seriously, even though he's trying to warn me about our grim, Asian-dominated future.

"You done here?" he asks, back in official mode.

"Yep."

Jim looks around. "Building looks good."

Yes, the building looks good, though I've felt better.

The contracting company hires security guards to protect the cubicles overnight. A mini-command center is set up in the lobby. Two guards alternate nights, each with his own crime-stopping method.

The younger guy, a little plump, takes his responsibilities seriously. He checks the locks on the office doors hourly. Records his thoughts on a tiny tape machine. He strides in a character known only to him. Says little, behaves officially.

Sweeping and mopping the lobby one night, I see him leap from his desk chair. He swiftly turns to me.

"Did you see that?" he asks excitedly.

"See what?"

"Out there!" He points to the glass doors. "There was some kind of movement. Someone's on foot."

I see nothing but empty parking spaces.

"Maybe it's ninjas," I offer. "Though if they were any good, you wouldn't see them."

The guard ignores me. He speaks into his tape machine, marks the time, then marches to the doors.

"Stay here," he instructs me. "I'm going to check the perimeter."

"The perimeter?" I reply. "You mean the parking lot?"

The guard signals me to be silent. He pulls out a tiny baton and creeps slowly outside.

I don't see him for an hour. I go back to the janitor's closet, dump dirty mop water down the slop sink drain, grab my jacket and lock it all up. I reenter the lobby. He's back at his desk, jotting notes.

"All clear?" I ask.

He glances up. "For now. But something's going on. I can feel it."

I shrug. "Well, good luck."

"Be careful out there," he says as I leave the building.

I think about falling to the pavement as if I'd been shot. But why pretend?

The other guard is older, more resigned. He likes the job because he can read and think. He makes his rounds at a relaxed pace, returns to the desk and his classical music station.

We chat now and then, mostly when I clean the lobby. He is a gentle cynic; distrustful of humans; soft on animals. He believes that reality is mystically shaped. The mind can alter anything.

He tells me about a woman who could mentally slow munitions, create pauses between explosions and debris. Enough time to save people. Added time to see through time.

"Her mind was so strong," he says. "It made the inevitable less so."

I lean on my mop handle and smile. I like his stories. His sincerity makes them plausible.

He takes dark turns. One night he appears drained. Gray face fallen, and sad.

"We won't kill ourselves accidentally," he says. "It'll be intentional and conscious. It will be the end of fear and hatred."

"It'll be the end of everything."

"Exactly," he suddenly smiles.

Maybe he is crazy. Or a doorway to something unseen. But he doesn't seem wrong. After several months, he quits, wants to try something else. He's replaced by a young woman fascinated with swords.

JOHN WILCOCK: NEW YORK YEARS

A SAMPLER-PACK of stories for the AMERICAN BYSTANDER

Since 2012, cartoonists Ethan Persoff and Scott Marshall have been collaborating on an extensive interview project with John Wilcock, an underground publisher of the 1960s.

The graphic novel biography, now in its eighth chapter, focuses a year-at-a-time on Wilcock's interesting and largely undocumented life, from co-founding the Village Voice in 1955, to becoming a member of Andy Warhol's Factory in the early Sixties, establishing the Underground Press Syndicate, and other interesting moments, until Wilcock left NYC in 1972.

The following is a small sampler of stories, compiled especially for the premiere issue of The American Bystander.

For more information on the Wilcock comic book, visit http://www.ep.tc/john-wilcock

DRUG MEMORIES OF 1961

1. MESCALINE via Air Mail

It's Legal, KIDS!

An auspicious scan of a mail-order catalog led me to a brief romance with Mescaline - EASILY and LEGALLY available from L. Light & Co, a British pharmaceutical. Brown bottles (one-gram) were $6, shipped by airmail.

But mescaline was a mere DALLIANCE when compared to the drug that I would ultimately use my entire life — POT. So, it's with gratitude I recall, in 1961:

2. My good friend SEYMOUR KRIM GIVES ME MY FIRST JOINT!

COUGH!!!

Puff it up, Johnny!

oh man this is nicer than EVERYTHING..

Good ol' Krim is one of the most UNKNOWN writers of the BEAT ERA, btw. Read "MAKING IT", a LIVELY bit of writing.

3. Pot's Aromatic SMELL AND THE ONE GOOD YEAR OF UN-INFORMED COPS

HEY, Put that CIGARETTE out!

4. THE SHOW GOES ON

one of the most rewarding places to smoke in public was in the lobby of Broadway theatres during intermission.

Is that a MENTHOL?

Turkish Cigar!

BA-DING!

an evening encounter with Leroi Jones

One night, I was a little glum, but invited to a party at a friend's apartment. Just the antidote for my blues. The special guest was LEROI JONES ... the POET!

JONES HAD JUST BEGUN publishing a magazine called YUGEN, a publication full of beat writers, including Kerouac, Ginsberg, Corso & Burroughs.

LEROI...I must say, I love YUGEN! I was in the worst mood, having just returned from Mexico, and --

Oh! You just **LEFT THIS COUNTRY?**

y-Yes, but I was going to say --

ONE 'THESE DAYS, You're going to return and **NONE OF THIS** is going to **BE HERE!!!**

bang!

So...THE PARTY DIDN'T WORK. And with depression still guiding my worst instincts, I headed for the GENTLEMEN'S CLUBS FOR SOME BURLESQUE.

Hi, boys

A notable MOMENT from that night: the one & only GYPSY ROSE LEE, who slowly pulled off a long glove ... in a tantalizing, gorgeous tease ... that ... STOPPED ... TIME.

I was in an INFINITELY better mood AFTER THAT!

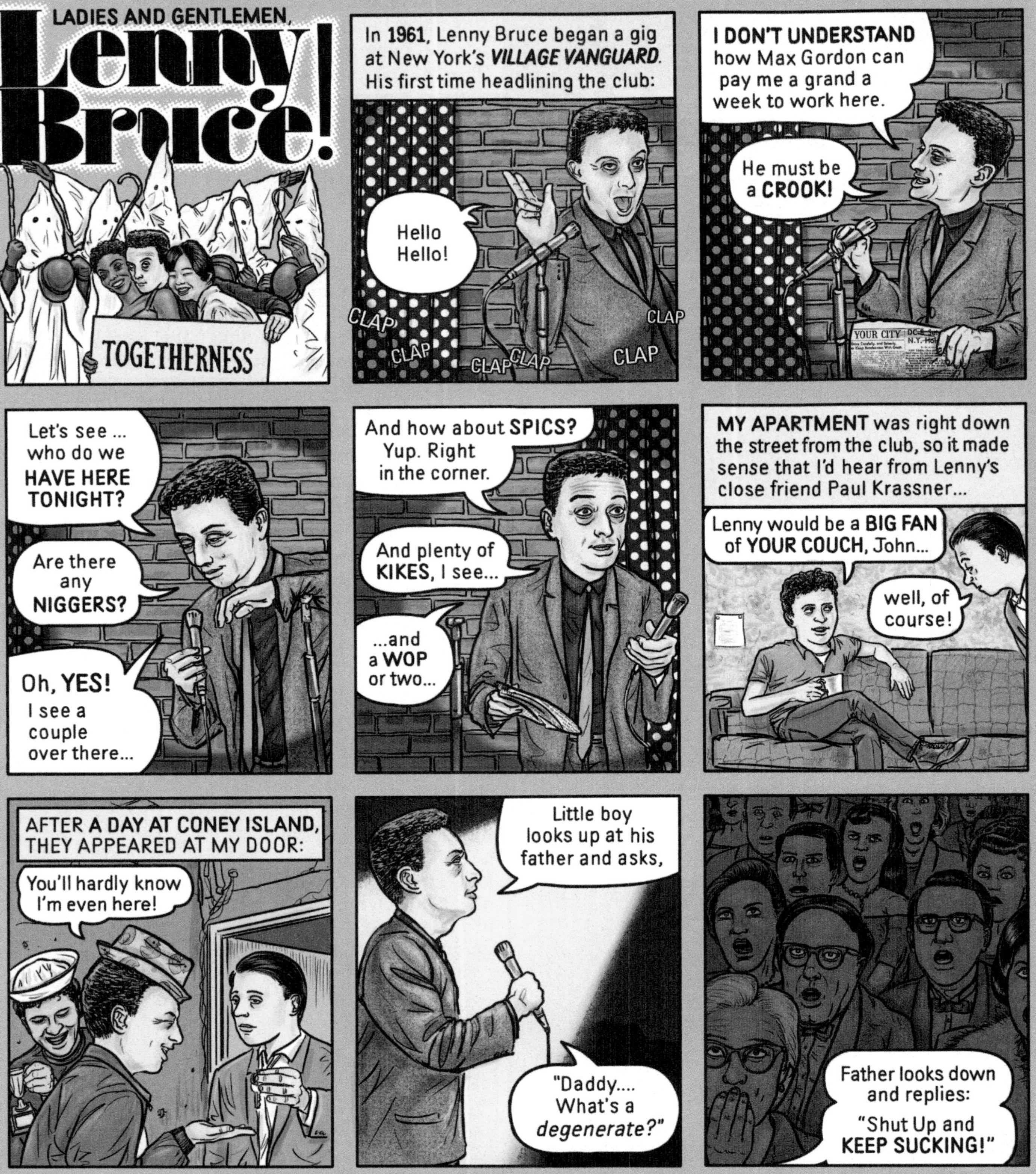
LADIES AND GENTLEMEN,
Lenny Bruce!
TOGETHERNESS
In 1961, Lenny Bruce began a gig at New York's VILLAGE VANGUARD. His first time headlining the club:
Hello Hello!
CLAP
CLAP
CLAP
CLAP
CLAP
CLAP
I DON'T UNDERSTAND how Max Gordon can pay me a grand a week to work here.
He must be a CROOK!
YOUR CITY
Let's see ... who do we HAVE HERE TONIGHT?
Are there any NIGGERS?
Oh, YES! I see a couple over there...
And how about SPICS? Yup. Right in the corner.
And plenty of KIKES, I see...
...and a WOP or two...
MY APARTMENT was right down the street from the club, so it made sense that I'd hear from Lenny's close friend Paul Krassner...
Lenny would be a BIG FAN of YOUR COUCH, John...
well, of course!
AFTER A DAY AT CONEY ISLAND, THEY APPEARED AT MY DOOR:
You'll hardly know I'm even here!
Little boy looks up at his father and asks,
"Daddy.... What's a *degenerate?*"
Father looks down and replies:
"Shut Up and KEEP SUCKING!"

Continuing "Ladies and Gentlemen, LENNY BRUCE"

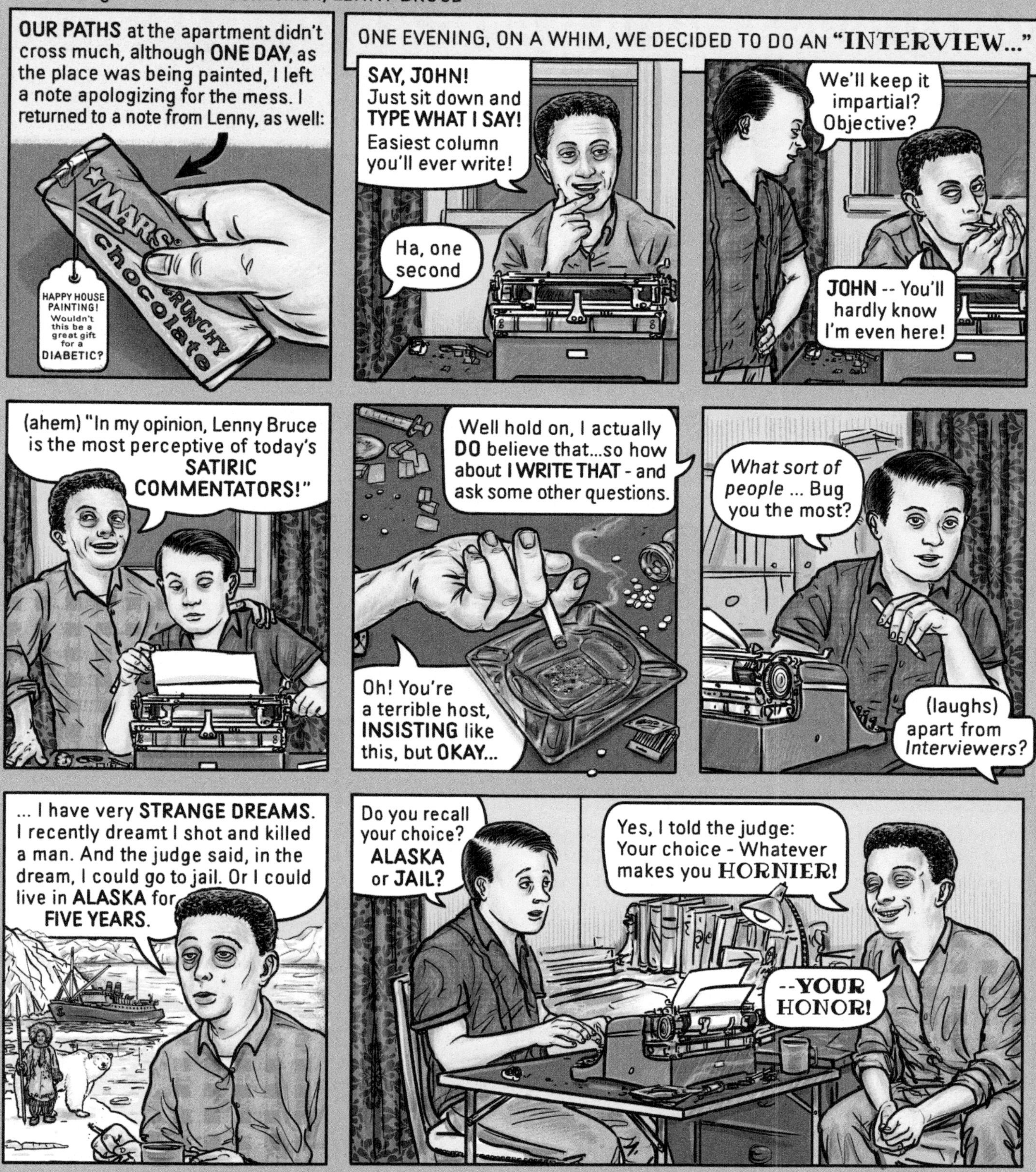

OUR PATHS at the apartment didn't cross much, although **ONE DAY**, as the place was being painted, I left a note apologizing for the mess. I returned to a note from Lenny, as well:
MARS CRUNCHY chocolate
HAPPY HOUSE PAINTING! Wouldn't this be a great gift for a DIABETIC?
ONE EVENING, ON A WHIM, WE DECIDED TO DO AN "INTERVIEW..."
SAY, JOHN! Just sit down and **TYPE WHAT I SAY!** Easiest column you'll ever write!
Ha, one second
We'll keep it impartial? Objective?
JOHN -- You'll hardly know I'm even here!
(ahem) "In my opinion, Lenny Bruce is the most perceptive of today's **SATIRIC COMMENTATORS!**"
Well hold on, I actually **DO** believe that...so how about **I WRITE THAT** - and ask some other questions.
Oh! You're a terrible host, **INSISTING** like this, but **OKAY...**
What sort of people ... Bug you the most?
(laughs) apart from *Interviewers?*
... I have very **STRANGE DREAMS.** I recently dreamt I shot and killed a man. And the judge said, in the dream, I could go to jail. Or I could live in **ALASKA** for **FIVE YEARS.**
Do you recall your choice? **ALASKA** or **JAIL?**
Yes, I told the judge: Your choice - Whatever makes you **HORNIER!**
--YOUR HONOR!

HE WAS A TERRIFIC GUEST. LENNY, WE ALL MISS YOU.

THELONIOUS MONK is alive AT THE FIVE SPOT

In 1951, BUD POWELL and THELONIOUS MONK were stopped by the New York narcotics division for sitting in a parked car ... on a street known for DRUG USE.

Sitting in a car ain't a crime. Is it, officers?

Let me tell you what's a crime and what isn't.

Yeah, stay STILL while we talk, slick.

The two jazz musicians were just there to visit Powell's grandmother, who had lived on that street for decades.

But unknown to Monk, Powell was holding a small bag of heroin. In a panic, he tried to throw the bag out the window, but missed, tossing it right onto Monk's shoes.

Hey, stop there, *shoeshine!* I see what that is. *BOTH YOU NEGROS OUT OF THE CAR*

MONK REFUSED TO SAY where the heroin came from. Held on $1500 bail, he spent 60 days at Riker's Island. His close friend Powell was not charged, and went free.

While in jail, Monk's NYC Cabaret Card was suspended. Without one, he could not perform in any city nightclub.

It would take years for Monk to recover. Finally, his license was restored (drug charges dropped!) and he had a regular gig with John Coltrane at the FIVE SPOT.

I'll never forget this: The night he was due to return, the Five Spot was packed, noisy with people's excitement...

WITHOUT ANY INTRODUCTION, Monk came in, stage right, strode to the piano (six paces), PLUNKED DOWN, and started playing. It was so sudden, people were still talking until they realized in awe what was happening.

!!!!

???

WHAT!

I TELL EVERYBODY it was the coolest thing I've ever seen a musician do onstage. Back then, *everybody was announced,* or at least they greeted the audience. To suddenly APPEAR and PLAY, was just so electrifying.

AND THEN, BABY, HE WAS GONE!

MICHAEL HOLLINGSHEAD TURNS ON THE WORLD

1960: On a tip from **ALDOUS HUXLEY**, drug researcher **Michael Hollingshead** purchases 1 gram of powdered LSD from Swiss-based **Sandoz Labs**, for **$285.**

LSD is **LEGAL** to buy for medical use. The sale is facillitated using borrowed hospital **LETTERHEAD**, claiming the drug is for **BONE MARROW** experiments!

Alone in his **KITCHEN**, Hollingshead recklessly **IMPROVISES** a mix of the LSD with sugar and distilled water. He stores the end result (5,000 doses!) in an empty mayonnaise jar.

tastes perfect!

He consumes **FAR** too much

NEVER having encountered LSD, he spends the next day delirious.

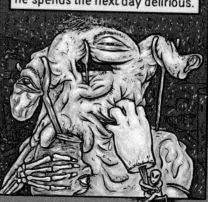

1961: My phone rings. Michael is leaving NYC, and introduces himself.

tell him you're a friend of a friend of a --

you're on a mission

i HAVE something

ARE YOU THE WRITER FROM THE **VILLAGE VOICE ??**

gotta share this!

MICHAEL has contacted me because he's interested in sharing his acid with people I'm known to frequently visit: local artists and musicians. I'm there with my friend **SOPHIE**, who has a car. We agree to pick him up at the post office.

I wanna meet him, John

THAT NIGHT, Michael and Sophie hit it off. I won't see the two of them for two years. During that time they will marry, have a child, and divorce.

Upon exiting New York, Michael travels to Boston to meet **TIM LEARY** in Harvard — Providing the doctor with his <u>first acid trip</u>!

EPILOGUE: Over the next five years, Michael's **GOOD JAR OF MAYONNAISE** will reach the likes of William S. Burroughs, Allen Ginsberg, Charles Mingus, Alan Watts ... As well as both the Beatles and the Rolling Stones ... Many others.

All of which is...to politely suggest:

Boom!

"...And then there was the time I took the subway to Harlem (IRT Lenox Ave line) to interview Langston Hughes..."

SUBWAY RUSH HOUR

Mingled
breath and smell
so close
mingled
black and white
so near
no room for fear.

-- L.H.

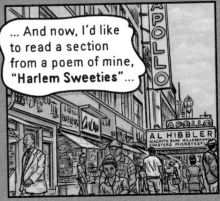
... And now, I'd like to read a section from a poem of mine, "Harlem Sweeties"...

... Blackberry cordial, Virginia Dare wine — All those sweet colors Flavor Harlem of mine!

BZZZ!

Walnut or cocoa, Let me repeat: Caramel, brown sugar, A chocolate treat.

hi John, come in

Molasses taffy, Coffee and cream, Licorice, clove, cinnamon ... To a honey-brown dream ...

Ginger, wine-gold, Persimmon, blackberry, All through the spectrum Harlem girls vary—

So if you want to know beauty's Rainbow-sweet thrill, Stroll down luscious,

... Delicious ...
.... fine ....

Sugar Hill.

bye bye, now.

RACHAEL SCHAFER is a well groomed illustrator + hand letterer + designer and you need her work for your books, ad campaigns, magazines, websites. She's an experienced, educated former hillbilly with a worldly joy de vivre that will add an irresistible charm to all your printed or web based projects. **rachaelschaferdesigns.com**

SPIRITS OF SUBURBIA - a webcomic! Do you like comics? Do you like crime? Well, why not read Spirits of Suburbia - a new webcomic about two kid detectives and their trusty pig hunting down spirits that done wrong. It's kids! It's pigs! It's a real good time! **www.spiritsofsuburbia.com**

GAMING PODCAST
Weekly Blizzard Entertainment fan podcast covering all games in addition to upcoming Blizzard media. **www.thegroupquest.com**

***LEAGUE OF MORTALS* BY** Duncan Cross. A raw & darkly comic novel... "a masterful storyteller, surprising us with plot twists, and evoking his world with humor, sly observation and depth"; "a witty and engaging voice"; "an addictive page turner". Available as ebook from Amazon, iTunes, Nook, etc.

RICHARD RAMIREZ got married on death row. Michael Jackson got married...twice. Even Gomer Pyle had Ms. Poovie. "The Celibate" takes you on one man's search for his Ms. Poovie. Catch all the action (or non-action) at **www.thecelibate.com**

JOHNANDNICK.COM is a comedy web site by John Carroll and Nick Klinger, the first two white men to blaze a trail into comedy writing.

RODGER ROUNDY
Humble Painter of Amazing Shit!!!!
www.rodgerroundy.net

THE MONA LISA SPEAKS by Christopher Angel. "The perfect caper book -- high art, high tech, high suspense." "The height of intrigue." A fictional update of the little known, real life theft of the Mona Lisa from the Louvre. Sometimes life is even crazier than art. **www.themonalisaspeaks.com**

LOOK KIDS! *ART!*
Nobody's Blues: a Flickr photoset by Casanova Frankenstein.
http://bit.ly/1NnFjbe

I have **A BIKE** i wanna move. $10.00. Firm. Im excited.

FOLLOW @RIVERCLEGG on Twitter. Comforting jokes for uncertain times.

THE CODE ZONE Gobs of free games for your mobile gizmo. Lots of good puzzles and card games and such. **TheCodeZone.com**

THE INTERPRETATION OF CAKES
www.facebook.com/allanteggauthor

MINERAL SCHOOL Writers residency near Mt. Rainier, Mineral School (www.mineralschool.org) will open up applications via Submittable in December 2015/January 2016. Spend two weeks enjoying room, board, the fishing lake, visiting authors, and good times in a rural setting in June, July, August, or September. Four full fellowships available.

HELLO FROM MANILA I am Apol Sta Maria and I make comics, too. Please look for **@apolsm** on instagram if you have time. And if you have more time, you can see more of my drawings at this website from the very popular internet: **apolstamaria.com**

THE BEST YOUTUBE channel no one is watching: DebbieDoesDaleks. Many videos under 2 minutes. Perfect for your inner attention deficit child. Sporadically maintained. Mostly work safe. **www.youtube.com/user/DebbieDoesDaleks**

TRAVEL ROUND THE WORLD TWICE—
first as a luxury travel writer, then using the travel-writing money to help the working poor worldwide. Both are surprisingly fun!
"The International Bank of Bob" by Bob Harris.
http://bit.ly/BankOfBob
"Give this book your time. It will pay you back." — Joss Whedon

ANDYDOTCOM.COM
A personal website that lists various projects. Limited spelling errors gauranteed!

WITHIN REACH follows two funky 30 somethings on their pedal powered transportation across the country as they search for a new home, looking for a way to free themselves of a tedious 9-5 life. Along the way they find old friends. unexpected hospitality, melt downs and survival: in short: life! Download a copy of the film at **www.WithinReachmovie.com**. Winner of the Orlando Film Festival's Eco Warriors Award Executive Producer and Co Creator Joanna Folino

I WILL PAY ANYONE $5.00 if they can tell me what is going on. **jon.schwarz@theintercept.com**

CLASSIFIEDS

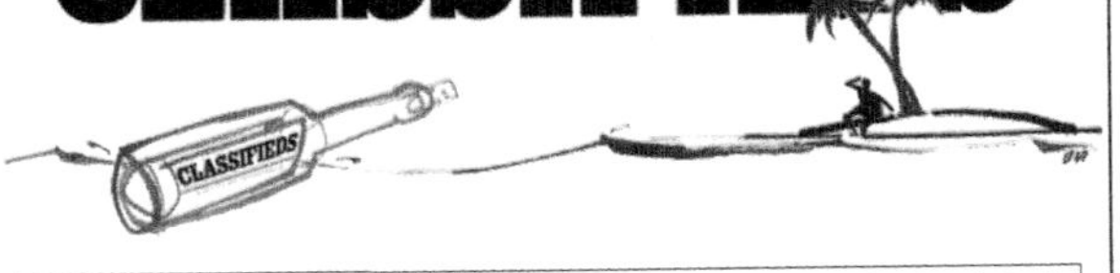

Interested in placing an ad? Email **Publisher@americanbystander.org**. *The American Bystander* reserves the right to reject any ad for any reason. We do not guarantee the quality of the items being sold, or the accuracy of the information provided. Ads are provided directly by sellers and are not verified.

YALE. AT ONCE A TRADItion, a company of scholars, a society of friends, a cabal of freemasons. Or at least it used to be. 'the bull report' is here to fix that. Announcing Yale's only satirical news show: 'the bull report.'
https://bit.ly/bull-report

INTRODUCING STEVEYOUNGWORLD.COM
the personal website of comedy writer/speaker/photographer/songwriter/author etc Steve Young! Supplying all your Steve Young needs at competitive prices. Voted "One Of The Things On The Internet" by steveyoungworld.com. Mention this ad and get blank stares!

WANTED: Readers for funny books. Fatties welcome, encouraged! All inquiries: **devastatorpress.com**

WALLS CLOSING IN, but you're already out? Eye floaties spell "S-U-R-R-E-N-D-E-R"? You see the fnords, but tinfoil hats make you look fat? Take arms against a sea of troubles, and by opposing, end them! Advice so bad it's good from Uncle Sort-Em-Out, unregistered dietician and named inventor. **unclesortemout@gmail.com**

BALING WIRE, a novel.. Two boys, a home-made airplane, and a mysterious spiraled house in the sticks of Oklahoma. Read it, and you'll be happier'n Cooter Brown. Download for Kindle: **http://amzn.com/B004H8GUDC**

WELCOME TO KUTSHER'S: The Last Catskills Resort" is now on DVD & VOD! Exploring the full Dirty Dancing-era Catskills experience through a close up look at Kutsher's rise and fall, this award-winning documentary captures a last glimpse of a lost world as it disappears before our eyes. **Info at Kutshersdoc.com**

MULLET TURTLE COMICS
Humorous self-published comics and books by Steve Steiner that have nothing to do with mullets nor turtles!
mulletturtle.storenvy.com

WILL DRAW FOR MONEY
Brooklyn-based artist/cartoonist Lauren Purje, **www.laurenpurje.com**

AMERICAN BYSTANDERS ... Quit standing by! If you want coaching with a twist of Irish to achieve your career, creative or life goals; I can help you chase the rainbow and find your own personal crock of... [insert key performance indicator here] **liz@realize.ie, Dublin, Ireland**

COMEDY WRITER LOOKING TO CONTRIBUTE TO CHARITY
Award-winning TV comedy writer wants to help world with narrative skills. Sick, poor, and disenfranchised in need of three act stories, zany characters, or simply a blow joke to end their scenes, please contact **JayKogen@aol.com.** (Multi or single camera, whatever works best for the children in crisis.)

If You Love Pop Culture,
COLLECTOR'S SHANGRI-LA
is your Paradise!
Visit CollectorsShangri-La.com for the finest Autographs, Classic Movie and TV Memorabilia, Sci-Fi, Horror, Comic Books, plus fantastic Lowbrow, Comic, and Illustration Art. USPAP-compliant Appraisals and Authentication. Lifetime money-back guarantee of authenticity on everything we sell!

HEY YOU!
Yes, you. I'm on to you. You can't fool me. I know what you're doing. Need help? **@gadgetchaser**

DESERT ISLAND COMICS
Your source for illuminated manuscripts. And weird comics. **www.desertislandbrooklyn.com**

POPE STREET RECORDS AND GAMES
Music by Drew Bancroft and Laura's Invention, Mad Science the Card Game, Serum Z, the Transylvania Star series of dice games, YA novels The Invisibles of Normal and Tooth, and Skateboard Heroes the comic! **www.popestreet.com**

NEED STORIES TOLD? Well, friend, I'm your teller! Check out my work and let me know if you'd like to work with me:Danny Mendoza - **https://vimeo.com/user4344710**

SHAKESPEARE STORIES. NPR Best Forthcoming Fiction. Desdemona, chair of an English Department whose only claim to diversity is Othello, is running an affirmative action search. "An Incarceration of Hamlets" concerns an inmate in a maximum security prison in Kentucky playing you-know-who. Taking What I Like (Godine) by Linda Bamber. **lindabamberwriter.com**

LOOK, THAT ISN'T MINE, I didn't do it, and I've never seen that woman before. **King Cormack**

RAMSEY HAS A TIME MACHINE
A webseries about an idiot with a time machine. Guest starring Chris Elliott, Julie Klausner, Josh Gondelman and many more! **www.ramseyhasatimemachine.com**

PETER BAYLIS: *STILL PHOTOGRAPHING PEOPLE*
Cannes Film Festival, 1975: Alongside a documentary film crew, I photographed Dustin Hoffman. After a fun two hours he invited us to dinner. I got great pictures, and learned a lesson in kindness and generosity. 40 years later I'm *still photographing people*, and I also support those learning photography.
peterbaylis@live.co.uk

COMEDY WRITING FOR LATE-NIGHT TV: THE BOOK
He has written and produced comedy/talk shows for over fifteen years. Now four-time Emmy winner Joe Toplyn reveals his proven methods of writing for late-night television in this one-of-a-kind insider's guide. Buy it now on Amazon: **http://amzn.to/1jXffof**

GRAVE-ROBBING. Spacesuits. Scientology. The Bloop. Shipping Containers. Dragons. Self-immolation.. Visual investigations of these subjects and more await you at **PrimerStories.com**, updated every week.

SIGH. Amaze your friends, startle your enemies, lose your best girl. Learn how to solder. Make electronic music. Poly bags of odd bits for you since 1969. **www.paia.com**

LEARN TO SPEAK GEEK
The Geek Primer is a fortnightly video series that helps you understand geek conversations. **http://geekprimer.tumblr.com/**

COMIC STRIP OF THE DAY.COM Good comics don't come along every day (unless you know where to look). Celebrating the best in syndicated and web comics, with rants and raves posted every day for more than five years. **www.comicstripoftheday.com**

TRUMPET BOYS COMEDY TRIO!
The Trumpet Boys are Connecticut's Premier Comedy Trumpet Trio! They've performed all across the globe, from New Haven Connecticut to Darien Connecticut to Wilton Connecticut to Brooklyn Connecticut! Check out their website **www.thetrumpetboys.com** to see if they are performing a gig near YOU!

HOW DOES THE OTHER HALF LIVE?
You know, the poor half in New Hampshire leading lives of quiet desperation. Find out by reading a blog which resides at **timhulsizer.com**, a website which is mine. We're not so different, you and I. Or are we? We probably aren't. That's 50 words.

THIS MIGHT SOUND CRAZY
Help me build the definitive directory of abandoned insane asylums. **www.atlasobscura.com/categories/abandoned-insane-asylums**

MULTIVERSEROS Do you speak Spanish? No? That's too bad. You are missing a great site to talk about comics, films, books, toys and other funny stuff. **www.multiverseros.com** (all the way from Uruguay).

THE DRAWING BOARD
Open discussion of new business ideas **www.thedrawingboard.net**

THIS MAGAZINE IS FULL OF JEWS
But Jewish genetic health is no laughing matter! Visit the Center for Jewish Genetics and get informed about recessive disorders and hereditary cancers more common in the Jewish community:
www.jewishgenetics.org.

LOOKING FOR: WHAT Were You Thinking?" stories — personal essays describing that moment in a relationship when, no matter how much you think it should work or want it to work or need it to work, it becomes clear to you that it's not going to work. **wwitonline.com**

EVERYTHING'S COMING UP Profits: The Golden Age of Industrial Musicals"--the lavishly illustrated book by Steve Young and Sport Murphy that celebrates the hidden world of insider-only corporate musical theater. **A surprising, hilarious chunk of 20th century American culture!** A perfect holiday gift, or treat yourself! Available on Amazon!

SELFIE SHTICK Instagram @timkleimancomedy. Stuff with captions. No duck lips.

DAVID KAZMIERSKI
Los Angeles
Comedy Writer
Co-writer of "Bigfoot: armed & dangerous"
Davidkazmierski@gmail.com

ILLUSTRATED FANTASY/ adventure chapter book for ages 7-12! With Mermaids! A young Bahamian girl learns she can communicate with sea creatures. Determined to understand her roots, she takes a risky journey to the undersea kingdom of Atlantica, where mer-people rule, humans are slaves, and dangerous and thrilling surprises await her. **www.thegirlfromatlantis.com/**

THE COVERT COMIC
isn't like you. The Covert Comic is love you.

HI! I'M ANTHONY Cusumano, aspiring comedy writer moving to Chicago sometime soon. I'd love to line up a job in advance. Any leads on video editor/writer jobs there would be appreciated! Email **anthontherun@gmail.com.** "Anthony Cusumano is probably the greatest creative genius out there right now." - Paul McCartney

---

JASH

PETS KNOW that the arrival of *Other People Exist* zine means a fresh cage lining for them, followed by weeks of superior comfort and leak protection. Birds, bunnies and guinea pigs are comforted by OPE's familiar feel underfoot. It's why I work to make each issue as thick and absorbent as I can. **K.A. Polzin**

THE NORMA GENE — the hilarious new novel by **M.A. Roufa.** Just another guy meets girl, guy runs from government, guy gets girl suspense thriller about Abraham Lincoln and Marilyn Monroe. **Now available online and in stores** from Bitingduck Press.

IMPROV COMEDY in Brooklyn! After 28 years of fearless fun, Chicago's infamous Annoyance Theatre now offers year-round comedy classes and shows Thursday-Sunday nights in Williamsburg, Brooklyn. "... for the kind of people who hold out hope, that young artists will always find ways to do ludicrous things in ridiculous dives." – *The New York Times* **www.theannoyancenewyork.com**

"I recently found **pigeonmoviedb.blogspot.co.uk** and Id love to see a classified about that. Its basically sort of like Mr. Skin, except instead of naked celebrities its pigeons. Seems consistent with this project." — We agree, here's your ad.

DOCUMENTARY FILM NOW in production: "The Industrial Musicals Movie." A hilarious yet sincere and thought-provoking journey into the bizarre hidden world of corporate musicals. Starring collector/author Steve Young and industrial show vets Martin Short, Florence Henderson, Susan Stroman, Sheldon Harnick, and more! Visit **industrialmusicalsmovie.com** -- donations gratefully accepted!

LAUREN R. WEINSTEIN
Person who makes comics about things.
www.laurenweinstein.com

VNVS IGNIS QVIS CAPVT
VIR MVLTVM IN CORPORE SE DE AVDERE ET CLAMABAT: "STVDIVM FVGA, MEVM IMPEDIRE!"

UNREPENTANT SELF-PROMOTION
Greetings, I'm Otto. I roam G+ and Tumblr spreading good cheer and merriment. I look for the brightside of things and always try an be a gentleman. Should you encounter me, please say hello.
With Regards,
Otto66

MEDIA TRAINING for the Social Media Age. Got the meeting? Let me help you close the deal: Media, Presentation & Pitch Training, Personal Branding and Social Media Strategies with Abel Intermedia **www.abelintermedia.com** +1 718 403 0200 **bba@abelintermedia.com**

DON'T BE A TOURIST! P2P SIGHTSEEING
Share your town's hidden gems with visitors and make some extra cash to boot. Meet locals while travelling and avoid the tourist traps. Make new friends, see what you've never seen before. Know someone everywhere: **KIMBITRAV.SHARETRIBE.COM**

DOS POLACAS TO EXPLODE ON KICKSTARTER

Dos Polacas collaborate with indigenous communities, producing book-length celebrations of tribal elders, language, ceremony and stories of 21st-century indigenous cultures. Click **www.Dos-Polacas.com** for stunning images and intimate interviews. Sorry, but you'll miss sipping gallons of coffee in kitchens and smelling the cedar chips. Support our KICKSTARTER campaign **MARCH 2016!**

CHECK OUT Interstellar Overdrive — an online sci-fi comic that doesn't suck. **www.interstellarcomic.com**

ANT FARMER'S ALMANAC
"The Thinking Man's No-Brainer!" Writings, Random Thoughts & the Occasional Cartoon from L.K. Peterson **www.antfarmersalmanac.com**

GOING ON A PSYCHEDELIC TRIP?
Take me with you. Make your next psychedelic experience the best it can be. Hire a philosophically-informed practicing psychiatrist to assist in untangling thoughts, nurturing a positive self image and preventing paranoia. A debriefing session at the end will help you re-enter the world as it is. Individuals or small groups. Email **bonumitinere(at)gmail.com.**

THIRD DATE: NOT-JUST-Comedy Improv. Veteran actors Dan Sipp, Nancy Pekar, J. Chachula and Jenny Spencer create a one-hour improvised show about the comic and sometimes bittersweet relationships between partners, family, friends, and co-workers, and reflecting the joys, surprises and everyday frustrations of life in our weird, wonderful world.
www.facebook.com/ThirdDateImprov
bit.ly/ThirdDateOnYouTube

GANG WAR, the long-lost 1982 rock opera by F.M. St. Jude, tells the tale of a dystopian future police state set right HERE in AMERICA — WHAT?!? Like Rush, Ziggy-era Bowie and G'n'R; this is glam-prog that demands your SUBMISSION! Visit **www.dragcity.com** for ordering details!

AN EVENING OF HUMOROUS READINGS
An Evening of Humorous Readings is a show where literary humorists read their most literary humor. It's short pieces, like the ones in this book, read aloud by the people who wrote them. With two convenient locations: DC and NYC! Hosted by Brian Agler, Luke Burns, and James Folta. **www.HumorousReadings.tumblr.com.**

FREE ONLINE READS My *Print* magazine features on Seymour Chwast, *Mad Men*, Mimi Pond, *National Lampoon*'s Michael Gross, Andy Warhol and Pop Art, *Charlie Hebdo*, Harvey Kurtzman, political protest posters, the Bauhaus, Art Spiegelman, Netflix's *Daredevil*, the Black Dahlia murder, censorship of American comics, etc., here... **www.printmag.com/author/michaeldooley/**

NO. 1 APP IN HELL? RASGUARD anticipates violence/crime. Free at Apple App Store. Not allowed in Hell.

POP'S GARAGE Specializing in the restoration and modification of classics, muscle cars and hot rods. Located in Boulder, Colorado and serving enthusiasts since 1961 we can make your automotive dreams come true. **Call Doc at 303-875-4917** or email at **Pops-Autos@gmail.com**.

DID YOU KNOW it takes a sloth one minute to move twelve feet? Odd animal facts, and beautiful illustrations, in Elisha Cooper's new children's book **8: An Animal Alphabet**. A perfect stocking stuffer, a great birthday gift. In bookstores now, at amazon.com, and at **elishacooper.com**.

LOVELY ART FOR PEOPLE WITH DISCERNING TASTE
Greetings Discerning Taste People, taste the loveliness at: mondomosher.com Taste it, I say!

BORED? THINK YOU'VE seen everything? Visit celebrigum.com, the semi-legendary site created by comedy writer Steve Young, featuring photos of celebrities outside the Letterman show with the same piece of old hardened gum on a window ledge in the foreground of each shot. "A perfectly silly, genius idea"--Dave Letterman
celebrigum.com

AS SEEN ON TV Do you like PDX? Do you like Bergers? Then follow **@pdxberger** on Twitter for witty repartee and crock pot recipes! Featured on @midnight Tag Team Thursday. With your support, late night local access cable in Vernonia, OR is next!

OVERSIZED BEAGLE seeks tasty morsel to be his and his alone. Any size or shape welcome. Personality not important. Interested? Meet me at my food bowl, ASAP. **Ask for Clarence.**

GAME NIGHT! GET "THE JACKBOX BUNDLE"! Spice up your next party, game night, bat mitzvah, or funeral with this bundle of The Jackbox Party Pack and The Jackbox Party Pack 2. **Ten hilarious party games** you play using phones/tablets as controllers! Available on Steam for PC and Mac!

INNOVATIONSHIP
Design thinking taught and practiced around the world..
http://innovationship.com

HORNS BY BENJAMIN RUSSELL
Horns: Trumpet, Cornet, Rhinocerous, Unicorn, Devil, Dilemma.
www.smartovercoat.com

MORE LOST TIME On this podcast, I play rare records from my collection and tell you about them. Often you'll say, "Wow, that was a really good song. I'd never heard of that one." **(iTunes and morelosttime.com)**

NATHAN CALLAHAN
nathancallahan.com
Wishes to *The American Bystander* for a grand, glorious, frolicking, audacious, and fan-fucking-tastically gelastic long life.

THANKS TO ACJ II
who let me stay up & listen to *The National Lampoon Radio Hour* w/him on KADI.

"A QUIET MAN,
is a thinking man. A quiet woman, is usually mad." Demystify the opposite sex. Get **So THAT'S Why They Do That! Men, Women And Their Hormones** – "the one book to solve World Peace by enlightening couples about their bodies & solving gender disputes." (Huff Post) Amazon, Istore.

COMICS MACHINE NO. 1
A 16-page asemic/abstract comic book, full of secrets. Confusion guaranteed. $3 + p/h. **comicsmachine.bigcartel.com/**

A REBEL IN GLASSES
John Tesh once blogged about a piece I wrote. Beat that. **CRAIG PLAYSTEAD** (http://craigplaystead) Writer. Corndog Aficionado. Wise Ass.

BOOKHAIKU.TUMBLR.COM
Summations of books / In seventeen syllables / Brevity is King. Written by **Wesley Seaton Bolin.**

SLIGHTLY USED MUSIC, MUST GO. AS IS
From just another band with a Twin Peaks inspired name: **windomearle.com**

TENT STOLEN
Lots of sentimental value. Lost in get-tent-quick scheme. Please contact **AlanMulgorp@gmail.com**

METAPHYSICAL COUNSELING
Do your gifts feel like burdens? A cosmic perspective could help. Call Dr. Dalas Verdugo: **503-272-1723**

MEN WANTED
for hazardous journey, low wages, bitter cold, long hours of complete darkness, safe return doubtful, honor and recognition in event of success. No creeps. **jeff.muskus@gmail.com**

FREE TENTS!
Must supply own starter tent. Typical applicants triple their tents in first week. WOW! Direct inquiries to **http://modern-brit.co.uk**

DO YOU KNOW SOMEONE
who was a salesman, dealer, manager, or executive for a U.S. company between 1950-1990? New documentary seeks their stories about attending conventions and sales meetings that featured musical entertainment. Contact **Cactus Flower Films** through industrialmusicalsmovie.com. Thanks!

NOBODY PLAYS FEWER HITS!
Listen to the Shuffle Function Morning Show, weekdays from six to nine a.m. CST on kmsu.org! Pop Music as Pornography! **shufflefunction.blogspot.com**. Also, Norman Carl Odam says 'Howdy!'

DERMATOLOGY SIMPLIFIED:
Outlines and Mnemonics by Dr. Jules Lipoff. A new dermatology review guide with all the essential facts to study for in-training and board examinations. Perfect for medical students, residents, and clinicians. Now available on Amazon and Springer.com!

THE INSTITUTE FOR THE
Separation of Theory from Practice (ISTP), in conjunction with Wegway Primary Culture, is concerned that what we like isn't necessarily the same as what we think is good - for example, The Communist Manifesto with all Words Functioning as Nouns Removed. Read this, and more, at **wegway.wordpress.com**

INVESTORS WANTED
Silicon Valley startup seeking angel investors for exciting B2C opportunity. We connect hungry customers with drivers of vehicles for hire (independent contractors) who transport hot baked potatoes. Still searching for suitable name. (Mash for Cash? Tater Freighter?) Inquires please email: **Spud@Pototoe.com**

CUSTOM GAMES, RPG'S,
LARPS Thought of a game? Don't know how to get it made? Damocles Thread Development will help you make it a reality. Contact us at **DamoclesThreadDevelopment.com**

LOST & FOUND DEPT.
One misplaced dinosaur found, in congo basin, in Drums Along the Congo. The rarest duck in the world located while dabbling in India, in The Search for the Pink-Headed Duck. Entire world of the independent commercial fisherman lost at sea, in Down at the Docks. Plus more gone missing in these books by RORY NUGENT...
rory@rorynugent.com

THE ANNUAL: HUMOR REGULARLY
After you've refreshed Facebook 40 times, head over to **TheAnnualOnline.Com** for your latest comedy fix! We've been bringing the jokes for 3 years, and we remain the web's best kept secret.

INTELLECTUALLY CURIOUS
people + vacation destinations + discussion of great books, music, and art = Classical Pursuits. Details at **classicalpursuits.com**. "Adventure for the mind, travel for the soul."

ANDY PALEY
To hear an infinite variety of great music please go to Andy Paley's official website... **www.andypaley.com**

CALVIN'S GIFT
Calvin, I know that because we've hit hard times, we said we wouldn't do Christmas gifts, but I love you too much not to show it. So, I've decided to sacrifice my most valuable possession, this ad space, to promote your ad space. Everyone go check out Calvin's ad space!

JEREMY'S GIFT
Jeremy, what fools we are! I have sacrificed my most valuable possession, my ad space, to promote your ad space. But we've gained something far greater than any gift we could receive: We now realize how priceless our love truly is!

WILL I EVER ACTUALLY
post on this? I don't know! Find out with me! **www.probably-nocomics.tumblr.com** But seriously, I probably will post comics on there! It's just a joke on my name, which is Paul Robalino.

FIND LIVE COMEDY NEAR YOU!
Stand-up comedians are performing near you. But where? Visit **www.dead-frog.com/live_comedy** to find upcoming shows from your favorite comedians (and future favorites).

NEED A CUSTOM WEBSITE?
You need a web platform. Not just a social media presence but your own unique home on the web for all your endeavors... humorous or otherwise. Check out my portfolio at **www.toddjacksonworks.com** and let me know how I can build your new web home.

PUBLISHED COOKBOOK
Author & Food Writer available for food writing projects, professional recipe testing & writing. Wrote bestselling "The Wiseguy Cookbook" for Penguin-Random House. Contact: **soya1919@gmail.com**.

IDIOT MAKES ART
Or maybe "Art". Definitely at least art. Here's some pictures: **www.weaselspoon.com**. I also make music. Listen to it here: **www.onceinamoon.com**. Alternatively, listen to these guys. They're much better than me. **tovesigurdsson.com** and **nickgill.bandcamp.com**. I ought to be on commission.

WWW.SARAHWALKER-INTERNATIONALSUPERSTAR.COM
(no hyphens necessary in the URL) "Sometimes God does give with both hands." --Daniel Day Lewis on co-starring with Sarah Walker, International Superstar. *Vanity Fair*, 2020.

KINDLY SEEKING VALIDATION
via web hits and minor humor-based art and design merchandise sales. Contact Mark* at:**markmattson.net** and **mattson.etsy.com** for a good time. *real name

MAN OF WAR
by Charlie Schroeder. One man's adventures in the world of historical re-enactment -- and the Civil War is just the beginning. "An offbeat, occasionally insightful, and funny memoir." -*The Wall Street Journal*. Available at all online booksellers from Penguin/Plume.

MR. B. SPECKTOR
will be drawing a #DogADay in 2016. If you'd like a free illustration of a dog you know (or wish you knew better), reach out to Mr. Specktor at **bspeckto@gmail.com**. Thank you very ruff.

A GIRL WALKS INTO A
magazine...Well...humor & immortality for such a reasonable price. All I ask — as an architect/designer/producer and all round feminine enthusiast of warm intelligent life on earth — is to share this new immortality with a mortal male...who makes people laugh with his insights! What better a pool of wise fools to fish in than this one, to land someone in his 60's early 70's smart enough to support the launch of this magazine! (Photo upon request) **bonnie1911@gmail.com**

THE INTERNET IS A NIGHTMARISH HELLSCAPE
But you NEED a web presence these days. That's why smart authors and other creative types turn to The Hot Brain to design and develop custom web solutions. (Is print dead? Probably! But we'd love to help with that too.) **More at thehotbrain.com.**

ENOUGH WITH THE FUNNY
Already! OK, if you can handle just a little more, please visit saltinwound.com. Jack Silbert will amuse you with satire and silliness, enlighten or enrage you with movie reviews, and give you such detailed information about his internet radio show, you'll swear you were actually listening. That's **saltinwound.com**, thank you!

MONTHLY COMEDIC PODCAST!
A monthly podcast of comedy, interviews, gags, curiosities, laughs, bloopers, boners, cuddling sessions, medical oddities, long stories ending with a funny pun, from the author of *Poking a Dead Frog.* **www.doinitwithmikesacks.com**

Check out these **AMAZON KINDLE SINGLES** by Emmy-winning *Simpsons* writer Mike Reiss —
Tales of Moronica —
a satiric tale for smart kids and dumb adults
I Conquered Kilimanjaro — Nearly: the hilarious true adventure of the worst vacation ever
Just 99 cents!
FREE with Kindle Unlimited
Only at Amazon.com!

WHO IS EVELYN WANE?

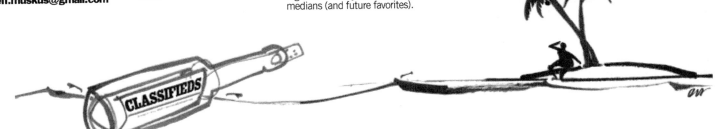

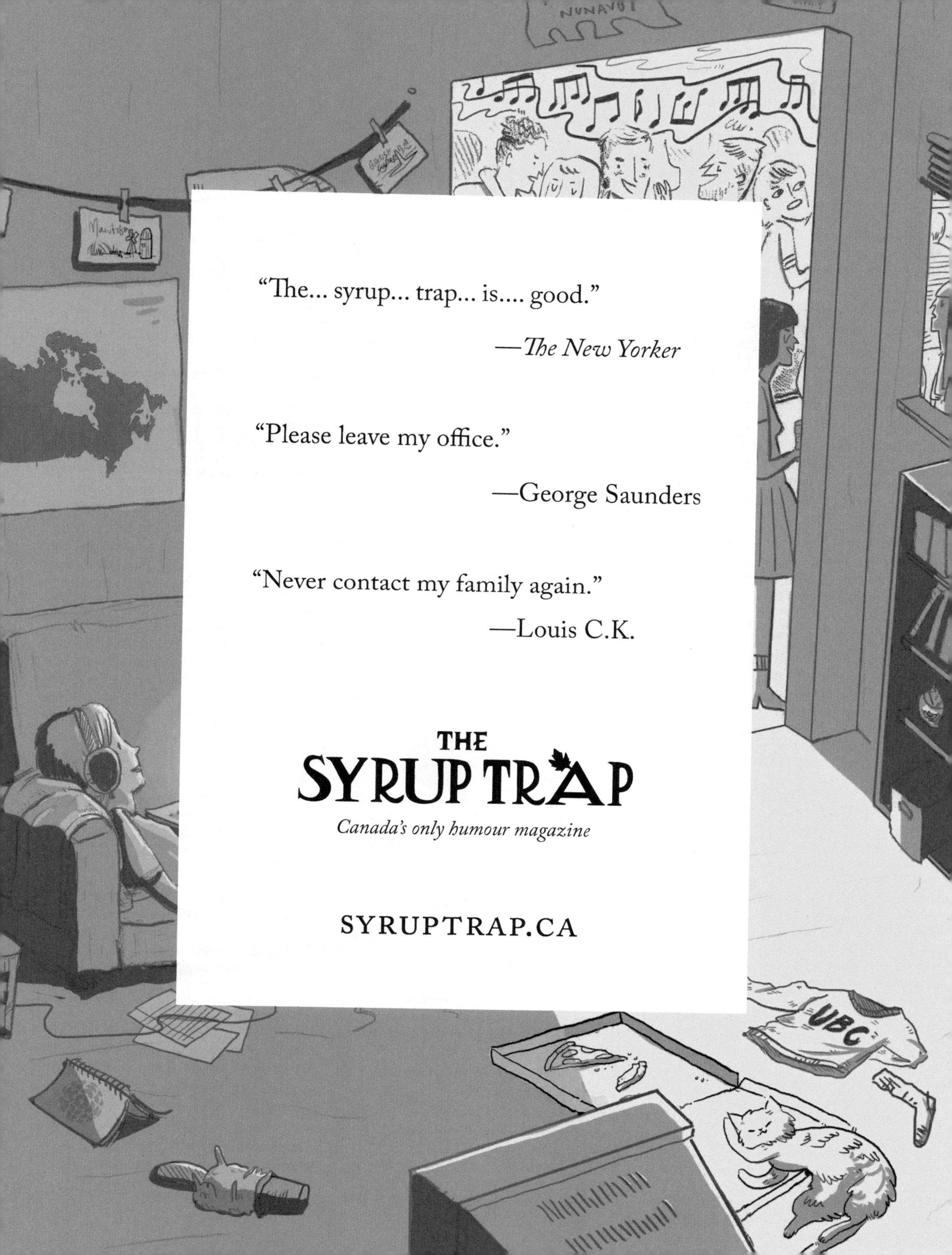
NUNAVUT
Manitoba
"The... syrup... trap... is.... good."
—The New Yorker
"Please leave my office."
—George Saunders
"Never contact my family again."
—Louis C.K.
THE SYRUP TRAP
Canada's only humour magazine
SYRUPTRAP.CA
UBC

BY BRIAN MCCONNACHIE

JOHNNY BULLWHIP

"Leave the anger in the corral, and just pay attention to the whipping."

Johnny Bullwhip. He was the fastest bullwhipper in the territory. He was fast and accurate and amazing. No one could beat Johnny Bullwhip in a bullwhip fight. No one handled a bullwhip like him. And if you weren't too particular about spelling, he could bullwhip your name right into your face. Unless you had a name like Alexander or Jedediah, which might not fit. But he could make an "Al" or a "Jed" if you really had your heart set on it.

Long ago people stopped challenging him to bullwhip fights. No one stood a chance. Johnny Bullwhip could bullwhip the down out of a baby's ear without waking the little darling. And did, too (with the mother's permission).

He wore a bullwhip on each hip, another bullwhip, like a belt, at the small of his back and a little, teeny bullwhip—actually, it was more like shoelaces—on the side of his boots.

If Johnny Bullwhip had worn a number, they would have retired it.

But these days he spends most of his time lecturing about bullwhips and taking care of your bullwhip, bullwhip registration, bullwhip safety goggles, proper cleaning, oiling and winter storage of your bullwhips.

Still, there's always some kid, some punk, who comes along and has to challenge Johnny Bullwhip to a bullwhip fight. Johnny usually says, "Put your bullwhip away, son. I don't do that anymore." But do you think they listen? Of course not. They have to learn the hard way. In a bullwhip fight. Against the fastest, sharpest, nicest, toughest bullwhip cracking guy in all of bullwhipdom. And small leather beltdom as well—if it ever comes to that.

But it never does.

I caught up with Johnny last month, at the Woodward County (OK) Regional Bullwhip and Pontoon Boat Show. Johnny's getting on in years, as we all are, and there are those who would say he's losing his touch. "His touch," no. His bullwhips, sometimes. He'll forget where he puts them.

…But if you're thinking of challenging him, I wouldn't count on it. —BM

Have you ever whipped a bull that didn't deserve it? That's a good question. You know, you start out whipping bulls and then you get to a point where you have to ask yourself, do any of them really deserve it? You don't know. You get the call from your agent and he gives you an address of a farmhouse somewhere in west Texas and you just show up and start in. "Tell it to the whip." That's a question everyone who's ever cracked a bullwhip has to answer for him or her self.

What's the main difference between bull riding and bull whipping? Another good question...In one you actually get on the bull and try to ride him around. Try to get him to go where you want him to go. Maybe even get the bull to do a little high-step prancing like show horses do. With the other, you just beat him, bam, bam, bam.

Do you, Johnny Bullwhip, make your own clothes or do you find someone who can make them for you and threaten to beat them, whip them thoroughly, if they don't make you a nice suit of clothes? I've tried that. Yes. I think all bull whippers have tried that at one time or another. It doesn't work. And it's wrong. You beat someone with a bullwhip and they're not going to sit down and sew you a nice suit of clothes. They're shaking. Their judgment is off. No, it doesn't work. It's wrong on a lot of levels.

Is it always wrong to bring anger to a bull whipping? I think so. Yes. Some people say, "use that anger." But I think it's something you leave outside the barn door. Or what's that place outside the barn.

The...barnyard? No. Like that. The, ah...

thing with the wood...and the gate.

The corral? Yes! …in the corral. Leave the anger in the corral and just pay attention to the whipping. Some people have to keep reminding themselves: It's business. It's not personal. It's not about you, it's about the bull and the whip. And the lessons you can only hope the bull is learning from the whipping you're giving him.

Johnny Mango once said, in a rare encounter, that he... Please. Johnny Mango! **He said that he hit you really hard on the back of the neck with a mango, and you were all disoriented and then blacked out before you could get to your bullwhips.** Not a word of that is true. He missed me—completely. And it was a papaya. How more wrong can one sentence get? **Well, his name is Johnny Mango. He's noted for throwing mangos from secret hiding places.** No. His name is Something Something Cabrini. Do you know how he operates? He either hides in the bushes, up in a tree or in a ditch by the road and when you're facing the other direction, he throws a papaya at the back of your neck. And then resumes hiding. He does throw hard but his aim isn't any good. As to why he does this, hey, your guess is as good as mine. I see nothing heroic in this.

If you ask him, he'll roll out some line of crap about fighting crime. What he needs is a normal job and someone to teach him the difference between a mango, a papaya and a guava. Different members of the *plantae* family. Ask him about that.

That brings me to the question: in the family of Johnnys, you and Johnny Guitar are generally regarded as the most senior and respected members. What do you think of this new guy, Johnny Mimosa? Yeah. I think I've heard of him. What does he do exactly?

He orders a double mimosa, then throws it in somebody's face and gets into a fight over it. He wins about half the time. That sounds promising. There's a place to plant your flag. I think we're done here. No more questions. I'm not going to comment on Johnnys gone rogue.

Thanks for your time, Mr. Bullwhip.